NOV 05 2018

D0971626 ⅢⅢABCL

Generously Donated By

Richard A. Freedman
Trust

_____

the PUBLIC LIBRARY
ABQ-BERNCO

CHRONIQUES

ALSO BY KAMEL DAOUD

The Meursault Investigation

Withdrawn/ABCL

CHRONIQUES

SELECTED COLUMNS, 2010–2016

KAMEL DAOUD

TRANSLATED FROM THE FRENCH
AND WITH AN INTRODUCTION BY

ELISABETH ZEROFSKY

Other Press
New York

© Actes Sud, Arles, 2017
© Éditions Barzakh, Algiers, 2017

Originally published in French as
Mes indépendances: Chroniques 2010–2016
by Actes Sud, Arles, and Éditions Barzakh, Algiers,
in 2017

Translation copyright © Other Press, 2018

Production editor: Yvonne E. Cárdenas
Text designer: Julie Fry
This book was set in Prensa with Futura.

1 3 5 7 9 10 8 6 4 2

All rights reserved. No part of this publication may be reproduced
or transmitted in any form or by any means, electronic or
mechanical, including photocopying, recording, or by any information
storage and retrieval system, without written permission from
Other Press LLC, except in the case of brief quotations in reviews
for inclusion in a magazine, newspaper, or broadcast. Printed in
the United States of America on acid-free paper. For information write to
Other Press LLC, 267 Fifth Avenue, 6th Floor, New York, NY 10016.
Or visit our Web site: www.otherpress.com.

Library of Congress Cataloging-in-Publication Data
Names: Daoud, Kamel, author. | Zerofsky, Elisabeth, translator
author of introduction.
Title: Chroniques : selected columns, 2010–2016 / Kamel Daoud ;
translated from the French and with an introduction by Elisabeth Zerofsky.
Description: New York : Other Press, 2018. | Originally published in French :
Algiers: Éditions Barzakh, 2017, and Arles : Actes Sud, 2017,
under title: Mes indépendances.
Identifiers: LCCN 2018005172 (print) | LCCN 2018016504 (ebook) |
ISBN 9781590519578 (Ebook) | ISBN 9781590519561 (hardback)
Subjects: LCSH: Algeria—Politics and government—21st century. |
Middle East—Politics and government—21st century. |
Daoud, Kamel—Political and social views. | BISAC: POLITICAL SCIENCE /
Colonialism & Post-Colonialism. | LITERARY COLLECTIONS / Essays.
Classification: LCC DT295.6 (ebook) | LCC DT295.6 .D3613 2018 (print) |
DDC 965.05/4—dc23
LC record available at https://lccn.loc.gov/2018005172

To my wife, upright in my storms

To Brahim H., because to dream is also to build

CONTENTS

INTRODUCTION

"What do you say about your little invisible country?" Kamel Daoud wrote during his first trip to Manhattan, in the fall of 2015. "How do you make your country be seen by those who don't know that it exists?" Of course when Daoud arrived in New York that November, he was, in reality, the most conspicuous of foreign writers. His first novel, *The Meursault Investigation*, had been published in America five months earlier, preceded by a luminous profile in the *New York Times Magazine* (and by my own brief but adulating clip for the *New Yorker*). By the end of the summer, nearly every U.S. publication of record was lauding this North African writer who had seemed to emerge from nowhere, for the singular music of his prose and his ability to upend accepted historical and literary narratives. Still, the novel's success in the United States was due at least in part to the fact that it operated within forms and structures that are easily recognizable to American readers—it played on the work of Albert Camus, and delivered Algeria to the reader in the guise of the country's 130-year relationship with France. That the second half of Daoud's novel shifts registers into a testimony to the writer's disenchantment with the Algerian nation for the unfulfilled possibilities of liberation is a clever maneuver, made to go down easy.

It was while Daoud was in New York that fall that the Islamic State struck Paris, on November 13, 2015, leaving 130 people dead. Daoud had, by that time, already become a kind of guru for the French-language press—he was a Muslim and an Algerian, a member of a postcolonial society but somewhat distanced from it by the privilege of his position and his intellect. In other words, a commentator who could both speak for and critique the "so-called Arab world," as Daoud likes to say, from the inside and from the outside. After the November attacks, the demands for Daoud's insights seemed to come from everywhere, a spotlight trained on him wherever he went. So it was that less than two months later, he published a column in *Le Monde* entitled "Cologne, Scene of Fantasies." The article took up the events of New Year's Eve in Cologne, Germany, in which some six hundred women were allegedly assaulted near the city's train station by several hundred men, the majority of whom appeared to be of North African or Middle Eastern origin. In his column, Daoud exhorted his Western audience to put aside their *bienpensance* and accept that if they were going to take in large numbers of refugees from this Arab world, as, he argued, they should, their new guests would essentially need to be reeducated—lifted from the backward sexual mores of their home countries and initiated into the enlightened ways of the West. The backlash against Daoud from the leftist establishment was quick and merciless; nineteen academics signed a petition against his "orientalist clichés" and "colonialist paternalism," igniting a transnational dustup that eventually drew in the prime minister of France.

When, a few weeks later, Daoud announced that he was taking a break from journalism (one that didn't last long in the end), he explained that the decision was not only so that he could regain some serenity, but also because he felt that the argument wasn't really about the words that he had written. What was going on, he felt, was that he was being used, instrumentalized within a broader political debate, one that was symptomatic of the kinds of virulent cultural confrontations that would explode elections across Europe and America over the next two years. The *Affaire Daoud,* as it was dubbed, seemed to cement in the European imagination a certain idea of who Daoud was, to reduce him to a caricature in a debate that many casual observers don't necessarily grasp the nuances of in a meaningful way. When I moved to Paris at the beginning of 2017, I would mention to French writers and journalists that I was translating Daoud. The reaction would invariably be a display of reverence followed by a charged silence. "Ah. So what do you think of him?" would come the question.

This collection, a selection of Daoud's columns mostly from *Le Quotidien d'Oran* between 2010 and 2016, will open up his thinking about upending world events, and about everything, beyond the handful of his pieces that circulated widely in the American press. I think that Daoud is a humanist. He is an anticonformist. He is instinctively suspicious of the dominant consensus in the press or in public discourse, and he takes pleasure in confronting his public with it—not for the sake of being reactionary, but to deconstruct the conclusion and the rationale, to better understand where it came from, and to urge readers to be more rigorous. Daoud is idiosyncratic. He is fearless. He is also, in many ways, a populist (though not in the sense that the word is now being used to describe right-wing reactionary and illiberal movements across the world). That is, he is a tireless defender of "the people," without being blind to the whims, failures, and shortcomings of popular will.

That populism is perhaps most discernible in his urgent writing in support of the Arab Spring revolutions that unfurled around him, beginning in late 2010 and early 2011. Daoud watched from Algeria, a nation paralyzed by its memories of violence from the "Black Decade" of the 1990s, and suppressed through monetary incentives from the government, while in neighboring countries, years' worth of resentment exploded in the streets. To follow Daoud's writing over this period is to follow the emotional trajectory of the Arab revolutions. At the beginning there is surprise, excitement, a simultaneous incredulity at what appears to be happening alongside a deep recognition of the impulses from which the movements arise. The path of the revolutions becomes bloody and complicated, and Daoud defends them against the cynics and the critics, both internal and external—those who say that these countries would have been better off leaving their dictators in place, that the revolutions may overthrow them but will never succeed in creating anything better. That's not to mention Daoud's impatience with those who blame "the West" for all ills. He is a tireless advocate for personal responsibility in all matters both private and collective, but also for the justice owed every inhabitant of this planet. As he watches the Syrian revolution surge, wither, mutate, he turns to those who hide behind their laptop screens. "The Syrians are alone," he wrote in May 2011, surely not knowing how the magnitude of the sentiment would multiply exponentially over the next years. "They can be killed en masse, executed in front of the whitest walls, people can watch them die between two detergent ads, hear them screaming before turning out the bedside lamp to go to sleep. Almost no one is concerned." Six months later, he denounces the conspiracy theorists, writing that "for the Syrian, the equation is simple—he's the one getting killed, dragged out, tortured. There's no NATO, no IDF, no conspiracy—just the dictator," and concluding, "the least they deserve is our respectful silence." In December, watching Syrians die on YouTube, he writes with his singular acumen: "Horror is something unknowable, something that each person carries alone in his own personal nighttime. On a screen you can listen and you can watch, but you can't know." He admonishes the obscenity of this Facebook world, where we can watch these people who are "just numbers" for a few seconds on an iPhone—if this new connectedness is supposed to make us feel closer to people on the other side of the world, well, what good has it done them? "How can you convey to each viewer the precise sensation of the screech of an arrested child," Daoud writes with some desperation. "A child who's had his elbows ripped, his eyes punctured, his honor violated, who consumes his last breath utterly alone in his pain, for whom the promised nation will be nothing more than his tomb, whose martyrdom has meaning only for the survivors?"

This collection also has the capacity to open up to Americans this mysterious Algerian nation, long inaccessible to them. As Orhan Pamuk did for Istanbul, Aleksandar Hemon for Sarajevo, so this writer can introduce Americans intimately to a place that remains—because of history, because of cultural and religious apprehension—entirely unknown to them. As Adam Shatz wrote in his *New York Times Magazine* profile, Daoud is a frequently harsh critic of his countrymen, to the point of being accused of racism and self-hatred. But, if this is the case, as Shatz wrote, and as Daoud argues in his own self-defense at moments throughout this collection, the criticism comes from a place of deep love, and of desire—to see his country surpass the fragile balance struck between the occult strongmen who run the country and the Islamists who threaten its peace, which, Daoud argues, has kept the country immobilized for two decades. This truce that has prevented Algeria from flourishing, offering itself to the world, defining its unique role and ambition. What Daoud calls "ambient Islamism," he insists again and again, has kept Algerians estranged from their own bodies, suppressed women, and therefore society. The country depends on its oil economy for its financial livelihood and peace, while neglecting other resources. Daoud's Algeria is in the stranglehold of a single historical narrative—that of the colonial liberators—and he wants to reclaim that history, to re-endow it with richness, to acknowledge the sacrifices of the liberators without being obligated to sacrifice the self to them; to rediscover a language, a power in the country's Mediterranean geography, its Ottoman origins, in religion as a source of transcendence not confinement, to pull away from dogma in search of personal, individual deliverance.

But a funny thing happened over the course of the months that I was working on this collection: America inaugurated its first would-be strongman and kleptocrat as president. I left for Paris in early January 2017, and watched from abroad as my friends, in their early thirties like me, flocked to the streets with an urgency, a sense of foreboding and helplessness, without recourse to anything other than physical bodies in public spaces, as we'd never before experienced in our lifetime. As I worked at Daoud's words of encouragement to protestors in Cairo and Tunis facing down family dynasties, the blatant exploitation of power for the benefit of personal bank accounts, and the use of humiliation as a lethal tool—this reigning wisdom that leaders could get away with whatever they pleased, without even trying to hide it—I felt a glint of recognition. That is not to suggest any sort of parallel between the political, historical, and cultural context in Egypt, Tunisia, or other North African or Middle Eastern countries and the particularisms of the United States; only to suggest that American readers may find certain familiar elements within this book that, a year or two earlier, they might have regarded as unfathomably foreign.

E.Z., Paris, October 2017

CHRONIQUES

2010

DECOLONIZE THE BODY, LANGUAGE, AND THE SEA

It is facing the sea, perhaps, that one feels the confinement of Algerian history most deeply—in the immediate taboos of the body, its liberties still missing even after the last colonists have gone. I have a vague intuition, still hazy, difficult to articulate, of an identity more vast than the controversies of the moment, overstepping the country's many colonizations—not denying them but reclaiming them as my history, too. In that moment, as I look out at the only trace of our heritage that is alive, the Mediterranean, the meaning of what it is to be Algerian becomes clear. It's not just any sea, it is this one. And in front of this sea one realizes that nothing is forcing us to experience the history of this nation simply as a story of violence that gave rise to cycles of rejection, to seasons of weapons and denials. Suddenly, in the colonial buildings, I can see that the French parenthesis was not something that came entirely from elsewhere but that it also belongs to me—to the succession of my history, and to my heritage. The buildings, the architecture, the public spaces, the churches that are still here, the synagogues that have disappeared along with the street names and the vineyards. They aren't just French—they are also mine, part of my history. Colonization, like decolonization, is an act; they are my acts, which I endured or enabled, and for which I, too, take responsibility. French colonization is part of Algerian history, and what was born of it is mine. And so, standing before

3

the Mediterranean, I retrace my steps even further, and I come up against this reality: if until now I've been unable to find the Mediterranean, it's because the other colonization, the Arab one, prevented me from finding the body. It is still the case today.

The body, my body, is the second trace of my Mediterranean and African history. The body is shared; it's the spirit that's solitary, that seeks companionship in the invisible.

Each body is experienced as two.

It's our law. And so I rediscover, I reclaim, I take pride in, I throw myself into my Ottoman period, or what's left of it. It stares us in the face in our language and our customs but, strangely, we don't see it. And after that, the same. Right up to the Roman stones where Albert Camus believed he'd found the remains of the true inhabitants of this country, when in fact those inhabitants were right next to him. Camus saw correctly, but he misunderstood. Unions are possible in this country: Tipaza is Algerian, and its Roman period is mine, too, not evidence of some external origin. Why does an ex-Egyptian get to claim to be both Muslim and Arab, without ever giving up the ruins of the pharaohs, while I'm supposed to be ashamed of my Roman ancestors, the colonial buildings, the Ottoman expressions, Andalusian cuisine, Spanish walls, Amazigh languages, olive trees, and my traditional dances? The columnist recalls his schoolbooks as one remembers an illness: a story that takes us back to Okba Ibnou Nafi, and, before him, to an empty plot of land where religious awakening and a future of fast food awaited us. Nothing about what there is in me that's Roman, Amazigh, Ottoman, Spanish, or French and Arab. Nothing about what, confronted with the Mediterranean, makes me Algerian. Why do I have to experience my history as a skin disease, or as a kind of prehistoric culpability, when it is an immense, magnificent tree, more than enough to provide me with an address?

And how did I get here? On a beach, facing the Mediterranean, forbidden access to my own body by the sick taboo of religion and by a withdrawal into false origins. If you look at an Algerian man or woman, uneasy and uncomfortable with his body, you realize that he *was* free, and that since the last colonists departed he has been unable to liberate his own body, to make it natural, to accept and rediscover, to assert through conquest and flexed muscles, to launch it into a triumphant orb. At the sea, this sea and not any other, the columnist vaguely understood that we are still sick because of this history which stole our land and our bodies. The body is not yet as Algerian as its history. There is another decolonization to achieve: that of the body. Colonization is not only a history that came from elsewhere, it's also within me. I don't have to hide my body to save it, and I don't have to hate it out of love for the unseeable. And there—in this confusion, in a kind of Camusian union, starting with beach umbrellas rather than Roman columns—the columnist understood the course of the future: to rediscover the Mediterranean, the body, and language, the real one. The three paths left by our ancestors, our real ones.

THE END OF AN UNCOMMONLY VIOLENT MONTH

Ramadan was murderous and violent, staggering in its level of violence and corruption, wholly inhuman. People stole, killed, assaulted, lashed out, lied about prices and about their souls. But they also prayed, made sure to plead before God, bankrolled soap operas like the "Knights of the Koran," circulated religious songs, and announced that Islam is ours and that everything else is against us. Even the presidential pardon, the power to free people imprisoned by the courts, was, to the exclusion of everything else (such as building a satellite, or converting to humanism, or works for the common good) only applicable to the casting candidates for "Knights of the Koran." What does it prove? One thing: Islam is ill, and Islamism is well—very well, even—because Islamism is an affliction of Islam. Just as fundamentalism is an affliction of truth, and truth is an affliction of scientific exactitude. It's the only way to explain the schizophrenia exhibited by this country and its people, and by a government that has grown mystical as its president ages. It explains the many mosques and the few bookstores, the ample donations for prayer rugs and the lack of money for clean buildings, the numerous fatwas while not a single rule is respected internally—there are plenty of people who pray, but practically none who follow the rule against smoking, even at the newspapers.

The truth is that it's not a national problem but a global one. Take the most recent Koran-burning affair. An American evangelical pastor announces that he's going to burn the Koran, the world of Allah gets mad, the rest of the world responds to this intolerance with fear or sadness. In the end, the pastor backs off and the controversy ends with no murder, no fire, no flying pages. Except it's not tolerance, or mutual respect, or dialogue, or calls from both "cultural" sides that win out. It's extremism. In the world of Allah, it reinforces the paranoia that the rest of the planet doesn't respect our religion, and that we are in a religious war, even if Obama says we aren't. Though there was no burning, there's an ambient Islamism, passive or active, that emerges triumphant, "martyrized" and therefore a martyr, proving that it is right that the West is an evil power. The same goes for the other side, with fundamentalist evangelicals, Iranian messianists, or the Israeli Orthodox; there's always a sense of wrong to avenge, a conviction that "the Muslims" are imposing themselves by force, that it's a trick, a global threat, or a war rather than just difference. This kind of spectacle by Western extremists only serves to reinforce the paranoia here, energizing Islamist recruiters. If you add to that nationalisms which are in a crisis of age and myth, presidents concerned with the firmament, the undereducated Arab world, and the increasing archaisms in the name of Allah, you end up with societies that are sick, Talibanized, murderous, and capable of a brutally violent month of hunger, all while claiming that this month is a gift from God.

According to ancient alchemists, the world is composed of four elements: earth, air, fire, and water. Those who live off the water are fishermen, and those who live off the earth are farmers. Those who live off fire are metallurgists, industrialists, or manufacturers. And those who live off the air? They are the extremists of every religion, gossips, and politicians. Not pilots, who can give the sky with just a bit of kerosene.

SEPTEMBER 20

DIALOGUE BETWEEN
AN OLD MUJAHID AND HIS PAL

"Everywhere I go, people ask me only one question. It's in the eyes of children and adults, in books, on signposts, everywhere. They don't ask my name, or what happened the day the Mountain climbed my back, or what I felt when I fired my first shot, tying myself for the rest of my life to my first corpse, my first kill. Nothing about that. No one cares anymore. All they want to ask me is this dreadful question, which doesn't even allow for a response. It's a trick question. It doesn't permit you to speak, it cuts you off and rebuffs you. It makes me wish I were back at the exact moment when I believed I had a fate, which I would now swap for a simple cup of coffee or a shrug of the shoulders. Should we have liberated this country? Today you can buy off an entire people with deliveries of frozen meat. You don't need a Constantine Plan, or even threats. Just a kind of exported de Gaulle and a few fake invoices, and it's settled. Oh, right, the question? It's simple: 'If you're a real mujahid, why aren't you dead?' Everyone seems to be waiting for me, with this question at the tip of the national tongue: Why aren't I dead? People came to accept the idea that those who fought are dead, and those who aren't dead deserted or hid out. So I'm a corpse who didn't even have the courtesy to decompose. Not only did I fail in life—even worse, I failed in death. And if I die now it won't resolve anything. I would've had to die before. What I did is unforgivable. I've felt guilt and shame, and I don't dare to meet people's gazes, not even those of the tough kids born thanks to me, while I try to explain myself by way of the painful chronology of this country and its national history. Everyone says it: 'What are you doing here? Your friends are on the other side of the painting of time. And you? Why are you still alive? Can't you see that you're a wrong note?' No, I don't see it. Or at least for a long time I didn't. I thought the roles were clear: God awaits the dead, the people await the survivors. But I was mistaken. Today I drag myself around like an insolence, a withered insult, a hymn sung through dentures. I feel practically naked in a crowd, as though I were sticking my nose into things that don't concern me—life, independence, this land. Why are you still alive? The worst is when the guy who asks is so craven that he adds insult to injury: 'How much did we give you? How much did you take?' Which is to say, how much did you take before independence, so as not to die? And how much did we give you, after independence, so you wouldn't say anything or denounce anyone? We got rid of the harkis, but we were full of resentment and history made us take on their roles, which has consumed our flesh. So I feel superfluous. I go for a walk. And I repeat to myself: it's easier to kill colonists than to kill time after they leave.

"There's nothing to do when you liberate a country except watch it go, become far away. You can listen to it tell you that you don't exist, that you can't have both eternal life and an income, both a hymn and a pension. I'm not sure what to do. Even God says that martyrs have a better fate than survivors. Is that my fault? I don't know. I'm not dead. It's not because of caution or cowardice, but maybe because death skips lines when going through its books. Even my sons seem to ask the question: Why am I still here when all my peers are waiting for me on the other side, looking for me, wondering why I'm late. I can't even hang myself or kill myself, it would be shameful to do it at my age, with my history and my past and my faith and my great-grandsons. What would they think? That I have something to atone for? No! So I'm stuck. France didn't kill me, and neither did life, nor a car, nor old age. I'm still here, and I don't have the answer. In this country, a real warrior shouldn't be older than his grandsons: he should have died at twenty-two, in 1958, leaving only a son and one photograph to keep him forever in his youth, spare him wrinkles and insults. Why am I still alive? I'm not alive. I'm stuck, turned away everywhere."

A GENERATION THAT DOESN'T
REALIZE THAT FRANCE IS IN SWEDEN

The day before yesterday, Jean-Pierre Chevènement, a French politician from another time—and maybe a future time, if he decides to run in the next presidential election—was invited to speak in Oran. He talked about Algeria according to history, about France, about both, about memories, Islam, and *laicité*. Knowing he'd been invited to a country that had turned postcolonial sensitivity into a booming business, he was polite, agreeable, generous, universalist, and pedagogical. His lecture was interesting, if a bit too controlled. But it didn't prevent the degeneration of this spectacle into a spectacle: yet again, when a French politician comes to Algeria, even as a civilian, he brings a message, recalling the best and admitting the worst, but always falling into the same trap. He's addressing an Algeria that basically no longer exists, in the name of a France that is more or less indiscernible, in the name of a relationship that is so tired and forced that it's kind of like a muscular tic or spasm. There are still Frenchmen who are nostalgic for Algeria, that's true. But even more complicated for us, there's a nostalgia for nostalgia. Meaning that there is a yearning for the time when France and Algeria were in a true bilateral communion—a stare-down that inspired the passion and bitterness of intellectuals—locked in a relation of power and mutual dependency, treating and experiencing history as a breathing body, not as a book. A time when there was Algeria, there was France, and then there was the rest of the world. And as you listen to a temporarily retired French politician speak in Algeria, what's fascinating is this gap between the tradition of devoted passion and the reality, which is no longer truly engaged with this memory, and hasn't been for a long time. What happened in the lead-up to this speech, which mixed analysis, appeal, a light mea culpa, and an avowal of a neighborliness in which the Mediterranean plays an intermediary that is older than the ancestors of each side? First, there was the *harraga*; second, Islamism, both passive and active; and also, as a general rule, there were the inhabitants of the South. In Algeria, a proposed law seeking an apology from France was as much a flashpoint as was the language of bilateralism on the other side—which is to say, not very much of one. France has been absorbed into the geography of this West, where the immigrant is headed, illegally or not; which the Islamist hates, or pretends to; and where the poor Southerner wishes to settle. Chevènement, or any of the others, always seems to be addressing the FLN generation in a country populated by a cable-TV generation and an al-Qaeda generation. Here, we want so badly to enhance a war memory that everyone understands is a trick to go back to the time when the current regime was young, beautiful, and armed, with all their teeth intact, and had meaning and true glory, and to stay there. On both sides, there is a curious kind of third nostalgia: for a postdecolonization Franco-Algerian relationship. French politicians and many French intellectuals can hardly speak of anything else, and Algerian nationalists don't want to hear about anything else.

Should we have expected anything less? No. Except that this new relationship between Algeria and the West, in which France plays only a supporting role, has not yet been deciphered; it is neither perceived as fundamental to the present nor as a prism for reading the future. France speaks a pre-1990s language, and we respond in one that is pre-1962. What has happened since 1990 is barely taken seriously, whether as a topic of discussion or a subject of study, and is excluded as a kind of minor news. It's like being stuck in the Andalusian period, when all the illegal rafts are headed toward Alicante. Despite the millions of Algerians who live there, France is a foreign country, part of a West that is either a destination or an object of grievances. It's a country that has its secularists, its Islamists, its identity and memory crises, its own problems. We can follow what this country says and try to understand, though all the preambles about times past are a little long. It might be nicer to listen to the young people who are complete strangers to it all, and are thus pleasantly interesting. There are so many French people capable of seeing contradictions or offering deep analyses who instead, when they arrive in Algeria, walk into the same pitfall: they become pilgrims despite themselves. Just as we become former combatants when we feel we have to respond. Gaullists versus FLN-ists in the rearguard of a world of satellites, *harraga*, multinational corporations, and jihadis, of the impulsions of the body and the muscles toward freedom, of money, violence, fantasies, and exclusion. "Do you want to go to France?" "Not particularly, and only if it's in Europe," is how the modern immigrant would respond. France could be in Sweden for all he cares.

GENERALIZED DEBASEMENT

In Mostaganem, one of the biggest waves of *harraga* left on the second and third days after the celebration of Aïd. There were nearly two dozen vessels, and dozens of voyagers. Most were intercepted, upon landing, by Spanish patrollers, who weren't on holiday, as we were. Others perished at sea as a result of overcrowding, their friends later recounted. Knife fights broke out among the clients during boarding, according to testimonies gathered by the columnist, and the smugglers had to let too many people on. "Up to twenty-six people per raft," one of them said. There were many deaths, and for a week the sea carried the corpses back toward the coast from which it had first taken them away. It's the kind of thing that happens in the country of shadows of the departed. Because, like in the Egypt of the pharaohs, we have one country for the living and another for the dead. You can pass from one to the other, according to myth, with a small boat and a guide. Once there, the body is embalmed, the spirit weighed and judged.

Why speak of Egypt in relation to the *harraga*? Because last week, in the ex-Egypt of the present, the Egyptians marched against Mubarak. Thousands took to the streets to denounce the expected coronation of Mubarak's son. They marched in a country where the police can rape an accused person, where they torture and kill, and Arab-style dictatorship has reached the height of cruelty and absurdity. Egyptians protested in the streets despite the batons and the state of emergency. It's something we no longer do here, no longer dare to do. How long has it been since Algerians went out in the streets to demand democracy? Twenty years. Why? For many reasons: the trauma of terrorism, and the state of emergency (the new synonym for dictatorship in third-world countries), to name two. Thousands of analyses have been offered for this mummification of Algerian society by its pharaohs. However, there is one more: so-called debasement.

Algerians were punished for the vote of the 1990s, and then beaten, scattered, and reduced to either committees or rioters, but that still doesn't explain everything. For two decades they've endured a process of degradation that has led them to conclude that they don't exist, ending in self-denigration.

Their political parties have been emptied out, their officials bought off, their public spaces shut down, their newspapers taken hostage, their national history torn apart, their means of expression privatized. We used to say "police state" to describe a government devout in surveillance and attacking liberties. Maybe it's something new now: the biography state, which hears only its own story. A state whose goal is to degrade people, in addition to monitoring them. It's pretty unbelievable that, after a great war of liberation and years of fighting for real democracy, everyone—elites, tribes, and former members of the regime—expect change only through biological expiration dates. There is a general fatigue among those who are fighting for freedom; everyone else wants the calm of a lamb. So there is a connection between the capacity for protest in your country and the number of *harraga*. Algerians don't emigrate: they escape. They do it legally when they have a visa, but also secretly, or on floats when they have no other way. Algerians flee. It's no longer our country, but the villa of someone who has indicated that he doesn't want us, despises us, and gives us food to eat only so he can look down on us while we're chewing.

OCTOBER 3

WHY I'M GOING TO BE PRESIDENT
OF THIS COUNTRY

"There's no other choice"—it's a story told to me by a friend, who heard it from Kateb Yacine. Someone had asked Kateb why he couldn't just live like everyone else, with a house, a salary, a birth certificate, and shoes handed out by the government. Why do people feel the need to fight, after the liberation, for freedom—to oppose, to say no, to denounce—even at the cost of their daily comforts, their lives, and those of their children? Why do they feel responsible for the rest of the world? The truth is that we don't feel any more responsible for the world than anyone else does; we don't have a world, not even the small piece of the world that the world owes a person. Kateb said that he, like everyone else, did want a house with a garden, a street, and trees. Except, he said, to have such things you must first have a land, with a country around it that has some sense. You can't build something on water, as the proverb goes.

This explains a little the long detour that great men take to come home. Before they start to build a home, they have to begin with a country. It's not some kind of fate, just the logic of masonry. To have a house, a tree, a good salary, a little respect in government offices, and the right to speak on television you need not just a residence but a country. What good is a home when you don't have the right to hold your wife's hand when you go for a walk outside of it, or if you can't let your children play in front of the building without worrying? What good is a garden if it doesn't span the entire country? What is a house if you can't feel free and happy when you walk through the door?

Which brings me to my story: I decided to become president of the republic sooner or later, because it's the only way to be a citizen of my country, or to even have a country, and, therefore, a home. Once elected, I will build a country at last, starting with independence, and then I will go home and labor on my land. I swear it isn't just a whim—a long reflection on my life has led me to this conclusion. I've waited for the construction work to be done by the parties, the businessmen, the administration, and the ex-generals, by elections, riots, or attacks, but my life is short and my desire vast. So I will build the country that I want for myself, instead of waiting for it. Is it even possible? Yes. I know I didn't fight in the war of liberation, and I risk ending up like Benflis. I don't have the "decision makers" behind me, and I'm an unknown born after 1962, so, essentially, never born at all. I know you need money, a party, credentials, endurance, a formidable ability to create consensus without upsetting anyone, and, finally, a life span that can outlast all the bureaucratic blockages. But I don't have a choice. What I want is a house, and, since I can't have a house in a country that doesn't exist, I will begin by building a country. I will make it modern: it will have respect for women, Algerian as the official language, the separation of mosque and laziness, and a national history that stretches back to the night of time and ends with my heartbeat. I'm not kidding: I'm running, even if I have only my forty years, my shoes, and my car. I have no choice: I have nothing to lose. I'm not going to wait for death to run and make history and live better, or for the constitution to change, or for them to decide to let me, or for the rules of the game to change. The only way to live in this country is to build it, and the only way to build it is to be president and do the bricklaying that the ex-warriors don't know how to do. I will be president because I want to have a house.

OCTOBER 4

TAKE THE DAY,

GIVE US BACK THE NIGHT

What is the national night? It's this half of the country that's lost. Since the 1990s, the night hasn't been Algerian. During this time, which isn't really time, *le pouvoir* has been content to have the police make their rounds and keep the embassies, the state residences, and the chauffeurs of late-arriving cars under surveillance. So it's not even half the country but a kind of lost space, a vague land where the laws are suspended and history retreats into prehistory. Night—the Algerian night—is frightening. People hurry home, shut themselves away. It's not a time for going out but for coming back. All Algerians have experienced the mute fear of going out at night in their own cities, which haven't belonged to them during this parenthesis. Night hasn't belonged to us since the civil war of the 1990s. We rush through it—we can't have fun, we're afraid. Women are pursued—some are snatched, surrounded, packed up, and carried off toward the mountains. Despite one rogue democratic minister and several billion dinars, *le pouvoir* has not succeeded in populating the night, making it inhabitable, opening stores and shop windows, holding soirees and concerts. Recently, a few thousand streetlights were allocated to all the villages, and they were quickly broken. Why? It's clear: we have not yet arrived at a national consensus that enables a country to let its women go out at night without their being lost. It's still a country of strong arms, of force and violence.

So billions were spent to repopulate the country during the day, but the night remains the territory of instinct and abduction.

Why talk about it? Because we've all experienced it: in the evening—when night descends and humanity descends, too—the public spaces and the gardens fill with crazies, alcoholics, glue-sniffers, random aggressors. Even the town centers, the heart of urbanism and of the cities wrested from the colonists, do not belong to us: you hear screeching, people running, a mouth that asks your name. It's frightening. *Le pouvoir* and the conservatives have succeeded in robbing Algerians of their night, and all that's left for them is the day. That's how you imprison a people.

So why this subject? Because the day before yesterday, in Oran, some people made an attempt to repatriate the night to the inhabitants of the city: Nuit Blanche was a program introduced by a cultural center and its supporters. The APC of Oran was invited to help but hedged at the last minute, saying it was because of "the new *wali* that's being initiated," and therefore because of this culture that tells us we only have to worry about the country during the day. Night is for sleeping. The list of participants in the event included mostly Lebanese cafés, a few Algerian ones, dance and musical groups, entertainers, and exhibits. Somehow a piece of the night was pulled out of the darkness and given back to the residents. It would be enough to make you dream about this city, if you didn't know the 1990s, the coups d'état, socialism, and Islamism. But it lasted only one night—actually, half of that night at most. The next day, the nocturne was returned to its ferocious owners: *le pouvoir*, the flashing lights, the mental illness, the homeless wanderers, the aggressors and the hounded women. Except for this one evening and the last days of Ramadan, the Algerian night remains a savage world, a lawless country. We could build big highways, import airplanes and Swedes, but it wouldn't make us a desirable, modern country so long as we haven't recaptured the night and given it back to Algerians.

OCTOBER 17

A MANIFESTO,
OR WHEN THE MOUTH SPITS
ON ITS OWN TONGUE

A people without the right to its own language—that can't speak it, is forced to treat it like the howl of a monkey and degrade it like a stutter—is not mute but ill. A people that doesn't speak its own tongue among itself cannot seize objects, bend reality to its will, name things, give its history a geography or vice versa. And when a people can't name things it can't reinvent them, it can't transform the cycles of seasons into wheels, or gravity into vapor. Which is to say that when a human being lives in his own country as a mute the world is deaf to him. Because when a people treats its own language as a dialect, it treats itself like a secondary character in a story that it cedes to someone else. Through language we surrender, and it is in language that identity finds a refuge when it no longer has land. That's how it is: all the great histories of small peoples started with language: it's what allows you to possess the center of the world in your palm, to lift up crowds, to restore confidence and birth and to take ownership of the cosmos. Even Adam, the founding father, started by naming things, before having children. And the day when the Algerian language is no longer treated as a compendium of historical accidents, or an amalgamation of loans and deformities—the day when we accept the truth that a people without a tongue is not mute but blind, and that we will never be anything on our land with-out our language—on that day we will finally arrive in the world. We will wake up and begin to understand things, identify things that for a long time have surrounded us like useless air. The day when books, songs, the TV news, our politicians' speeches, and our posters and our papers are in Algerian is the day we will finally be Algerian and will finally begin to build the country, beginning with the essential: giving our own nouns and verbs to our own land.

Of course that will take a century, not just a handful of years: the colonizations were harsh—the most violent were those that con-vinced us we don't exist without the colonizers and their beliefs. We are in our own Middle Ages right now, and it will end by fin-ishing off itself. One day, we will speak Algerian in Algeria, and we will finally be cured of this feeling of not being in our own home, of living in a kind of second-class country, of not being able to touch objects, or own them, or transform them. We will be cured of failure and inferiority and self-denial. It's what the Arabs did fourteen cen-turies ago, when they awoke: they gave themselves a language and made it sacred. As the Romans did before them, and the Turks most recently. What, in fact, is a language? It's wrong to think it's some-thing that connects the mouth to the ear, or a man to his neighbor. Language is what connects a nation to its universe—to the universe. Man invented language to create order in his world, to populate it, to allay a primitive fear, and to remember, thereby softening death with memory. You take away a man's memory, his courage, order, and strength when you say that his language is a dialect or slang. You kill a nationality when you give it subtitles.

The Algerian language today is poor, weak, despised, and dimin-ished. We killed its poets, threw away its first dictionaries, emptied its words and disfigured the names given to cities and towns. It is lacking power and recognition, but one day it will begin to flourish. Is it an impoverished language? Yes: give it the world, and it will name and unname things and beings one by one. Algeria will awaken the day it cuts ties with the dead languages and realizes that there is nothing shameful in being itself. Western countries left the Middle Ages and woke up to the direction of history the day they understood that they could speak their own language instead of the Latin of the church, and that they could do so without destroying the church, the heavens, the holy, and the past. What will be destroyed is the profit that each "sacred" language promises to those who use it, those who adhere to divinity by saying that it speaks their language, and those who are paid to teach a dead language. The end of Latin in Europe was not easy—it happened only through audacity and violence. The church was rich with alms as insurance for its sacred language, and excluded the proletariat by reducing them to inaudible serfs, turning voices into a mutter, memory into a rumor, speech into a dialect. We still have all that, we know it and we live it: in Algeria, the clergymen of the "authentic" culture and elite ideology, of the *khassa*, prescribe a dead language while imposing on us the false idea that our own language is worthless. And thus that we are too, and so is everything that we do.

Malek Haddad was right to be unhappy living between two languages, except that he cheated on his wife while accusing his mistress: his war booty was French, certainly, but his true, native language was not classical Arabic, but Algerian. It was on the tip of his tongue, but he was blind, because he was deaf.

IDLE VARIATIONS
ON THE MYTH OF SISYPHUS

A man named Sisyphus, who betrayed his deepest instincts, the laws of nature, and the Greek gods (their ancient analogues), was condemned to push an enormous boulder up a hill; it would roll back down as soon as it reached the top. Then he would do it again and again, and it would never end—not even when he died, because punishment continues after death.

Albert Camus made the story into a more modern myth and an illustration of the absurdity of the human condition, whose sole consolation is the dignity of effort. Man is man, and the boulder is his universe: he is condemned to meaninglessness for as long as possible in a world without sense. It's a fascinating illustration that offers different variations on the abyss.

You could imagine, for example, a Sisyphus who believes: he refuses to lug the boulder and instead sculpts it into a likeness of God, then kneels before it to beg God to make the stone roll itself, without effort, calmly and miraculously defying gravity. You could also imagine Sisyphus refusing, and sitting down at the top of the hill waiting for someone to pass by, as the third world has done since decolonization. Or the opposite: he sits on top of the hill, colonizes a country, takes its men, and forces them to push the boulder in his place, as the West did. Or you could imagine the enormous stone rolling over Sisyphus, killing him without making him die, running over him again and again while he tries to get up, as is the case of those who live poor and mean in dirty countries without rights or democracy. Finally you can imagine a more intelligent Sisyphus: he tries to flatten the hill rather than push the boulder forever. That's the West's solution, and the source of its technological development, from the ax to the satellite. You can also find a genre of Sisyphus with a suicide vest, who, in the name of Allah or Jehovah or Jesus the Warrior, blows up the boulder along with himself. As the boulder embodies pain, one cannot change one's condition except by refusing it and putting an end to it: a kind of ready-made TNT Buddhism.

There is an even sicker Sisyphus: the type who questions himself endlessly about the weight of the rock, the diameter of the hill, and the nature of gravity. Is it the boulder's mass or the hill's slope that matters? Where does the boulder come from, and where does the hill lead? A Sisyphean politician would stand at the summit and give a speech to the enormous boulder, seeking to mobilize it with words or convince it to roll into the palm of his hand.

A mystery: what does Sisyphus do when he's asleep? Does he find himself, beneath his eyelids, with a different boulder and a different hill? Maybe the gods saw to it to fill in the gap of sleep, like a hallucinogenic herb.

Sleep is not a solution to absurdity—it's a revitalization of the human condition without muscle or progress. From it come the clearest realizations about silly but contemptuous questions: you don't push a boulder any faster or slower with a beard. You can stall it for a while with a book, give yourself time to think. You can't do much better with a rope: you're alone in the universe. With a machine, the boulder becomes bigger and the hill becomes steeper. Even geology is futile: the stone can be studied but that doesn't make it easier to move.

Last question: why did the myth make Sisyphus a man, and a solitary one? Because each person is him. Sisyphus's rock is cleanliness or death or birth or love (the essentials): you can only experience it alone, and sometimes you don't come back. Nothing replaces actually carrying the boulder: not sacred texts, or preachers, or mass ideologies, or avoidance. The only things that can help man's decisions are faith, a sense of dignity, and the challenge of filling the void or defying solitude by singing, or with community.

MOKRI, LIEBERMAN, AND
THE PALESTINIAN SANDWICH

Should we talk about it? Yes—it's a moral obligation to bear witness to history. The subject: the Social Movement for Peace deputy Abderrazak Mokri's declarations, aired on Channel 3 last week, about what's happening in Western Sahara. When asked about the Islamists' tepidness, if not silence, on the events at Laayoune, he came up with the most tragic response, heavy with meaning. He didn't say that it was a matter of decolonization, or a crisis concerning Morocco and the Polisario Front, or even that we should prioritize Algeria's interests ahead of any form of engagement. Angry with the Channel 3 journalist for stressing that the Islamists supported Palestine but not the Sahrawi Arab Democratic Republic, he said simply, "We shouldn't put the Saharan question and the Palestinian question on the same plane, because they are two different things. The Palestinian conflict is first and foremost a religious one. The Arab-Muslim nations cannot ignore this. They must defend and support the Palestinian people." We should note that rarely have the Islamists so obviously admitted to the way they use the Palestinian question—for religious and propaganda purposes. In the same way that the Palestinians were a cause for the Arab nationalist regimes in the 1970s, they are now caught in the trap of Islamist propaganda on both sides, Sunni and Shiite: Ahmedinejad promises to liberate Jerusalem, just as Saddam and Zawahiri and bin Laden did.

Other colonizations don't concern the Islamists. They know that the Palestinian question, emotional and passionate, is a booming business. But the simultaneous use of the "religious" offer of Islamism and of the Palestine issue is rarely confessed to; there must be an impulse, a certain loss of control, for an Islamist to admit that his motivation isn't the human being, the Palestinian, colonization, or injustice—it's the Palestinian "cause." Which is to say not Palestinians or Palestine, because the difference between them is that between a living being and an idea, the goods and the drama. So one arrives at the conclusion that there is no difference between an Arab or Algerian Islamist and Avigdor Lieberman and the messianic ambitions of the racist Israel Beytenou party: one side wants Palestine in the name of Allah, the other wants it in the name of Yehovah. Both insist on the "religious significance" of the conflict, imbue "the cause" with devout emotion, and work to develop the "holy war" dimension that sidesteps evidence of the problems of colonization and decolonization. If you take this religious currency away from both sides, they have nothing more to sell or offer. The Algerian Islamists, like their tutors in the rest of the Muslim world, understand that Palestine is one of the major reasons for their survival, and they have succeeded in monopolizing it and making it into a registered trademark. This explains the anger of Deputy Mokri: it's that of a merchant who has been asked to give up his principal product. Irritated, trapped in the posturing of permanent and renewable compromise, the Arab regimes ended up entrusting this asset to the Islamists, who invest it with noise, media attention, martyrs, by-products, and party logos. It would mean little to the Islamists if the rest of Africa were to revert back into colonization, if the world were to burn, if Mandela were put back in prison or the last Indians exterminated. Their cause is the Palestinian cause, not humanity. Humanism was never part of Islamism, and the inverse is true, too.

Mokri's reaction is important: it's that of an era, a more insidious business and negationism that have taken over. We need to point this out, draw tireless attention to it, for our own conscience and for the rest of the world, which already confuses Palestine and the war against the mullahs. Palestine has been done a disservice by being labeled the "Arab" cause, and even more so by being transformed into a religious one. Both prevent it from being a human cause.

QATAR, OR HOW TO SUCCEED AS A COUNTRY BY TRANSFORMING INTO A BUSINESS

Qatar has just won its bid to host the 2022 World Cup. This has brought immense joy to Qatar and elsewhere. Some people see it as an Arab victory; others, as the triumph of an Arab and Muslim country; and still others see a rich country's feat. So it depends what you expect from the world—revenge, proof, or recognition— but that's perhaps not where the heart of the matter lies. If you saw the explosions of delight in this country on TV, and the big, proud smiles of the royal couple, you could end up feeling a kind of secret jealousy and sadness. Here is a country like ours—not part of anything, but with a supply of natural gas that has succeeded in becoming the center of the world despite having the surface area of one Algerian province. Why? There are many reasons. Let's put aside the analyses saying that it's because of international lobbying, the American military bases there, or friendly relations with Israel, as well as those that reduce it to a money issue. Let's start at the beginning. Qatar is a small country that barely even has a national history—something like a million and a half martyrs, that's all. It's so small it can't even allow itself the vanity of presenting itself as the best example of twentieth-century decolonization. It has natural gas, but not as a sickness. Like us, it's been governed for years by an old-timer who didn't know how to use a keyboard until his son put one in his room and suggested that he not confuse his own age with the country's.

The emir of Qatar succeeded, first of all, in creating an image, and a media empire, with *Al-Jazeera*, which gave this country of 11,427 square kilometers the surface area of the entire planet. The *Al-Jazeera* revolution is undeniable. You can say what you want about the network—about its reach, its deceitful games, and its manipulations—but its owners understood the mechanisms of modern times: the empire of images—their impact, industry, and profit. Qatar exported an image of a country where people can speak, where they take responsibility for international relationships—even with Israel—without hypocrisy, where the debates are relevant and the royalty is not at all ridiculous, where religious freedom is not just a hunt for quick satisfaction, where women's rights are the most respected in the region. The *Al-Jazeera* revolution ended up marring the rest of the Arab world even further by way of contrast, exposing its medieval calendar.

The monarchy thus succeeded in creating, first and foremost, a so-called Qatari dream, even for Arab intellectuals and their sellers. The "Qatari way of life" is both a myth and an image. Even with the world's critics at its heels, the country has a positive image, being known for understanding how to use its resources to further the needs of its national brainpower rather than its army, its militias, plunderers, or for electoral frauds. In this way, things appear with clarity: natural gas is not a scourge, the monarchy is not a fake republic, free expression is an industry, not a caricature of a ban, the skyscrapers represent an urbanism that seeks the sky, not displacement, and the economy is astonishingly modern.

The truth is that Qatar understood an essential reality: for a country to succeed, it has to rally around an international enterprise; an enterprise with an image, a logo, advertising campaigns, media channels, unique packaging, free initiative, transparency in accounting, a delegation of power and speed in fulfilling orders. It's a company-state (like Taiwan, Japan, and South Korea) that, once again, by contrast, relegates the other Arab states to museums of monstrosities, managed like tribes or barracks, where the kings and the presidents worry primarily about asserting their ownership rather than having a healthy balance sheet.

DECEMBER 6

WIKILEAKS: THE SOUNDTRACK
OF LOCAL REGIMES

It's become a morning ritual: get up not to make sure the country's cities and cars are whirring but to see if WikiLeaks has said anything new about us. A little something that explains mysterious phrases, like "the president discussed affairs of common interest with the special envoy from...," or confirms a suspicion, or provides sound for the famous silent sequences that ENTV shows when a foreign chief is received in our presidential palace. There is little that hasn't been said about the enigma of WikiLeaks, but we haven't said enough about the pleasures of the texts it obtained. What you discover reading them isn't really about America's diplomacy or its vision of the world. It's about something else: it shows how power, ours and that of many Arab regimes, is a biological being—with claws, ears, and fur that expands or contracts depending on its mood; with desires and the disposition of a daughter-in-law in thrall to an alpha male; with caprices when confronted with jewelry or the opposition of the international harem. This is the true pleasure of WikiLeaks for people like us, in countries where the media are domesticated goats, and PR is the regime's personal secretary. The border between Algeria and Morocco? It's closed because Bouteflika can't stand the whims of Mohammed VI, who was only a child when he, Bouteflika, was already a star of nonalignment diplomacy. Western Sahara? Algeria will never allow the president of the

Sahrawi Arab Democratic Republic to fire a shot. Franco-Algerian relations? It's always a story of wheat and the local *dey*. So we the people, along with our newspapers and our analyses, take pity on ourselves for the vast abundance of articles and keyboards that consider these questions with a thousand brains, when all of it can be reduced just to these mundane realities. Through WikiLeaks, we discover the comic element of the Saharan president's threats to return to violence, or the humor in an exchange of greetings between a president and a king who hate each other. We begin to daydream about all the blah-blah-blah that was served up to us for decades about what our regime was up to, about what they think and what they say. And so we get carried away and start to fantasize about a domestic WikiLeaks—an Algerian Web site that tells us what's happening in Algiers, what the creators of presidents think of their current tenant, their ideas about UFOs, khalifa, Abane, Boudiaf, riots, and Saadane.

There is a kind of Algerian WikiLeaks domain that's not yet public. The former oil minister Khelil's laughing response to a question about the possibility of prosecution revealed that he had read some of these secret archives. When the boss of the Social Movement for Peace mentioned "the decision makers" and then retracted his statement like a dull blade, it showed that his name was somewhere in the archive. Could an audacious Algerian ever give out all the country's dirty laundry to the secondhand shops? Unlikely: the Internet remains a minor network compared to the mosques and the *kasmas*, and *le pouvoir* has always known how to keep control over the quotas of the illiterate, the educated, the intellectuals, the Web surfers, and the media. For a Wikileaks.dz, there are a few homemade formulas: call a journalist in the press service, distribute photocopied letters of denunciation of a regional administrator around his region in order to depose him, launch rumors, or give a targeted interview. When Adami and Betchine pelted Zeroual, who was subsequently dismissed, it was a kind of WikiLeaks before WikiLeaks. The methods have been updated a bit since then.

So WikiLeaks can only be international, like any possibility of change—in regime, in democratization, in the price of oil, in opposition, or in pressure. For now, WikiLeaks hasn't said anything that could change the *dey* or the *bey*, but it has given pundits a taste of reverie. Real or fake, manipulative or not, it doesn't matter: when it comes down to it, the Arab regimes are entertaining!

AN AMERICAN AMBASSADOR'S
GUIDE TO ALGERIA

Among the most striking phrases in the debris of the WikiLeaks explosion was one used by our American ambassador to describe Algeria: "An unhappy country." Not a poor country, not just your standard dictatorship, or a country at war, or even simply a country, period. No: an unhappy country. Which is to say a sad country suffering at its own hand and lacking in self-love, where the people, the land, and the walls constitute only half of a thing they've never really had, and for which they've run out of hope, confined and immobile in their own hearts. In the columnist's mind, it is the shortest and most poignant biography of a nation. The reasons? We know all of them. One analyst summed up the effect of WikiLeaks perfectly when he wrote that the site reveals nothing but confirms almost everything.

But to return to the American ambassador's telegram about Algeria being its own widow: the reasons are admirably summarized.

(1) The distance between the land and those who walk on it. You could say that people here pay attention, all day every day, to votes, the constitution, mandates, and dissidence, while nothing is said about the country, the populace, the riots—in other words, nothing is said about what's real. Everyone wants Algiers, and no one wants to bother with the rest of Algeria.

(2) The pipeline mentality: the only economic policy we've known is one of spending, cement, and profitability. Capitalism is uncontrollable, but socialism is even more statist. The projects come to nothing, because the center of economic thinking is not the company but the budget. Wealth isn't created—it's distributed by an overly bureaucratic network of administrations with a deep pathology of distrust, the birth mother of excessive centralization. Oil isn't a form of wealth, but pocket money.

(3) Systematic hesitation: everyone who visits Algeria discovers at least one thing about it: this country doesn't know what it wants. We had a particular kind of socialism, then socialized capitalism, then a controlled market economy, then the neosocialism of national sovereignty. There is a "lack of vision at the top," the American ambassador wrote, explaining, "Bouteflika and his team don't know whether they want Algeria to integrate into the world market economy, or if they should persist in the social contract of the 1960s and 70s."

(4) Mistrust: the basis of the political and social system in this country, an Algerian businessman told the columnist, is "the psychology of mistrust," and not "win-win consensus." The American ambassador can only see this insofar as it weighs on the famous security cooperation between his country and ours. He does, however, grasp one of the most troubling facets of Algerian psychology: paranoia, the younger sister of independence, acquired through armed battle and the clandestine *maquis*. According to the press, the American ambassador describes Algerian intelligence services as "prickly and paranoid," and "not in a hurry to cooperate with the FBI" in the fight against terrorist networks.

(5) The lag time between the country and those who govern it with nostalgia and undereducation: the ambassador remarked, pertinently, that "Bouteflika is his own minister for the exterior, and his political conception of the region hasn't changed since the 1970s." Note the year: 1970. It's when the country was young and beautiful, when the minister for foreign affairs was rich, well regarded, without

wrinkles, and apt at dancing between the Eastern and Western blocs in the name of nonalignment. That date, 1970, explains everything: why the country is stuck, and why everyone wants to go back to that time.

So how do you survive in an unhappy country like ours? What should you do? How do you walk on the moon? The American ambassador doesn't have an answer. He isn't paid for that, it's not his role. Here's the only good news he has to offer, according to his "secret" telegram to the American secretary of state, who was planning a visit to Algiers at the time: "During your visit, we are expecting a teachers' strike. School closures will ease your movement, thanks to more fluid traffic, Inshallah." This seems to reveal the innermost fantasy of the Algerian regime: the country is inhabitable only when it's empty.

ANGEL ASSANGE

It's an easy verbal trick: when you don't have a subject, you turn back to the verb. What should I talk about today? Angel Assange. The prophet of a new world in the form of a glass house and a global keyboard. Is that simplistic? Yes, but fabulously so. People everywhere dream a little of seeing Assange descend from the sky, or dream that the two Assanges who exist in every living being will make the secret dossier of every other living being public. But Assange chose five newspapers in the West and not a single one from the third world, which is the principal source of this digital deluge. Why? Familiarity, culture, or perhaps a certainty that Western media are less parasitic and opaque than those in Arab and Muslim countries. So here, on the planet of Allah, no one says or does anything to save this man or to denounce what Western politicians have in store for him. And yet he's done more than bin Laden without killing a soul. He has announced a final judgment, the end of an era, exposed the neocolonial reality of commerce and of monarchist nationalist independence. Mowed down by a media Tora Bora, hunted, condemned, and dirtied, Assange aroused no pity from the Arab world that owes him so many new convictions and evidence of murder.

There has been no show of support for this man in the Arab capitals, no prayers for his liberation alongside those for the liberation of Palestine, no prayer for him in the mosques, no show of thanks from the last stragglers of the pan-Arab left. The man is alone, and he barely exists in the so-called Arab world. Why? The Arab world is divided: when it isn't the kept wife of a dictator or a crowd of people with their heads bent like sinners it's a voyeur. An exercise in modernity for people who see themselves disappearing into sacks of grain and oil pipelines. So Assange didn't do anything for us? In the immediate sense, no. Because we are myopic and well trained, and we watch his succession of revelations when the main point is right beneath our noses: Assange himself. That is, his actions, his gestures, his jests, his philosophy of uncompromising transparency, and its consequences. One could invent a myth for future generations using these dream fragments. Except that, as they say, when you reveal to fatalistic people that the world is unjust, it doesn't change their reality, only the volume of their whining on the sound scale of history.

In the monotheistic traditions, there were prophets who lived through the same history and then ended by turning to the great beyond, rather than the earthly kingdom and its heavy souls. Gutenberg invented (or reinvented) the printing press around 1450, but it wasn't until the beginning of the twentieth century that Muslim clergy authorized printing the Koran on paper. The delay? Almost five centuries. That's how long you have to wait between a revelation and its first imprints. And yet Assange may be the angel of a revelation on the order of divine enlightenment.

THE FAMILY ACCOUNT BOOK
AS CONSTITUTION

It's terrible, this story about Arafat's wife in Tunisia, revealed in an American cable in the latest WikiLeaks dump. Even if we can't know for sure that the story is true, we can at least confirm that it's plausible. Think about it: the wife of the last leader of a so-called pan-Arab cause, an icon for nationalisms and local regimes, was expelled from Tunisia and lost her Tunisian nationality because of the wife of Ben Ali, the neighboring dictator. The cause? There are two versions. First, a power struggle, regarding an investment in this country, between the woman who supposedly rules over Tunisia as though it were her kitchen or her hair appointment, and Arafat's wife. As a result, Suha Arafat loses her nationality, her property, her belongings, and her home, and is expelled, just as her husband was, from everywhere and by everyone, first and foremost by his "brothers." The second version is more richly layered: one of Ben Ali's nieces, an eighteen-year-old, was to wed a sixty-one-year-old emir from the Gulf, who was already married to a relative of the queen of Jordan. According to this version, Arafat's wife alerted the Jordanian queen, and Ben Ali's wife got upset and took revenge. It's a kind of pathetic pan-Arab sitcom, where the countries and the kingdoms serve as set pieces. Is it true? Possibly. It's believable, the type of story where the states and the people are dishes and dish towels, mixing together an eighteen-year-old virgin, a jealous wife, and weddings and hatreds, which are the real state secrets over here. WikiLeaks just delivered one episode.

But that's not the most interesting part. What's worth retaining from all this is a new law that's been governing the Arab dictatorships for the past ten or twenty years. These days, each dictator is mirrored by a kind of second dictatorship, one that's more intimate and more violent: that of the wife or the second-oldest son or the brother. Historically, when a dictatorship ages it becomes a family affair, including a wife and a mistress. In Tunisia's case, this has been taken to an absurd extreme. It's painful to imagine the best of our Tunisian brothers seeing themselves presented to the world in this way, dressed up like ten million abused dolls by one woman who consumes all their daily bread. And if that's a caricature it means that other Arab countries are the norm. In a kind of curious revenge on twentieth-century geopolitical destinies, the Arab republics have turned into monarchical dynasties in precisely the places where the Arab monarchies have attempted reforms toward controlled republican democratization. Between age, illness, and the greed of successors, the old dictators serve merely as a label on vicious family holdings, because they are constrained neither by appearance nor by international pressure, not by political morals or even the obligations of image. Nothing. Alongside these new forms of governance, the shadow governments of the secret service and the lobbyists are an outdated joke. The family account books have replaced the constitution, theft has taken the place of infiltration, hair-pulling has replaced the spy imbroglios of the old days. You don't take power by force in the barracks but through hair salons, businessmen who lend their names, company registries, monopolies on imports, and a regular percentage on large contracts. These are platter governments, or slipper governments, or, even better, genetic governments.

2011

I DREAM OF BEING TUNISIAN

Ah, to be Tunisian today! Because really it's the only way to feel Algerian. The columnist generally avoids writing in the first person, but today I'm going to do it. I've often dreamt of this moment. Of turning on the TV and seeing the current president sputtering excuses, seeking compromise like a mouse caught in the jaws of a dinosaur, suggesting freedom of the press, of the Internet, of assembly, and of speech—access, in other words, to our own country. To see him abandoning his wife and his corrupt inner circle, throwing his favorite interior minister out the window. To hear the president say over and over again, "I've understood you, I was mistaken, I've misled you." (Oh, the Gaullist sound of it!) To see the "Zinochet" (a Tunisian Pinochet) of every Arab country explain that he will not run in the next election—not him, nor his brother, nor wife, nor brother-in-law, nor his prime minister—all the while organizing a private jet to take him to hide out in the Emirates, just in case. Yes, I've dreamt of it: to see the entire country put on their shoes, go out in the morning, and head toward the capital to demand that it choose one beloved, and one only—either the Zinochet of the moment or the people forever. Because what's happening in Tunisia is making the entire Arab world dream. Yesterday, surely, the Forty Thief-Dictators of the Arab world (if you count the kings, the presidents, their wives, their sons, and their brothers) didn't sleep well; they spent the night watching the streets through palace windows, making calls, jumping at the slightest sound in the kitchen. A people has risen up, a Zinochet has apologized, and there may be a domino effect. Because although some have tried to reduce the Tunisians to their intestines, semolina, and sugar, they are all of us—Algerians, Moroccans, Libyans, Jordanians, Egyptians. We've all been handed the same lot, the same dictator and his same sons and relatives, the same speeches, the same police. The Tunisians, this people that we've reduced to our memories of characters in the Inspector Tahar films and a neighbor who steals our fruit, have, after decades of submission, shown that dictatorships don't win. Even if he lasts two centuries, a Zinochet needs an army to stay in power. An incident, a simple slap to the people can wake them up. Which is to say, there's only one way to change a country: it must take itself back. Fully. With muscle and mobilization, death and sacrifice. And so at home in my streets, with my country at my back, I dream of being Tunisian, of facing the Forty Thieves—surrounding them and making them lower prices, then their eyes, their heads, and their arms, and to hear them say they'll leave, will give the country back to its martyrs, and let me and my children live here, even if I have to eat my shoes for dinner, or swallow my ancestors to restore my courage. I dream of it. It's the best offer to come out of Tunisia in decades: a five-star revolt, protests and batons included, for seven days and one night. At the end, you get a Zinochet paper doll. Yes, here in Algeria I dream of being Tunisian!

STANDARD FORMULA

FOR AN ARAB DICTATORSHIP

Arab dictatorships have become an intolerable routine: again and again you get all the same characters. First, a president who came to power militarily, maintained it by election fraud, and who, the older he gets, needs a higher and higher percentage of yes votes to satisfy his empty caprices. The dictator is generally older than sixty-five, presents himself as heir to some Father of the Nation figure who's been dead for a long time, and has an elder son who has been promised power, or a wife who already possesses it, or a brother who maintains half of it. In this cast you'll also find the famous interior minister, who, from the Gulf to the Sea, always repeats the same phrase, one of total nonsense. Known for supporting the unsupportable, he recites laughable statistics after each election, and explains that the protestors are delinquents or that nothing can destabilize the state, which is to say, him, his master, and their few allies. Within this established order you'll also find a "majority" party, which is the trendy way of saying only party. This party is managed, maintained, and muscularly propped up by a team of people who are generally of the same age as the president, and say idiotic things about the nation, reform, loyalty, and the past, while the government uses them like a private club of political house-maids. This structure is consolidated with subservient unions that steal money and contributions and put out fake competitors to the president. They serve multiple roles and are tolerated for the color they provide. There is also, under the aide-de-camp, an army, whose members are indoctrinated by the cult of stability, and are often implicated in the national gluttony.

Le pouvoir also, typically, counts several newspapers among its assets; with the media under its heel and a stranglehold on strategic markets, it can guarantee the West's collaboration. In this pan-Arab blueprint, the dictator himself is usually minister of defense (you can't steal from a thief), and his son, his wife, or his brother takes care of the business community and the employers, who are weak or complicit. When demonstrations break out, or opposition parties are born, the dictator keeps quiet, the better to highlight his own sovereignty, which doesn't deign to get into the little intestinal details of the country. The interior minister sends the police to beat them or ban them, explaining that they're just delinquents; a communication from al-Qaeda is made public, along with the dismantling of a jihadist cell, to get the message across to the West. And then the people are divided in two: half will receive more semolina, the other half more pummeling from police batons. This is what's been happening, from Morocco to Yemen, for ten years, twenty years, thirty years. It doesn't change, even if it's indecent, laughable, murderous, funny. Even if it's a ruler's final moments. Even if the people are at the palace doors, and they curse the dictator every time he appears in public. Because the dictator, after so many years, has finally said to himself that if the people have tolerated him for this long without saying anything, it's because there is no "people," and just as his interior minister says, nothing can really happen.

So what's the conclusion? There's a joke circulating on the Internet, which in its biting humor says something about the sad reality: when God sent the angel Azrael to Mubarak to gather what was left of his soul, the angel asked him, "Aren't you going to say goodbye to your people?" Mubarak responded, "What! Are the people are going somewhere?" The joke can be easily applied to any of the other twenty-one dictators of the Arab League.

WHERE DO THESE MONSTERS COME FROM?

How do you rip a dictator out of the land, how do you tear away the country that he has gripped in his jaws? Ben Ali's pathetic escape has made it clear that Tunisia is small fry compared to what's happening in Egypt. There the local dictator is prepared to do the worst: murder and divide a people in order to plunge it into civil war, then intervene as mediator, release dogs and delinquents into the crowd, make the confrontation go on and on to wear out the protestors, lie, reform the government by changing out the Hadj Moussa figures, etc. Mubarak has tried, and done, everything against his people, from F16s to media stunts.

The goal: to keep the country his, his sons', and his wife's. To consume it, alone and according to his desires. Which is to say that a dictatorship sometimes has deep roots, vast means, and a private conviction that the country is a property, the protestors illegitimate occupants who want to take over the house. Listening to Mubarak say the day before yesterday that he'd never wanted power, nor the presidency, and that he didn't want to run in the next presidential election, is a cosmic assault of words and lies. These simple phrases reveal just how little esteem these dictators have for their cattle, to the point that in official speech they suggest that the land has attached itself to them, begs them to fertilize it with their enlightened vision. It's absurd, unthinkable, incredible. What world do these people live in? How do they dare steal from us, all the while telling us it belongs to us, when in fact everything is in their pockets? As people with money and chateaux in Europe, double nationalities stashed in drawers, militias at their fingertips, and billions of dollars in their grasp, do they really dare tell us that they've sacrificed their lives for the country and are only here to serve us at our will? How have we arrived in an era in which, for an Arab country, the only way to change presidents is with a million demonstrators, hundreds of deaths, and billions in economic losses? Where do these monsters, whom you can get rid of only by tearing off a piece of your own skin, come from? Saying no, telling them to get lost—apparently it's not enough.

The dictators are organizing a resistance, too: they are also stuck—between the palace and the jet. They've learned a lesson from Tunisia, and the Fathers of the Nation do not wish to find themselves chased out of their countries and in heaven without kerosene, their bank accounts emptied by former friends in the West. They want what Mubarak wants: time to secure their retirement and their children, put their fifty-five-billion-dollar fortune somewhere safe, and, before leaving, make the country burn, as revenge. The Forty Thieves' Club is going to play all its cards in the coming months. So will the people. No protests, no end to the state of emergency, no democracy, no change—this is Algeria's off-the-cuff response, in a country that's been privatized by and is dependent on force. It's a sad state of affairs when Algerians can't march in their own country—except on water, or in their sleep!

FEBRUARY 9

COUNTERREVOLUTIONARY METHODS

How do you stop a revolution? Here are several well-established methods:

(1) Direct police repression: a method that dates back to the invention of the baton. It also, unfortunately, has a tipping point: ten suppressed rebellions can provoke fear; eleven can provoke rage, martyrdom, vengeance, and widespread revolt. Exercise with caution. The baton is more effective when wielded as a threat, rather than when actually striking.

(2) Criminalization: accuse the revolutionaries of being rioters, terrorists, Islamists. To strike fear into fearful people, both in the West and inside the country. "It's not the people, only a few dozen individuals."

(3) Counterprotests: for, against, anti. To highlight for the West that this is not the people who are rising up, but merely a fraction of them. Mubarak did it. In Algeria, "spontaneous" counterprotests are already being planned for February 12.

(4) Oedipal guilt: the revolutionaries are presented as ingrates before the benevolent Father of the Nation, who "built roads, provided housing, handed out grain, and chased out the colonists." The revolutionaries are infantilized, made out to be children who are manipulated by foreign powers that seek to destroy and take over the country.

(5) Cover-up: the dictator "is" the country, the nation, the state. "Why are these people attacking the country?" say the dictator and

his staff, who are working to speed up the repression. The revolutionaries answer: "We are the country. You are the power."

(6) Corruption: in record time, they pay the delayed salaries, the pensions, they register the unemployed, hand out empty housing, stop revoking drivers' permits, increase public communications of elected officials, and call upon "civil society" to engage in dialogue.

(7) International manipulation: an al-Qaeda cell that has been threatening Europe is conveniently dismantled, a bearded chief is arrested, other bearded men are filmed in the streets and among the protestors, with the explanation: it's either us or the terrorists.

(8) Displacement: the revolutionaries want to see the end of the dictator and his circle? The dictator makes his own offer: a change of government and ministers, a purge, an investigation into corruption. The dictator instates himself in the transcendent role of arbiter, above the fray: it's a crisis between the government and its opponents. "I can be the judge and repair things because I love the people and the people love me."

(9) Breakdown: "What do these young people want?" the official propaganda demands. "We can't have dialogue with them, because they don't have any representatives." The system responds obliquely: by revising an article in the constitution, or organizing dialogue, offering proposals, etc. The goal is to gain time and cause fatigue.

(10) Banalization: the regime forcefully restores normal life. The banks reopen, there's traffic in the streets, fish and bread. The goal is to break the momentum and confine it to one public plaza, then to one bench, then one foot, then a toe.

(11) Dialogue: with whom? With fake parties, which the system has maintained for decades. In reality the dictatorship talks with itself, in a discussion with its other face. The street, the people, the revolution are excluded. Pluralism is only possible within the framework of a single pluralist party.

(12) Cosmetic assimilation: at the end of all these different efforts is an attempt to integrate. "Yes, these young people are heroes who

are altering the history of this country." Television propaganda gets involved, inviting the youths on air, saluting them like the national heroes of a new jump-start for the country that doesn't target anyone in particular, only the future. They erase the "Get Lost!" slogans, and from inside their effusive exclamations of "What courage!" they kiss the activists, listen to them transform their stories into an epic that has been emptied of any political demands. They say the country will come out of this stronger and more unified. Against what? It doesn't matter.

Can all this succeed? Yes, sort of, for a while. But as a general rule, dictators fall. They always fall, and they never change.

THE WORKER'S CHOICE,
THE HERO'S BET

A country is a land plus a myth. A national dream with shoes. The columnist spent the night channel-surfing on Egyptian and Tunisian TV. The takeaway is painful: these countries may be experiencing fear, disorder, the messiness of rebirth, and anarchy, but they have one thing in common—they dream. People there have revived anthems to be nontoxic, hymns, the freedom to speak and shout, and enthusiasm. There's a pile-up at the door to tomorrow. That's the big difference between them and us: the fear of chaos in Algeria has led to submission in everyday life. It's a choice. An Algerian proverb tells us that the fortune of the fearful is slim, but that doesn't seem to bother most people here. Everyone knows that in the end the future has a price. We can pay it now, and see our children live freer and better than us, or we can do nothing, and watch our children live the same flat but secure life that we have. Faced with the possibility of revolution, Algerians react with the miserable lucidity of an employee deferring to his boss at a private company; everyone knows that smugglers are interesting and employees make for boring conversation partners. On the scale of transgression and maturity, we are far from the spirit of 1954, 1962, and October 1988: the glint of fire ended as embers in the hearth.

Of course we shouldn't judge: there are people, like the Swiss during the Third Reich, who are able to hold on to their pennies and their neutrality. But that arrangement is a tepid one, not very sweet, lacking in flavor, and also without risk. The disillusioned arrive at this hard reality. And that's what makes renewed countries like Tunisia and Egypt brilliant, with a taste for risk: the possibility of enchanting the world, with a mix of the naïveté of revolution and the entrepreneurial spirit of the moment.

At the end of each decolonization, the distance shrinks between the hero and the guardian of traditions, the single-party liberator, the regime acting alone. And so, two months after Egypt's victory over the old Egypt, which the country rid itself of like a shameful plague, the columnist goes back to watching TV in his country: you see people talking, agencies crumbling, ministers put up for judgment, unions that finally represent the people, journalists who dare, demonstrators not intimidated by the prospect of disorder, liars repenting, analyses, banners, pictures of people walking on the moon and on hope. Hope, this wild animal conceived in the heart, grown out of the countdown between the self and heaven. Hope is far away from Algeria, whose only action has been to oppose a no-fly zone over Libya, where Qaddafi is murdering his people with bombs. Oh, the misery of a country that ages badly!

APRIL 4

BEN ALI, LIVE FROM
MULTIPLE ARAB CAPITALS

"*Ben Ali h'rab!*" the Arab shouts in the dark streets of his capital. "Ben Ali has fled!" His voice is loud, it carries far into space and deep into the collective heart. As in the time of colonization, the guy has no name: he's called "the Arab." Camus murdered him, decolonization finished him off. The dictator, chased out and watching from far away in the heavens, surveys the scene and then turns toward the future that he failed to share with his own people. Is he finished? No. After Tunisia, Ben Ali appeared in Egypt with his teeth sharpened and his fists clenched. He tried to do better there: he brought out the planes, the camels, the bludgeons, and the Molotov cocktails. He killed a few more people, but despite help from abroad, he was still a little lost.

Still dragging around his sons and his wife, who are burdensome to carry and feed, Ben Ali ended up slipping out through the air, this time in a helicopter instead of a plane, landing a bit farther away like a wasp, and wallowing there in his melancholy. At least that's what everyone thought, and what he made everyone believe. In reality, when Ben Ali left Egypt, he headed west. Toward Tripoli. There, a little more restless from drugs and disguised in the getup of a Bedouin thug, he started another war with surveillance and bombs. In Libya, he killed a few more, tortured more, injured more, and then isolated himself among the rubble and started a genocide with a song, *"Zengua Zengua."* Completely crazed from lack of sleep, paranoia, and his supporters' hurrahs, he was erratic, eating all the children of the future and stamping out dozens of towns with his missiles.

Surrounded and bombed by practically the entire world, he finally passed through a tunnel, with the help of hundreds of mercenaries, and came out the other side in Yemen, where he would often appear in the form of massacres. Ben Ali decided to be uncompromising and nonnegotiable at that point: no surrender, no compromise, no emotion—he'll stay. He'll do so by shooting, talking, giving speeches, slipping in and out. The source of his certainty was that the world is largely uninterested in the end of the earth that is Yemen, according to and because of him. The trick was that by appearing in the form of Qaddafi in Libya, he could make people forget the presence of Ben Ali in Yemen. It's a good formula, but to keep hold of history you have to be everywhere in these times of rebellion and insolence. That's what explains the unexpected appearance of Ben Ali in Syria, his mustache thin like that of an unruly juvenile. There Ben Ali finally understood, which is why he decided not to give the "I have understood you" speech. It's not necessary when you know where it leads. "It's an international conspiracy, and we'll see about reforms," he said. In Damascus, Ben Ali struck hard: nighttime arrests, abuse, counterdemonstrations, torture, and forced disappearances. Damascus is not Tripoli is not Cairo. It's a lot of hard work and effort, because there are twelve Arab capitals but only one Ben Ali to govern them all.

"Ben Ali has fled," the Tunisian's magnificent voice cries out at night in his capital, filmed with a cell phone for posterity. "Ben Ali has arrived," others reply—in Syria, Yemen, Libya, Saudi Arabia, and beyond.

APRIL 26

IS REVOLUTION NECESSARY?

Is revolution necessary? "Explain it to me," someone says insistently but with sincerity. "What I see most of all is chaos, disaster, and misery. Did you see those Tunisians on Lampedusa? We hailed them as revolutionaries, they kicked out their dictator, and now they're being humiliated on their lifeboats and chased away just before they get to Europe. Did you see the Libyans? I'll never be a prostitute for the West. I will never call for the French or English flag in my own country. Tell me what good it did to start a revolution if we can't even go out safely into the streets of our own country anymore?" he says, exasperated. "Tell people. Don't talk only about revolution, talk about reality." And it's true: postdictatorship in Tunisia, Egypt, and elsewhere has hurt: things are going badly, the economy has slid backward, there is total insecurity, no bread to eat, people are fleeing by sea, score settling and delinquency have reached new heights. "No matter what they say, it was better with Ben Ali than without him," our conversationalist concludes. Is it true? Maybe if you're not Tunisian. But it depends on what you're seeking: a better life for yourself, or a better life for your children and grandchildren.

The Arab revolutions have been and will be violent. After those first days of glory, the whole of society comes to realize what it is and what the dictatorships have done. So the question remains: is revolution necessary? It depends what you want. The Arab peoples did not turn to revolution because they were bored, because they wanted to break windows or live in anarchy, but because their country was stolen from them, their politicians were fakes, their hopes lies, their economies violated, their resources sold off. Revolution appears as a painful solution, to decolonize a country long after the departure of its foreign rulers. It costs a great deal, risks everything, and can turn blindly in the direction of indecision. You can trust a revolution or not. It can betray or be betrayed. In any country where people see that they are not a people, where democracy is a scam, corruption a necessity, injustice the rule, and power struggles the law, revolution ensues. Sooner or later. Women know that you don't give birth with a smile on your face. And in every country where the young cannot be born and the old don't die, the result is violence. Every "Arab," every Algerian has dreamed of revolution at one time or another: in front of a post office, at the seaside, watching an official speech on TV, faced with an abuse, or when confronted with one's own dreams. The only distinction is that with revolution, everyone pays, and without it, you pay alone. Maybe the better question is, does a revolution always have to be violent?

The columnist recalls the answer from the sociologist Lahouari Addi when he was asked why the War of Independence was violent. "Because colonization was hard and murderous." You can only get rid of the intruder with violence. Of course, fear and doubt are understandable: a democratic transition would be better than the promise of democracy, obtained through murder and NATO. But in this case, it isn't the choice of the people who want change. It's the choice of their dictators, who constantly refuse because they don't want a smooth transition. Was Tunisia better with Ben Ali? Yes, except that if Ben Ali had been better, Tunisians wouldn't be on Lampedusa. Even when he's thrown out or killed, a dictator continues to murder the future for a long time. Violence is avoidable. Revolution is not.

MAY 14

SCENES FROM AN
INCOMPREHENSIBLE DEATH

When the bullet hit me, I fell. And with me fell buildings, a faraway tree, two innocent birds; the noise of the entire world faded. That's how I died: a bullet in the chest and a giant exclamation point inside my head. Except that I was still there. Practically nothing changes when you're killed. When I opened my eyes again I saw the tarmac of the street and, farther away, a dozen pairs of shoes walking slowly. So I didn't hesitate, I knew I had only a few minutes: quickly, as when I used to steal fruit from the neighbors, I stood up. There next to me, stretched out, dead indeed, wiped out, gone dark, I discovered it: my own body. A slogan still in my mouth, fumes spilling out with my words. I was angry, as though someone had pickpocketed me, or stolen my shoes at the entrance to the mosque. Being killed is a betrayal, and you experience the hereafter as a moment of great anxiety, awaiting the final judgment. And so, as I said, I was angry, and I decided to take my corpse and move on so that I could drop it off at home, in my bed, let it rest. I walked straight toward the police cordon that restrained us, and the unmarked cars into which they had already crammed half the people in revolt. In any case, a voice said to me, you can't kill a man twice. I wanted to shout that in the government's face, and then bring my body somewhere so I could retie its laces, allow it to catch its breath, and then go home when the protest was over. Fragments of glass hung in the air, a cry with droplets of saliva. A young man was bizarrely entangled with his slingshot, frozen like a statue; a white wall had turned red from the light of a siren. So after the first bullet, I walked with my own body on my back, feeling its weight, shoes dragging and hitting against my back because I was holding it by the waist, slung over my shoulders, head hanging down and buttocks toward the sky. Oddly, no one seemed to care about me—neither the police nor the snipers on the roofs, nor my friends who had come to make a revolution with me. And yet I was the only murdered dead man when the police charged us, and no one seemed concerned with what I had on my back. Far away, people surrounded a puddle of my blood, but I was behind their backs, yearning to pull them by their jackets.

Then I became weary.

It was like when music stops, or when you go home after a futile search, or when a wedding becomes boring.

So. I decided to go home.

In the street, suddenly, there was no one. It reminded me of a day when I was seven years old, I came home from school and when I opened the door of the house I found it empty. Everything was there: the coffee cups in their place, the bread in a bag hanging from the window, and the silent tree, but no one was there. It was my first real panic. I called out my mother's name, searched the rooms, and then I was extremely scared. Years later, I saw a film about a man who outlived all of humanity. It was the same thing. The stores were open, the windows ajar or broken, cars were stopped in the middle of intersections with their doors open. But there was no one else.

I could hear behind me the noise of the protest, which was winding down. As though I were leaving the city, when in fact I was headed toward its center. I never liked physical effort, and the corpse on my back was heavy. I was thirsty, and I could smell my own odor as though it were on someone else's jacket. I wanted to go home, but I no longer knew where that was: the name of the city had escaped me for the moment. Where was I? In Khor Maksar's neighborhood, in Sheikh Othman's neighborhood in Aden? Maybe I'm still in the financial district of Manama. Much as I tried, it was difficult to see: because of a faraway mosque praying to God, I had the impression of Maydane Street in Damascus. I was beginning to forget everything except the weight of my body on my back. Maybe that's what death is: being everywhere without knowing where your home is, or your own mother. And then to walk endlessly, as everything turns to dust, without a trace of your steps...

MAY 18

SYRIANS ARE DYING
IN BETWEEN GOD AND YOUTUBE

The Syrians are alone. They can be killed en masse, executed in front of the whitest walls, people can watch them die between two detergent ads, hear them screaming before turning out the bedside lamp to go to sleep. Almost no one is concerned—not the UN, nor the global Rights of Man franchise, nor world opinion, nor NATO. The reason is clear: Bashar al-Assad and his regime are the best incarnation of the "useful dictatorship," which has ensured the fortune of other despots in the region. He's "our best enemy," as an Israeli columnist wrote recently, summing up the right's argument. No one knows what would happen in the region if the Rat of Damascus fell—"no one" meaning the region's rulers. The safety belt that has been assured for decades by Arab dictators could come loose. Arab democracy is the worst enemy of the Israeli right (the left being in a state of inescapable misery), and the only instrument of force for people without weapons.

Egypt is the perfect example. Before, you could insult the country with a bad word to its dictator; now you can kill thousands of Egyptians without changing anyone's opinion. And that explains why the Syrians are alone. As Bashar's brother wrote in an American newspaper, "Without us, the threat is against Israel." A clear, direct message. The facade of refusal is a joke, a con game with Hamas, a sanctuary offered to extremists; the alliances with Hezbollah and the turf wars in the Golan are for decoration, superfluous scams. Nothing that's been sold to us is true: the tanks that move across the screen aren't headed to Golan, but to Daraa to kill Syrians. So often, in fact, that the columnist can no longer follow the events without wanting to reach into the screen and pound the Rat's head with the biggest rock he can find. Syrians are being killed in cold blood behind the world's back, by the dozen, as though they were extras. With unprecedented courage Syrians are confronting one of the most ruthless regimes in the region, and the world. The genocide is only beginning and already mass graves have been discovered, despite the regime's Stalin-style propaganda. But Bashar has already fallen, and his brother, Maher, too, along with their cousin; what remains is the blood on their hands and the battalions of troops obeying the orders of minority rule by the Rat of Damascus and his brothers.

What remains is a scene of courage and a vast theater, empty of a world eating popcorn. Nearly a thousand deaths, hundreds disappeared, and thousands of arrests in Syria, without it yet being understood as both a revolution and a massacre. All because our dictatorships are useful to their democracies, and a stable concentration camp is better than a democracy that's disobedient, threatening. Seen yesterday on TV: a video that zooms in on a pair of dentures. They belong to an old Syrian woman, shot in cold blood by soldiers because she was crying for freedom. There was blood, a hunched body, and the dentures. God help them! We see everything. And YouTube, too.

CAN YOU SEND AN ALGERIAN TO JAIL FOR ATTEMPTED SELF-IMMOLATION?

A fascinating philosophical paradox: can you send a man to jail because he wants to commit suicide? In Ouargla, a city in southern Algeria that kills its unemployed with sandstorms, two Algerians were imprisoned for attempted self-immolation. So, wanting to go away, whether by sea or by fire, is a crime. Become a *harraga*, or burn. What is a young Algerian wanting to set himself on fire in protest guilty of? First, of reversing the roles: he is the victim, and, fatally, *le pouvoir* is the assassin. When you succeed with suicide by burning, it means the government has sold you the wind that's necessary for the fire, and someone didn't do his job: the president, the minister, the *wali*, the martyr, or the one who promised to sell oil to buy a patch of grass. Next, lighting a fire too close to the oil deposits is risky: "Don't play with fire" is a political command, but also a logistical one. You can try to set yourself on fire in El Bayadh, be saved, and go home to your mother. But you can't do it in Hassi Messaoud. There you threaten the oil, and therefore the general well-being. Next, self-immolation is a crime: you want to escape the punishment of the life of your nation, leave millions to suffer boredom and meaninglessness, subtract yourself from the sum total of pain, get out while no one else can move. To set fire to yourself is to leave without authorization. It's an illegal departure, an emigration toward nothing, because of everything. Immolation is a message to the world, a smoke signal from a drowned person on an island under siege, a defection, a denial that makes too much noise. And finally, self-immolation also sets fire to everyone else. The two culprits in Ouargla who were sent to prison are accused of giving ideas to others in the South who are out of work, and they are guilty of premeditation. So, it's a conspiracy by two ringleaders, even if they're headed toward death and ashes. You shouldn't rally people, not even to die, if it's not le pouvoir that kills you. A life of unemployment must be lived to the very end, swallowed whole like an unpleasant tonic, otherwise you will be punished and denied dessert. You can't die in one single shot like that, with the noise pollution it provokes; only slowly. You don't have the right to burn yourself—only with small fires in an unpaid job, or at the birth certificate office that doesn't have any forms.

Suicide is a crime for totalitarian regimes and imperial religions: it's a rebellion that's unacceptable to the spirit of domination, a refusal, as they say above, tax evasion of the body and the spirit. The two down-and-out culprits in Ouargla are therefore "guilty" in the eyes of national security—which is to say the security of the regime, which is to say its ideology. The trial of these Algerians is not to be missed: existential questions will be asked, and the old Camusian matter will be up for discussion: freedom through death, or clarity through suicide. It will lead toward the right interrogation: does a person's life belong to him and his own choices, or is it a wakf, a possession of the state? The accused can say: I didn't want to live anymore because I wasn't alive. The judge can respond: no, you weren't trying to die but rather to engage in politics through death. Furthermore (and this is not a play on words), the criminal charge that comes closest is "desertion," imbued with double meanings for an out-of-work inhabitant of the deserts of the South. The story is absurd, and reveals that regimes at an impasse always end up at the same crossroads: to the left, repression, to the right, ridicule.

JUNE 25

A LITTLE POETRY
IN A WORLD OF PRESS RELEASES

These are new times. Words feel as old as your breath. So, a dictionary for the modern era:

First, "revolution": it doesn't mean chasing out the colonists but the dictator, his sons, his wives, and his servants. Colonists are not always foreigners. They can have your nationality, your face, your documents, but not your skin. Revolution is an obligation, not a memory. You leave your bones there, not a bouquet of flowers. Its martyrs are yet to come, not to be commemorated. It's a way of taking back the land, not of walking on top of it.

"Liberty": to be distinguished from "liberation." You aren't free because someone tells you you are, but only when you say it yourself, to yourself. Liberty has a price. Otherwise, life is free. You're free when you're ready to die, and not when others have died for you before you were born.

"Protesting": not breaking, but smashing. You break a window; you smash chains.

"Marching": it's not using your shoes, but grabbing the road by the collar and telling it where you want to go, not just to where people tell you to stop. Protesting is a right because the country saw the birth of your fathers, and it's the way you can give birth to your sons. When you can't march, all you do is turn in circles.

"Slogans": they aren't labels, they're cries. The summary of all your books. The union of your name and your life. If you don't have one, hit a wall and it will give you the first words of your poem.

"Reforms": this is how they wear you out, by taking off your pants while stroking your hair.

"Fear": a sign that you're alive. If you're not afraid, it means you aren't alive, and you can't give life to those who will follow in your wake. During a revolution, the dictator will strike at you often. More and more. It's a sign that he is increasingly afraid. Think of this: fear is when you think courage is useless. And that's not the case when you want to live better.

"Chaos": on paper, it's a monster. You can't have a house if you don't have a country. And you don't have a house if it's built by the king's index finger. Is revolution chaos? Yes. Chaos precedes reconstruction.

"Islamists": a vapor, with a beard. The sky belongs to those who lift their eyes, not to those who prostrate themselves before it. God doesn't have a body, hands, a kami, or a chief of staff. Be skeptical of organized voyages to the sky: God is like death or birth, a unique kind of solitude, and no one can face him in your place. No one can speak to him by proxy.

"Elections": vote. Don't give in. You vote with your hands, not with a sigh of despair. It's your right, not your day off. Doesn't do any good? That means that, for the moment, you're serving the worst.

"The president": a man you pay to take care of the country while you take care of your children. If he does a bad job, get a new one. It's your right: you have a right to only one wife, but to four presidents. Otherwise, it's a ruse.

"The bureaucracy": they aren't any better than you, but they can be worse. Demand accountability, names not pseudonyms. The more unmarked cars there are, the more unmarked lives. Don't trust state security, it doesn't serve you. The police are your employees, not the other way around. You are more numerous, but they are better organized: reverse the trend.

"Democracy": not the name of a woman from a foreign country, but your right to be a president, a people, a woman or a man, a merchant, an activist, an architect, a calm sunset, a person who goes for walks alone. When you have democracy, you will no longer need to get a visa to go to Europe, to walk over the sea, to howl. Democracy is when we are all presidents of the republic, and the president of the republic makes dinner while you watch TV.

JULY 7

THE BUTTERFLY BYSTANDER

They're there, together, in the same country, but they don't know it: a doctor, a groundskeeper, an eternal student, a lawyer bleeding from the head, and a bystander in three dimensions. As we know, they all march, have marched, or will march in the future, because of salaries, lies, or the flaccid national dictatorship. The doctors, the groundskeepers, the lawyers, the students, and the bystanders. What's more, all five have the same worries and the same target when they talk about happiness and misery in the third person singular. They all go to the president's residence, by way of the same route (because there's only one), and they have the same slogan. The only difference is in the timing: each goes by himself, for himself, without the others. The five of them never march at the same time, or they almost don't, if you consider the particular case of the bystander. A stringent old Marxist would say that that's why it's easy to beat them up without provoking any notable change, except in the timbre of the collective sigh.

So, a question: what would happen if the groundskeeper, the doctor, the lawyer, the student, and the bystander all marched to the same place, together, at the same time, and with the entire world, too? *Le pouvoir* wouldn't be able to swallow them all at once, strike at them all at the same time, or push them back, because they would be everywhere: while the doctor took care of the injured, the lawyer could cry at the top of his lungs what the student has always wanted to say, while the groundskeeper tried to defend them all.

Passing by, the bystander can bring his incalculable number, his fact of being an entire people, his legitimacy as sole lawful elector, and his full weight, which gives life to the revolution. What can *le pouvoir* do then, even if they hide behind the police? Nothing. Or almost nothing. It can triumph over everybody, one by one, but never all at the same time. All that's needed to get rid of Mubarak and his brothers is concurrence, coincidence.

The people have the means to save themselves. They need only the link, the cord, the ancestral ties that create one man, without his feeling alone. It's what all the songs, the clairvoyants, the analysts, and logic, say. Furthermore, it's written in the agitator's manual: "Make revolution in the street and wait." Okay, but what if the street is blocked by a police cordon? The manual continues: it doesn't matter. The proverb is symbolic, it means to say that the street will always exist. All you have to do is fill it, and it'll take off on its own. But it must be shouldered equally as a cause. Not an effect.

What's needed also is to convince the bystander that he's not just a bystander. Tell him that he's like the Japanese butterfly that causes storms in South Africa: when the bystander lowers his head, the doctor gets hit and the lawyer gets beat up. The bystander's thorax is the future of the people.

AUGUST 16

THE SECOND DAY OF THE YEAR OF THE CAGE

The first day of trial for Mubarak and his sons, and everyone was sure that all the Arab chiefs, the shadily elected armed gangs and other kings, everyone was watching the same broadcast. Even from far away you could hear, clearly for once, what each of the Forty Thieves was thinking in his urn. You could feel their skin, see one eye calculating the distance between the chair and the escape jet, and you could feel their anxiety and their anger deep inside their chests. It was the first day of the cage. Mubarak, the most powerful in the pack, was stretched out there, pretending to be sick, with his two sons, one holding up the sky as it fell and the other a Koran. We even smiled: those who are powerful, even when they fall, still take us for idiots. The Koran in the hands of Saddam, Djamel, or Ala is intended for chauvinistic peoples, to soften them and their immensely naive piety, and arouse a pity that the former leader never had for his people's children. Someday, Qaddafi, Bashar, and the others will all find themselves in a cage clutching at a Koran. The path was inaugurated by Saddam the benevolent. Remember this tyrant and his sudden faith during his final days.

Saddam also invented the scenario: the bravado and the pride, the grandiose rhetoric of standing firm, the promise to triumph over the West like Saladin; and then the escape, the recorded speeches, the hole in Tikrit, and, finally, the cage, the trial, the Koran, and the hangman's rope.

And so yesterday was the second coming of one of the Mubaraks of our time, in his cage. There, too, the most attentive can hear the other Mubaraks thinking—a single blinding, tenacious thought: what do we do so that this doesn't happen to us? It's not the beginning of the path to accepting democracy, but rather the muffled awakening of a survival instinct. What do we do? Whom do we kill? How many? Who are our allies? What do we give to the West or sacrifice for them? What do we offer armed gangs of supporters? How do we avoid the mistakes of the Mubarak clan, without ever democratizing? What did Mubarak fail to do that he finds himself fallen from the palace and into a cage? The Forty Thieves' strategies after Mubarak's cage scene aren't a collective salute, but an individual one. No one thinks of how to save the country from ruin, only how to save power from falling. So let's bet that the cage will give a second wind to the Arab dictators, who know that they have nowhere to escape to, and who know how they will end up if they stay. Not much to celebrate, and it's hard to see them softening on our fate. The evidence suggests to them that it's a question of life or death. Some of them know it. That's where the monstrosity, the repression, and the great ruse of their delaying tactics come from. It's no longer about politics, but Darwinism.

So the list of fetish objects from the beginning of the twenty-first century expands: Gbagbo's vest, Ben Ali's plane, Mubarak's cage, Saddam's hole, Ali Salah's barbecue. What's next? We'll see.

SEPTEMBER 14

THOUSANDS OF ARABS "KILLED" BY CHINA AND RUSSIA

How do we understand the world? Answer: there's us, and there's the West. So in explaining the Arab Spring, everything comes down to this relationship: the history, the thievery, the soft colonization, immigration, love, rejection. For example, the paranoia about foreign interference is limited to Europe and the Anglo-Saxon world. A Chinese person could do the same thing as a Brit, set his sights on oil in the South, manipulate and corrupt, spy or not: he will never be accused of interfering, of seeking to colonize, or planning to destabilize. Then there is Russia, which sells just as many weapons as the Chinese do, Russia thinks of eating us too, as the Chinese do—but both are immune to public opinion. An American who takes a picture in Hassi Messaoud can be accused of espionage; a group of Chinese who dig a hole or install a pipe there would never be suspected of such. The Chinese can drown the country and its engines in fake motor oil, dressed up in Algerian packaging, and no one says a word. We prefer to get outraged about schoolbook covers with a symbol that resembles a Star of David. Corruption is institutionalized in Algeria with the Chinese or the Russians: it's normal, and no one gets offended, except maybe Algerian business executives who try to confront it.

With the Arab Spring, the high season of paranoia and manipulation, we accuse the West of everything; we watch and suspect them, we ask them to intervene or reproach them for not doing so. But never a word is said about the scandalous positions of China and Russia, who don't even bother with the courtesy of explaining that they are on the side of the regimes and the dictatorships. We remember very well that the United States supports and covers up the crimes of Israel; but we say nothing of the cover provided by the Russians for the butcher of Damascus and his massacres of women, children, and the Free Syrian Army. The Chinese covered for Qaddafi to the very last minute to save their contracts in Libya, and provided an umbrella for his massacres—but no one finds anything wrong with their predatory role in the Maghreb.

The role of these two powers in covering for the dictators and ensuring their immunity after their crimes will remain in our memory, however, even as they try to erase the evidence. Those who rebelled in our world will remember for a long time—just as they remember the Crusades or the colonizations to incriminate the West today. The opportunism of these two powers is scandalous, immoral, intolerable, and criminal. These two allies of our dictators are guilty of thousands of deaths, in the name of their interest, taking our money, and their strategizing.

This acknowledgment is necessary: it allows a kind of mental clarity. Why? The interests that want to benefit from the shifting plate tectonics in the Arab world aren't only in the West—there are other powers, too. Why say it? Clarity avoids manipulation.

To accuse only the West of trickery is to revive the selective blindness and hatred that aren't useful to us, the traumas of history that don't get us anywhere so long as they don't help us to understand better. Remembering that other powers are there to eat our crumbs and profit from our cries for freedom allows us to remain vigilant without drowning it in fantasy and myopic hatred.

Just as much as the West of yesterday, China and Russia today are killing thousands of Arabs for sugar, reserves, a well, or a contract.

THE FOURTEENTH OF JANUARY, AND ETERNITY

One night, around a fire with attentive ears, a group of travelers discusses how each of them has, will, or is presently making a revolution.

The Tunisian says: "I used Facebook. I posted the names and images of my life, my death, and life after death. That's how I made the dictator fall: he saw nothing, and I saw everything." The Egyptian says: "I have *Al Jazeera*. The station saw everything: the names, the faces, the images. With *Al Jazeera* the world can't pretend they haven't seen anything. And I saw myself from behind, from in front, from above, and from the inside. It helped me to believe that I existed: I had proof of myself before my own eyes."

The Algerian thinks a bit, and says: "I have my eyes. I never forget faces, images, or names. One day I will find myself, my deliverance, I will take my own hand and pardon myself, arm myself, and rise up." And the Syrian says: "I have my cell phone: it has the names, the faces, the images of all those who were murdered. My martyrdom is multimedia. My death is in three dimensions. You can press a button and feel everything: how I died, how they killed me, how I went from beneath a shoe to eternity, from crying slogans from the tomb to the end of the world, from submission to revelation."

---

* On January 14, Ben Ali fled Tunisia for Saudi Arabia aboard the presidential plane.

The Yemenite explains: "For me, it was a little of all of that. I remember filming. I spoke, cried out, then I was dead, but still I'm there. I burned a dictator and he's still alive. The dictatorship killed me, and I still exist. My story isn't finished yet. My only fault is to live in a lost corner of the world, no one pays attention even to the fact that we exist. I have to fight not only death but insignificance."

The Moroccan says: "I marched in the street, then I got caught up in the racket, which put an end to it. I wanted reforms; they reformed me."

The Saudi speaks next: "For us it's different. If you're subjugated to the king, you murmur 'Allahu-akbar.' When you're al-Qaeda, you scream it. In both cases you die for nothing. For the moment anyway. The king hides behind God and God is invisible. It's complicated."

An Iraqi walks by. He sees the group and sits down. "In Iraq there are three holes. In the first, we found oil. In the second, we found Saddam. In the third, we dug three more—one for the Kurds, one for the Shiites, and one more for the Sunnis." The Egyptian interrupts: "In Egypt, the revolution started when they tortured a youth at a police station, to the point of sending him to find God. His name was Khalid Saïd."

The Tunisian adds: "For me, it started when a police officer struck a banana vendor who set himself on fire. His name was Mohammed Bouazizi."

The Syrian says: "For us, it started when the children were arrested in Daraa and they pulled out their nails. When we went to see the head of the Secret Service, he told us, 'Forget your children. Make new ones, and if you don't know how, bring us your women.' The children had been tortured so much that they'd lost their names."

The Libyan, still sweating, joins the group: "It's the same for us. It started with a lawyer in Benghazi. He was arrested, then released. The people understood that they could receive the same privilege: release after forty-two years in custody. We didn't need any names. We knew our enemies' names."

The Algerian stays quiet for a long time, then responds: "For us it hasn't started yet, because we had too many names. We needed to listen to one single dead man, to follow him. The revolution will begin when, like you, we have the name of the dead man, and of the dictator. We don't have those things. There are two hundred Ben Alis, a million and a half old martyrs, and 200,000 new ones."

The Yemenite, seemingly distant, picks up: "In Yemen it began when we saw that it was possible elsewhere, even if it was on television. But it was the inverse: we had the name of the dictator, but not yet the names of the martyrs or the tortured."

Everyone turns, then, toward one last voyager—dark, silent: "And you—are you Jordanian? Bahraini? Qatari perhaps? Or Mauritanian? Tell us about your death, or your life, or the life that was promised to you, your torture, who walked on your bones or who stole your country. Tell us."

The voyager clears his throat and mutters: "I am the anonymous people. The wandering Arab. The rest of history. Volume II of the cries. Mason of the Granada of the future. Some call me Ibn Khaldoun." Each one nods his head. A bird flies above them in the sky, sign of the infinity of time. In the desert, the sand emits a sigh of love at the sight of a flashing comet.

OCTOBER 9

ALGERIAN BODIES ON FIRE

The Algerian body is under siege: accused of being a sin, of being too numerous, of being irritating for the purposes of statistics and speeches, of being everywhere and for nothing. We carry this body with self-hatred and chagrin because it's costly, with vanity when it's fat and well nourished or curvy and attractive, with discretion when it's the body of a woman. But it's also sick—it drags, is ill-kempt, neither fun nor amused, incapable of joy or dancing, out of sync with the music of the world. It's the first to be hit, or avoided, when it's part of a couple, or during protests. It's the location of all so-called social malaise. The finite space of infinite living beings. What's more, everyone has an opinion about the other's body. But it's also the last place where an Algerian can feel at home. Because of a lack of sufficient housing, of places of recreation, nonveiled beaches, a right to nudism, to have muscles that are healthy like Greek statues, for lack of an equitable country, forests with clean air, picnic spots and green spaces—the Algerian only feels at home in his body. Well—50 percent of his body. The other half of the body is a matter of too much religion, taboos, fatwas, inquisitions, or aesthetic merchandise. So you can understand why the Algerian fights with his body while holding it in one hand. It's his unique fortune.

When nothing is working and the Algerian feels rotten, betrayed, faced with injustice or violence or absurdity, he turns against his own body. Since he doesn't have any friends, he has only one enemy within reach: his body. So he burns it, immolates it, casts it into flames that consume, carbonize him. Immolation is an institution, and it's becoming widespread elsewhere besides Oran. Why? Everyone knows at least one person who's done it. The actual act is a simple combination of matchstick, weather, and thermostat.

When the Algerian doesn't understand, feels disparaged and punished, he punishes himself: because there's nothing mediating between him and the adversary, there's only one remaining institution that he can touch with his hand: the body. So the Algerian burns it. It's an act that allows him to set fire to history and geography at the same time. You resolve the problem by getting rid of the problem. You attack the only person you know to be incapable of defending himself: yourself. You kill yourself for lack of weapons or conviction to kill others. You get justice by doing yourself injustice. You accuse all other living beings of their own deaths. Suicide can—sometimes, often—be a crime committed by the collective against the individual.

And so self-immolation is an institution, the last one. Because there is no justice, no elected officials who are truly elected, no civil society or good consciences; no convictions, mediation, understanding, intelligence, congressional committees, listening sessions; because we see ourselves as disadvantaged, without rights to the fruit of our own labor. So we catch the first person to pass through our own perimeter—which is to say, oneself—and we kill him. Meaning that if the Algerian body is surrounded, it's because everyone has something against it. The Islamists, the religious, the conservatives, the skirt-chasers, the insecure, the historians, the martyrs who no longer have a body, age, usury, the sea, floods and neighbors and even, finally, the owner of the body itself.

THE SONS OF HASSI MESSAOUD

This is a story from Hassi Messaoud. It began in 1917, when a man called Messaoud discovered a well for his troops. Still today, in the center of the town, you can find the rim and the white cupola of a well that offered water to the caravans of the past. Messaoud died in 1926, so he never learned the value of the black viscous substance that also seeped out of the well, along with the water. In 1956, a Frenchman was digging next to it when he discovered the thing that Messaoud had seen: oil. Lots of it. An enormous amount. More than anywhere else in Africa. The French began to drill in 1958. In 1962, Algeria gained independence; but not the area around Hassi Messaoud, which made for a contentious chapter in the Evian Accords. In 1971, Houari Boumédiène nationalized the oil field and the town of Hassi Messaoud. In 1980, Sonatrach made Algiers the political capital of the country, and Hassi Messaoud the energy capital. Algerian businesses moved their managers there, along with their chalets and their problems. The residents of Hassi Messaoud, who hadn't discovered the oil, discover instead the concerns of big cities—of unemployment in the desert, of northern executives who come with their hairdressers or their families, their contracts from Algiers, their bids and their subcontractors, and the laws of multinationals. In 1990, Hassi Messaoud became the biggest magnet for Algerian *harraga*, who headed south in search of employment, salaries, and long-term contracts. The 1990s turned Algerian eyes toward the South: the state sought solutions there, with internment camps for Islamists at Oued En-Namous, and the unemployed sought easy work there, often becoming security guards.

July 13, 2001 (a Friday): an imam delivers a sermon in which he accuses the women who work in the oil industry in Hassi Messaoud, many of whom live alone, of being the source of evil, drought, venereal disease, dandruff, and cars breaking down. Hundreds of intoxicated men rise up and attack the El-Haicha neighborhood. For hours and hours, they assault women, rape them, drag them naked through the streets, rob them, kidnap them. Several years later, there will be a trial, with six defendants in the place of the hundred who committed the crimes, and three victims standing in for the hundred others who were threatened with retaliation if they testified. In 2006, the state decided to turn the oil well into a real city. That was the project for the new Hassi Messaoud. It would cost a great deal and attract a lot of people. Chakib Khellil resigned, the project was dropped. Then it was promised again for 2014, then 2017. The new city will have all imaginable facilities—roads, banks, green spaces, housing. September 2011: the unemployed in Hassi Messaoud protest, demand work or oil, and threaten to march to Ouargla, then to Algiers, and then on to the UN.

You might have noticed that throughout this whole story there's a group that hasn't said a word—the descendants of Messaoud, the founder. That is, until yesterday. They've been staging a sit-in for several days to demand accountability for their four square kilometers of land. In a statement to *Algérie News*, the tribe's spokesman was clear: "Take the oil, but give us back the land," he said. It's not a request for shares in Sonatrach, only justice. Declared a nationalized no-building zone, property in Hassi Messaoud has quickly become the object of unbridled speculation. In the very same space where the Messaouds have been told that the land belongs not to their father but to the state, others came from the North, bought up lots, are building parking lots and gas stations in anticipation of the city's skyrocketing rise. If you're going to take the land away from the Messaouds, why give it then to the brokers? That's precisely what the Messaouds are asking with their sit-in: of the six hundred family members, "only six are working in the oil industry," they say. That's a pretty good joke to make of Messaoud and his well. And the real well, the one for water? "It has fallen into ruins," the inheritors say, dismayed.

The moral of this story? It's obvious: the social contract is broken. Since ownership is no longer really collective, Algerians demand the restoration of individual property. Was old Messaoud a mujahid? A landlord, or the first Algerian to be screwed by Algerian history? His children have an answer. You can find them in Hassi Messaoud, in the center of town.

FOUR DAYS AFTER
THE TUNISIAN VOTE (I)

Everything has been said in the three or four days since the Islamist vote in Tunisia—or almost everything. It's been said that Tunisia is not Algeria, that Ghannouchi is not Benhadj. It's been said that the vote was a disaster, and the Tunisians will pay for it, as we did. It was said that people must accept democracy and the choice of the majority; that Tunisians voted with a civic mind, but poorly; that it's over, or that it's only the beginning. The question's been posed, what good is revolution if it means going from a dictatorship to Islamism? Everything, or almost, has been pronounced, according to everyone—everyone's pain, everyone's fear, everyone's hope. Except there's one more question, and in this columnist's opinion, it's the most useful one: Where do the Islamists come from? And where do the people who vote for them come from?

First answer: they are numerous, more organized, more aggressive, and they play the heavens against the earth, God against their opponents. That's all true, but it's just an observation, not an answer. Second answer: democrats are convinced, but don't know how to convince, whereas the Islamists have both. And that's true, but again an observation.

The clues therefore lie elsewhere. The Islamists didn't just fall from the sky, they didn't appear spontaneously. Rather they were created, little by little, as much by the failure of ideological alternatives as by Islamism and the dictatorships themselves. The Arab regimes combat Islamism to attain power, but cultivate an alliance with passive Islamism because it's a good way to seed conservatism among their people. The Islamists in this Arab world are born from the TVs of Sheikh talk shows, preachers, books on jihad, neurosis, our schools, academic programs, compromises, and this prevailing sickness that fixates on women's bodies as an evil, all the while everyone neglects to wash their own hands before eating, or to clean the stairwells in their buildings. The Islamists are the product of our education system, the biggest mosque in Africa. They are the last gift, offered postmortem, by the "Arab" dictatorships to the "Arab" people.

So, even when you throw a dictator out, his crime against the future remains along with the hysterical children it has produced for thirty or forty years. Libya is an extreme example: in their land, the Libyan people know only how to turn toward the sky. The wreckage from our forty years of dictatorship is immense, and will last for generations. A revolution doesn't finish it off so quickly. It takes time.

Being free is sometimes more difficult than being dead. Death takes only a moment, but liberty requires an entire lifetime. The Tunisians voted for Islamists who are Tunisians, plain and simple, homegrown over generations. The Algerian sociologist Addi Lahouari was right to talk about illusion. We Algerians can see it, the Tunisians giving in to it, despite the irrationality of such a choice in a country where employment and the economy depend on European tourism. We see the mirage, the foolish hope placed in prayer rather than effort, the return of old demons like "Arabness," identity, Islam, the caliphate, the hostility to the body and to women. We Algerians see it and we know it can lead to death and disaster. But the Tunisians don't know it, or they believe they can avoid it. The dictator punished their religion, and today they are reclaiming it. Ben Ali accustomed them to submission, and today they are choosing it in voting booths.

The illusion of the Islam solution remains strong, hypnotic in the faltering Arab world; it is espoused from places like Saudi Arabia, its finances distributed to parties like Ennahdha. The Turkish model gives it credibility, encourages it as a response to the rejection of the West and its false international solutions, or at least the image of such that it gives. This illusion is spread in the schools as an identity of self-sufficiency, as richness for lack of real wealth, as capital in the place of symbolic international capitals. This solution offers another dictatorship, another illusion, like verbal decolonization, and sovereignty purchased for a price. They will live it, endure it, and pay for it. It's the dream of the majority, bitterness for those who are most lucid. We believed for a moment that we'd finished the work of kicking out the dictatorship, but it seems there is need for more: we must continue to fight and advocate, to explain to people that the desert doesn't disappear on its own and heaven is not a question for ballot booths but a private one. We must continue despite the disappointment, despite the obstacles: we must fight against Islamism and the suicide that it represents, as we must fight against the local regimes and their crimes. The Islamists win because they believe, and those who see clearly lose because displaying intelligence often leads people to suspect that you're useless. So we must reverse it: I am, because I think ahead.

FOUR DAYS AFTER
THE TUNISIAN VOTE (II)

"Because they fear God." That's how a Tunisian woman responded when asked why she voted for the Islamists. It's an abyssal answer: it means the voter no longer believes in any principle other than divine punishment. An elected official must be an Islamist, because an Islamist is afraid of God. So what is a democrat afraid of, a progressive, a secularist? Voter's response: nothing. Therefore I can't trust him by voting for him. It's a question of guarantee: the Islamist official says that God is watching him. The democratic official says nothing. The Arab voter doesn't believe in the capacity of public opinion or civil society to hold the official, politics, public life, or spending, accountable. The official doesn't yet see himself as a citizen, who can be sanctioned; so he turns to the sky.

They pass from a single party to the party of Him Alone. What must be understood? The obvious: Arab voters don't believe that political candidates have morals, principles, or a system of values outside of religious ones. A democrat is someone who has no value system, no "fear" that can push him to do good, to improve and defend the interests of all. From which one arrives at something of a conclusion: the secularists are unable to convince people that you can be a citizen with principles, whose actions are founded on ethical convictions, without being religious. The dictator was bad because he didn't believe in divine punishment and didn't fear God.

Consequently, all those who aren't Islamists don't fear God, and thus have no reason to be honest. The only ideology that's a guarantee is Islamism. So, after they're gone, the dictators leave one last rotten fruit: Arab voters' lack of trust in the power of their own citizenship. The voters don't know what they're capable of, they believe only in what they can't do. They're not citizens, but believers.

A half-century of dictatorships created voters who are suspicious, fearful, hopeless, nihilistic, resigned, and tired of standing up for no reason. And that's the Achilles' heel of those who want to convince Arab societies that secularism is a right and a guarantee against totalitarianism and perversion, that democracy is an affair of men, not of religion, and that belief is an intimate choice and not a magic ballot. Democrats are unconvincing with their value system, their morals. They have not managed to explain to voters that it is possible to desire good for all, with a win-win formula, through consensus and common interest. They are unable to answer the question: What proves that you're afraid of evil, that there isn't a risk you'll become thieves and crooks, that you won't become Ben Alis? The answer is unclear, or too complicated.

Because Tunisians endured Ben Ali for a long time, today they vote for his opposite. For them, if a man doesn't fear the people, let's at least choose someone who fears God.

The failure of alternative ideologies to Islamism comes from this inability to respond to these simple questions of simple voters, who are the most numerous: secularism is persuasive for the upper classes and the business world, but not the benevolent people. The Arab voter puts his confidence in the systems of authority that assure his life: the army or the parties of God.

In Tunisia, Ennahdha will try to embody a consensus, but their method is fundamentally faulty. They're not Turkey. What holds the Ankara way together is the common interest of all—the economy, the oppositional forces inside the state. In Tunisia and elsewhere, they're letting the idea of citizenship off the hook, in the name of guarantee through belief. The incoherence of the democrats' response can be seen everywhere in the other Arab countries, and the lack of self-confidence among believers distorts the uneasy game of political transition, reduces revolutions to upheavals— for now.

After Ennahdha's victory, someone on the Internet rightly observed that where the Islamists spoke of the fight against corruption, of identity, and of moderation, and took ownership of big questions like those concerning women and language, democrats and their supporters were lured into debating, with an unwise magnifying glass, the details: alcohol, bikinis, homosexuality. Huge strategic error, in the end. The same mistake committed twenty years ago by Algerian democrats, who were made to debate with Abassi Madani as a "representative of Islam," and not just a simple politician, the same as any other.

THE BIGGEST DRAMA OF
THE ARAB WORLD: WAITHOOD

Waithood. A fascinating concept, discovered yesterday on the Internet, invented by political scientists who've dived into the crisis in the Arab world. Translated from English, "waithood" means the era of waiting. Waiting for what? For everything: jobs, women, leisure, laughter, money, power, success, life. "Waiting" was analyzed as one of the primary activities of young populations in the Arab world. And to understand the drama, you must remember, "the Arab region comprises the second largest percentage of young people in the world. Almost two out of three Arabs are younger than thirty, a level surpassed only in sub-Saharan Africa. What's more, the Middle East and North Africa have both the highest rate of youth unemployment and the highest overall rate of unemployment in the world," one of the studies says, quoted in some of the international newspapers that are trying to understand what's happening (and not happening) in this "Arab" world.

So Arab "Waithoods" are waiting, getting old in the meantime, and then they'll die. The few solutions are marriage (thereby having a wife who waits for you, and giving meaning to the wait to have children, who will wait to eat), or religion: transform the wait into eschatology or Messianism, transform life into a stage, death into a fulfillment, and the hereafter into life's goal. Other than these two solutions, if denial or libido keeps you from them, there's nothing else. Except revolution. The concept of waithood is indeed believed to be one of the keys to understanding the Arab Spring: the young who've been waiting for such a long time are the first to take up arms or to riot, because it gives meaning to their lives, to their wait, and gives them a chance to "go" somewhere, even out of disillusion. The Arab Spring is also a question of age: in the places where there are the most people under thirty, the old retain and control power. Yesterday, the columnist wrote about four new political parties...made up of elderly Algerians. There's not a single party for the young, and at the same time there is a crisis of meaning and participation among youth.

The Arab gerontocracies believe it's enough to give food to a young person looking for meaning, and the problem will resolve itself during digestion. A dietary vision to fill in for a lack of vision for the future. In Algeria, the waithoods are legion, they number in the millions. Those above seventy are a minority, but they are suffocating everyone else. Every legal reform is undertaken by the old for the old. They've taken history, the state, symbolism, time, and to the young they give a few dinars and a ticket to wait in line. The waithoods get bored, people eat poorly, they can no longer dream, they become violent, and one day they'll use arms, the sky, stones, or their teeth. Waiting can't be endless. At some point it turns into asking, then demanding, then revolution. When it isn't harvest, it's destruction.

The subject remains an abyss: how did we get to this equation where, with oil, natural gas, and the biggest reserve of youth on the planet, the Arab world is poor, violent, dirty, uninventive, fanatical, miserable, and bored to the point where the only resonant way to be amused is to blow oneself up?

NOVEMBER 14

BASHAR, THE DEAD WILL KILL YOU!

For a Syrian who has died, gotten back up, resumed marching until he's killed again, and then done the whole thing over again, the international conspiracy theories about geopolitical strategy, the calculations of Western powers, the armchair analyses, and the denunciations of NATO are all straw men, parasites on his combat jacket. For the Syrian the equation is simple: he's the one getting killed, dragged out, tortured. It's his mother who's being kidnapped, his daughter and his wife. For him there's no NATO, no IDF, no conspiracy—just the dictator, a tyrant and his militias. The analyses that come out of the TV screen have something inhuman about them—they're out of sync, almost indecent. This is not a conspiracy—it's men dying. Will the West benefit? Sure. And why not us? Either way it doesn't matter much to the dead Syrian. What he wants is his life, a better one, with freedom. These transcendent analyses are all well and good to understand, but their excesses are immoral.

Syrians have shown exemplary courage, singular, unwavering, admirable, and that at least deserves our respectful silence. Their fight exposed the mafioso networks in the Middle East, among Hezbollah, the apparatchiks of the Palestinian cause (fed and lodged by the Secret Service in Damascus), and the dictatorships in the name of Arabness and refusal. It brought closure to this era of pretend ideologies that use Palestine, Israel, Arabness, and a facade of disobedience to maintain power or win a little more with two or three gunshots and a homemade missile.

The end of Saddam signaled the end of the Saladin revivals, the type with mustaches who trafficked in Scud missiles. The end of Bashar, the butcher of Damascus, will be the end of this scam that has used Palestine like a G-string. We'll wind up in the unknown, but that's better than the old diversions and the fraud of half a century of devastating Baathism. An era is dead, Bashar is dead, his gang is dead; they're the only ones who don't know it. They're the only ones who kill others without realizing that they're bringing about their own death. The Arab League's decisions should be praised, after a half-century of being soft and months of wandering on the moon. There's no external agenda, no instrument of conspiracy, no servility. The butcher of Damascus is an illness to be quarantined. It's people like him who allowed the new colonizations. This man will kill until he's dead, and his death will be violent. May we not pity his fate, nor his lynching, which is surely coming soon, as we did with the others when we forgot their crimes at the sight of the criminal's first tears.

NOVEMBER 28

THE OTHER

I could feel the other's space, carved out of me; the need to move toward her, the charring from where she burned me, the pain left in the place where she was torn away. Without the other, I felt suddenly off balance, unsteady in my humanity, small, directionless in space now that I wasn't moving toward a face, turning to it in panic as in orbit around an enigmatic force. The other wasn't my second half, but my true self. In every direction I was traveling toward her, coming to her, coming back again. Everything could be explained in my gestures toward this endless center. Desire is an offer made to the sky, a sacrifice, the invention of fire for two hands, not just one; sexuality is its cry, art its exhale, the direction of all the rivers in the world are its confession, its narration, its story of coming and going.

Everything was a conjecture of the other: the trace of her steps, her noise during the night, the day not yet unbound from the future. The other was marriage, wedding, burning, fire, flame, pollen, the soft step of a wise creature approaching in the forest that watches over it with benevolence. What good is enjoying life without the other? For whom is your smile? For no one. So you must go and seek out this other. Wait for the clinching in her ears as she rests them against her skin. I follow desire that scalds me, the only one that's worth the trouble. The sky remains faraway, without her, and sleep deep in the earth, rest that turns an illuminated face toward darkness, I can't distinguish appetite from routine, nor understand my own path when I have nowhere to go. The other is a bow that I pierce, water around us or the deepening colors of the sky as the sun sets. I'm the announcement, and the reply. It's not that I'm looking for you, but for myself, as all the stories in the world tell you when you let them speak honestly, without interrupting in the language of your nationality, clan, tribe, or country. The other is what I want to attain in order to attain myself, get out of this shell with a momentum that will take me to the sky, to get the keys that have been left there for me before falling back to earth.

What do I call you? Angel, woman, child, or this waiting that leads me to fill pages? I don't know. I know only what stays with me of you when you've left: myself, sitting at the threshold of something that I don't have a precise name for. A curve of flesh hardened and charred from hurt. The universe slaloms between embracing and burning. Life is in the middle, I see it as an immense star. All language is nuance of the same fire. What I know is to walk and walk and walk some more until it lights up again. I want so much to speak the colors I've found: not their range but their deep light, the music they make with what they see, their form of prayer.

It's as though while I walk I push aside plants suspended in the air, and I head toward the center of a garden. Sometimes I can see it, I swear, and I want to weep, like someone on a pilgrimage. Are you there? Am I here, for once in my life? I've missed you so much that for a long time I experienced nothing, just so I could understand my humanity.

DECEMBER 4

BEN ALI'S HEIRS DIVIDED IN FOUR

What would be an honest evaluation of the first year of the Arab Spring? Fundamentally, the Arab regimes going forward can be divided into four.

First, the countries that did it: after the dictator's fall, secured through protests, public plazas, martyrs, Facebook, Internet, blood, and cries, the people discover that the dictator is gone but the dictatorship remains in place. It's slow to dissolve, defends itself better without a head. They discover also that the dictator's children are everywhere, along with his doppelgangers and his nostalgics, and that he ensnared the future with bad schools, populism, underdevelopment, and ignorance organized around tribalism or denomination or regionalism. And so the task is long. Generally, after thirty years in power, the dictator has destroyed everything: civil society, justice, citizenship, tolerance, and good faith. He leaves the country poor, divided, violent, and in flames, without harvest. Everything must be rebuilt, not just the presidency and its legitimacy.

Second, the countries where it's still going on. Syria, Yemen, Bahrain. The people there suffer, die, get back up, march some more, plead, demand, and mobilize. We don't know how to put an end to it, to rescue the hostage (the people, or the whole region) from the one in the suicide vest (the regime). Because it *is* a hostage situation, and force isn't enough. You have to deduce what the hostage taker wants, find a good negotiator, lay his mistrust to rest. The equation is very complicated: if the dictator stays, the country will disappear.

If the dictator leaves, the country risks disappearing. What to do? Choose freedom, and the bet is worth more than if you gamble on the opposite. That's stage one of the fight—history is still meaningful, the myth is in place. The battle is rapturous with blood, hymns, a new flag.

Third, the monarchies that try to make everyone forget about them. Saudi Arabia, for example, and its satellites. There the strategy is to deflect the international gaze by supporting activism in favor of the Arab Spring. However, everything necessary for revolution is present: the people don't exist, or only in the form of belief and constraint; there's oil and corruption, women are cattle and can't drive cars; rights belong to royal blood; the political police protect the regime from the people and not the people from thieves; the young are in cyclical unemployment and democracy is spoken of as a Western prostitute, a woman of loose morals that one ought not to marry. Are they safe then? No. Their turn will come. The repression will be even more brutal, they'll strike hard. Why? The sanctity of religion. Power hides behind Allah, the Kaaba, Islam, and the genealogy of the Prophet. Everyone knows that the greatest number of men have been killed in the history of humanity in the name of God. You can already see the hazy images on the Internet of the first protestors marching in Saudi Arabia (they'll be accused of being Shiites, in order to isolate them).

Fourth, the countries of fake reforms. Algeria, Morocco, and Jordan, for example. The domain of trickery. They invoke a state of emergency, but on paper: the political police change acronyms, but not mission. The game is open, according to the power rapport between protestors and tear gas bombs. The style is false reforms of the constitution, commissions, negotiations and conferences for national dialogue. Elections to calm the populace, without changing anything on the question of sovereignty (foreign affairs, ministers of the interior and money, the Secret Service, and Justice). They speak of democracy, but new leaders are harassed; they allow protestors to march once, but the second time they assault them. They suppress, buy, manipulate, equivocate, and joke with the West to gain time for themselves, and make the opposition lose time. Trickery is the goal and to make international opinion believe that the regime is serious about becoming a real state. In reality, they're hedging with all means available to them, and with the complicity of their Western tutors, in order to avoid a crash. Stability over protection (Morocco), security of supplies over understanding (Algeria), utility over assistance (Jordan).

Have they won? No. It's only a deferral. Confucius never said it, but it's what he would have thought if he'd worked for a think tank: fake reforms lead to more violent rebellions than straightforward dictatorships. We'll find out soon enough.

A YOUNG SYRIAN, ALONE AT NIGHT BENEATH TEN THOUSAND COMMENTS

Horror is something unknowable that each person carries alone in his own nighttime. On a screen you can listen and watch, but you can't know; you find yourself blocked, suddenly, at the threshold of absolute compassion. When a young Syrian is arrested by the butcher of Damascus's army, for us he's a number, a few brief seconds in a clip on a phone, an image. Then the speaker comments, you see the rest of the world looking for a solution, or a pretend solution, and after that we don't know anything more. What does the word "torture" mean? How can you convey to each viewer the precise sensation of the screech of an arrested child who's been tortured, his elbows broken, eyes punctured, honor violated, drawing his last breath, utterly alone in pain, and for whom the promised nation will be nothing more than his tomb, and freedom a draft of air? How can you explain the absolute horror of this tortured Syrian, the blinding pain, whose martyrdom only has meaning for the survivors, a stain on all humanity? One single person tortured, killed, in this Arab world is enough for all the dictators to deserve to fall, be thrown out, condemned, and hanged. What's happening in Syria is horrible, nearly inexplicable by politics. You can soliloquize about geopolitical strategy, conspiracy, whatever. It doesn't take anything away from the raw truth: death, torture, abuse, rape, theft, bombs. To speak of other things is indecent. It's a crime against one's own humanity, and complicity. The butcher of Damascus is a criminal and the Syrians in revolt are an example of the greatest courage against repression, embargo, collective punishment, mass graves, and governance by terror.

This regime is ready to do the worst, and they are doing it: international terrorism, kidnappings, falsified confessions, betrayals, and taking an entire land and region hostage. Everything is fair game to keep the revolt and the international community at bay. What for? To stay put. But what land, if you destroy it? We don't know. This regime has been dead for months, it can't be engaged with, it is alone, criminal, condemned, without sense, and yet it remains in place, with a gun pointed at the head of its people, threatening to explode everything if anyone gets too close. Firm in its belief that a people can be subdued with force and death. And the image stays in one's mind: this young man, grabbed by the neck, loaded into a truck with soldiers, crumpled into a ball with his hands on his head. We'll never see him again. We'll know nothing of his death, or his cries of pain when they break his elbows and jaw. He'll disappear under a slew of comments, analysis, doubts, debates, and polemics. Everyone talks, myself included, while he is alone hearing nothing but his own breath. Of all the people who've risen up against the Forty Thieves, the Syrian people are a beacon of admiration. Their courage is exemplary, and their future belongs to them because they've paid the price of it so dearly that they can attain it only in heaven. The Syrian regime has become hysterical, a danger to the entire region, incredulous, a modern case of the terror regimes of the twentieth century—totalitarian, duplicitous, pathological, and cunning. Assad, Makhlouf & Co. versus humanity.

This is the end of the column, but the image stays: this young man, the day before yesterday, put into the truck of a family army, shoved from the back into a tomb, head down, unnamed, collapsing under blows and ten thousand analyses, alone in his terror, and yet still illuminated from inside by the meaning he gave to his life, and to his death.

TUNISIA: THE ONLY TRULY ELECTED ARAB PRESIDENT

The Algerian stealth campaign against Tunisia has been indecent, unfair, and full of lies: some people quickly understood that it was necessary to make an example of our neighbor to prevent the contagion of revolution. And yet Tunisia advances. They predicted catastrophe, civil war, a crash, massacre: there was none. They convinced Algerian tourists not to go there, and yet the country remains standing. It continues to build itself post-Spring, to debate and search. Its elections were a lesson, its Islamists are obligated to seek consensus and be pragmatic, its civil society remains vigilant and attentive, and the people have pride, which allows them to walk on the moon even without a space suit or NASA.

And so on Nessma TV yesterday we saw Moncef Marzouki, long-standing opponent of triumphant Benali-ism, elected president of his country. There was applause and emotional congratulations. Some were against it, others criticized his alliance with the Islamists, but the man has integrity, credibility, and is a longtime activist in his country. The critics are of a Tunisian flavor, but we on the outside can see the essential: it's a powerful, moving moment because Marzouki is the first president of an Arab country to be truly elected, even provisionally, even by an assembly. It's the first time in nearly a century that an Arab president is not the bastard child of stuffed ballot boxes, massive fraud, threats, 99 percent victories, or results determined in advance. So Marzouki shouldn't expect congratulations from his Arab colleagues, neighbors, or other Arab brothers: he's a new species, a threat, a case apart, a singularity. And in the subjugated Arab world and the dictators' club, he'll be seen badly, proof that the Neanderthal dictator is going to disappear through the laws of evolution. For the moment he's a unique case, the first president of a liberated Arab country. See the representatives of the Tunisian Assembly on their feet, singing their country's hymn, proud of their new chance and their country's second life. Congratulations! May the Marzoukis be more numerous one day than the Assads, and may this horrible story of blood, pain, and sacrifice that makes martyrs of us for freedom be finished. May there be a day when all the Arab presidents are elected, without cheating or crime; may they be legitimate, strong, and not the perfidious, crazy, old-fashioned little princelets of their families, but filled with the song of their people.

2012

ANALYSIS OF
A DOUBLE IMMOLATION

"I'm not Bouazizi. I just want a place to live." That's what an Algerian who tried to set himself on fire told a colleague at *El Watan*. The phrase sums up nicely the crushing of life. An Algerian reduced to broken glass, mere fragments of demands. The guy has good reason: he doesn't care about springtime for everyone, he just wants a season for himself. It's the particularly Algerian situation: revolution that's individual, personalized, solitary, a matter of oneself. Multiplied by 36 million, that makes a request for one sprig of jasmine per person, with total handouts coming to zero. So the regime has succeeded: it doesn't beat anyone up, doesn't ban anything explicitly, doesn't kill or repress the masses, or shoot at the crowd; it just asks everyone to get in line. One Algerian behind the other, in front of the sole ticket counter for the oil-instead-of-food program.

The sentence is an extraordinary synopsis of the answer to the famous question: Why hasn't Algeria exploded? Response: nothing is my problem. The regime says, I'm listening to you, one by one. I will reply to each of you, one by one. So there's nothing tying those making the demands together, no common slogan, no unanimous cry, no "Get out!" in unison. It's a tremendous achievement, dispersing the crowd before it gathers.

The sentence also reveals a deep political nihilism: many Algerians don't see the connection between their misery and its cause.

They rise up against the mayor, but not against the fraudulent election that put him in power. They denounce a policy, without being willing to admit that that's what politics is. No—I'm not Bouazizi. I just want my piece, not my rights. A roof, not a country. A crumb, not the whole package of citizenship. I set fire to myself, but not to bother you too much. "I'm not Bouazizi" is my way of saying that I don't exist, and I want to say it so much and so publicly that I should be rewarded because I'm fulfilling your goals for you. Bouazizi is our common enemy. Yours and mine. You want nothing of him, and I'm telling you that I don't want to be him. Can we get along? This is well-calculated despair, negation of the self behind one's "Algerian" identity, abnegation of the right to say "no" because I am saying no to myself—which means, through double negation, a "yes" to you. And then it becomes comprehensible: the Algerian has been so depoliticized that he assumes this position as evidence of his nationalism.

This Algerian's words are a double immolation: I set fire to myself, but also to the potential Bouazizi in me. Furthermore, I burn him before I burn me. Or after. A sentence with real weight, a sign of true misery, in both meaning and act. They're the words of a man without a roof, the father of a disabled girl. So we must not judge him; just reflect on this astonishing testimony of sadness and denial. The man sets fire to himself and also to the meaning of his action. He understood the message: we'll only give you a roof or a barrel or money if you prove that you don't exist, that you're nothing. A choice between existing and living. You can have a roof, but part of the rent is conditional on negation of the self, and signed at the bottom in ash.

WHILE IT'S SNOWING OUTSIDE: THE REAL SECRET TO BEING A COLUMNIST

It's like a dog inside my head: it barks, and I write. Except it's not so simple. It seems to me that I'm the one at the end of the leash; it walks me, sometimes for half an hour per day, lets me prance through its universe and then leads me toward my blind spot—my everyday life. Let me explain: it's a giant dog made up of stars in a dark night that wraps him in its boundless skin. He barks out letters, I write. Sometimes I write well, sometimes not, when he goes too fast and I can only catch partial sentences. He's big, this black dog who jumps over me to go and drink water on the other side of the world and then come back. That's how I describe the things that happen in my head. Because to those who see me from the outside, nothing is happening. I'm bent over an enormous notebook filled with things that are crossed out, in front of a microphone, tapping at a keyboard, and I write endlessly, all the time. A scribe at a newspaper, paid to pretend to have courage. But no one knows that I cross things out incessantly between columns. It's kind of on purpose, my way of writing through my scritch-scratch. In fact, it's a pathway between my letters and the vast, cosmic barking of the dog holding me on a leash that hangs from the end of his paw, like a constellation above this miniature world. So my inspiration comes from a divine animal—he could even have been one of the twelve zodiac signs, if such a thing happened inside several heads turned toward the sky, and not just mine, which is too small for all that. What do I write? What I can't write in any other way: madness. Good madness, the one that holds the keys to an immense door leading to the sky, or into a library where the mass of all possible things is described: the colors, meanings, future, and purpose, arranged on the shelves with a Holy Book that constitutes the absolute instruction manual. That's how it is. I like the dog, and I know he'll murmur in my ear when I fall short in explaining the universe. He knows so many things, sometimes I'm virtually in love, like a woman whom a man has promised to protect from the world's thorns. It doesn't happen all the time, and eventually I came to understand that this is inspiration. That's what it is. The dog is my inspiration. Often I sense the great texts that arrive in my head first as melodies. Music, I swear, or the notes of a piano. It's sound before ink and notebook. I don't even know what I'm going to write. I just know that somewhere it's all in order, already in a head that's more expansive than mine. Then I begin to write, and the images arrive first. They make me laugh! They always have this way of giving me an angle, and adding a pheasant's tail to the ends of sentences that others have worn out. For example, when I write, "Baghdad has fallen," the idea of a pair of pants comes to me. The sky is a stork's leg. I get the impression that the words are waiting for me to fold their imaginary paper in a new way. I can feel the tired metaphors in my skin, the clichés, the lazy images. First I write a sound, and the meaning comes afterward. It's the dog who dictates it to me: large and black, but capable of romping through the immensity of things and then coming back to circle around me gently. I'm its translator. I've felt it since childhood: my head is someone else's fingertip. His pen rests on the corner of a notebook, the sky is a face in thought. I'm just the instrument. A drop of ink at the end of an idea about the air. For example, right now the dog is whispering to me: Why are you talking about this? Who will understand? People will think you're reciting a poem and no one will really believe you. It accomplishes nothing, he says to me, and then runs off. Where does he go when I'm not writing? I've never tried following him. It's too dangerous, not for me. I was four years old when I saw Dolma the dog for the first time in his Soviet spacesuit. He taught me to write like juggling, and to find solutions like stones collected at the mouth of a dried-up riverbed. It didn't scare me, but I was a little uncomfortable with the size of his presence inside my head, and because when he barked for the first time there were thousands of languages. *The Thousand and One Nights* was barely one and a half lines in the long story he told me. I think I've said too much. I'll stop here.

Since then I've known I had a book under my arm, that I was its author and it would be infinite. And each time I returned to it, the story would change, along with the hero, the landscape, and the ending.

APRIL 19

ARE THE PEOPLE CULPRITS
OR VICTIMS? (I)

Are the people victims of power, or of themselves?

It's a big debate among Algerian intellectuals. The left contin-ues to treat the Algerian people as though they had been subtracted from the equation of power. It's an antiquated vision of the people as poor, malnourished, colonized by others and then by themselves, naive, forced into illiteracy and to the edges of existence, good by nature, courageous if given the chance. On the other side, the right regards the people with contempt: what happens to them is the result of their sinful subservience to ritual and to their own failures. If they are who they are, on the margins of their own country, it's because they don't fight, don't rise up, don't criticize or protest, and they turn to the heavens and to fatalism to explain their disillu-sion and their fate as an empty bag that won't stand up. According to this almost neocolonial view, the people are indigenous because they deserve it. They are complicit in the crimes against them, and if *le pouvoir* despises them, it's because the people are greedy, weak, lazy, never satisfied, rude, lacking in civility, racist, disrespectful of women and stoplights, poorly educated, and lacking the desire to improve themselves.

So between these two visions, where exactly are the people? Who knows? Those we imagine in our heads, who push you over in a shop, enter last, put an arm over your shoulder and order a kilo of sugar. The paradox is that both visions entail culpability. On one hand, we don't like when foreigners criticize the people because we are of the people; on the other hand, we don't feel we are part of this people because they don't correspond to our aspirations or to our criteria for good manners. Everyone feels alone.

A week ago, while giving a lecture in Oran, the great sociologist Lahouari Addi explained that Algerians want to escape. Always to somewhere farther away. There are even a number of jokes about the Algerian who is seeking a place where there will be no Algerians other than himself. This land remains unknown and impossible, as we Algerians are everywhere and will be wherever we go. We are trying to escape ourselves in the name of the people, and the people in the name of themselves.

So are the people victims of this power, which in fact comes from the people, or of their passivity? Both. If we've become this way, it's because of "them," and Education Minister Benbouzid's twenty-two-year reign, the longest in the world. Are the people responsible? Yes. Everyone can see it. In himself, his neighbors, the guy who hands over control and the millions of other gestures that make us want to flee to everywhere where we are not. This is a giant debate. Two million square kilometers wide. It's inescapable perhaps because what we need is to rebuild the community and regain a desire to live together. Without that, all the visas in the world won't do, and neither will all the imagined lands.

APRIL 21

ARE THE PEOPLE CULPRITS OR VICTIMS? (II)

Are the people victims of power or of themselves? Both answers are valid: *le pouvoir* has made this people indigenous—illiterate, vain, medieval, superstitious, violent, and poorly dressed. They are everything that Meursault, Albert Camus's hero, saw in the figure of "the Arab," whom he ended up killing, gun in hand, on a beach in Algiers. How do you attain power? For Algerians, by turning back the clock: from the elite inheritors of the 1970s, to the zaouias of the 1940s, to the newspaper readers of the 1920s. Beyond that, the tribes in thrall to the dey of Algiers, and so on. Who is doing this? An education system with the goal of instilling general imbecility. "We think *le pouvoir* failed in education, but that's false: it succeeded, because its goal was to undo the literacy of the people and the generations," a colleague told the columnist. It explains Benbouzid's inexplicable permanence at the Education Ministry. What's more, if you add to this deculturation the FLN, UGTA, the ban on protests and on participating in one's own country, the 1990s, and the elimination of elites, it leaves you with this people as absolute victim of absolute power.

Except that, in the game of submission, the people are also guilty: power as currently practiced is not a foreign entity, as it was for millennia, but something local. It's the only product that's "made in Algeria," renewed every day, performing itself. The fatalist's dictionary offers the perfect axiom: "You have the government that you deserve." The people don't want to want anything, they say nothing and allow everything by their collective resignation, the sum total of each individual resignation. And here you start to see a solution to this desire to flee, to go far away, to leave and put the maximum distance between yourself and your nationality. What is it? To see yourself as all of the people, the sole inhabitant of an island, the only one in charge, and to act upon oneself: wash your hands before meals, don't burn red lights, don't be deferential to the measure of what's possible, don't see yourself as the appointed attorney for Islam, don't be intolerant, don't lie to yourself, don't be lazy, a thief, corrupt, weak...in sum, it's the entire catalogue of divine, good manners. And everyone else? The rest of the people who don't want to change? That's precisely the trap. The solution is to strive in life as in death, beginning at birth: protect, above all, the meaning of your life. Oddly, this behavior is contagious: through the total egotism of the man who wants a better world for himself, you get sooner or later the unforeseen generosity of a better world for all; or at least one that's less burdensome to carry on your back. You also get past the self-hatred that's been pounded into our culture, our official language, the denial of self and history. Is it a confusing and complicated idea? Yes, because it's counterintuitive and entirely new. Making peace is hard work for a people that knows only war. It's also counterintuitive to the current school of thought—the colonization, Arabization, the FLN, the general ignorance. One day we will travel the world to understand that you can't escape your own shadow in the light of the obvious.

MAY 29

CAN ARAB ARMIES BE ABSORBED INTO DEMOCRACIES?

What will the army do if it loses the Egyptian presidential election? The question is being asked in Egypt and elsewhere. The transition process will determine what happens next in the Arab Spring. Arab armies, these self-proclaimed guardians of borders and everything inside them, tutors of people who've only just been decolonized; they appear frowning, guns strapped to their backs, in uniform to distinguish themselves from the natives, bearing a savior's mission and their initiation into this secret cult.

These Arab armies have a strange profession: after liberation, they became guardians of freedom and anxiety. Their understanding of themselves as mentors has coincided with the development of fortunes, strategic interests, and corruption. Today it's easier to get rid of a dictator than to make soldiers go back to their barracks, get them out of the ministries, businesses, and administrative agencies: they have interests, industries, their own history, children, bank accounts, and convictions. That makes it hard to move on to democracy.

And so, as the most intuitive have understood, the Egyptian presidential election is of great interest to the chiefs of staff in this world that is no longer Arab. The Egyptian army can play it the Algerian way if it loses. It can also win elections in the Algerian way—with three-fourths of the presidency, or by putting a fake civilian in place just for show. They can't stay onstage, because putschists aren't made for polite society; but they can't go back to the barracks, because the Islamists are neither reliable nor fully developed. The army can't remain part of the show, but they can't retreat without guarantees.

In Algeria, the elite could have made up for lost time in a decade, but in Egypt time has already been taken into consideration and an immediate transition is needed. The other Arab armies are watching the Cairo laboratory, asking themselves if their fate lies with the dictator or with a successful transition. Should they speak out, or should they go silent? Invest in politics, or create a kind of vassalized personnel for the grunt work and smokescreen societies, as in Algeria.

The armies are watching: in Turkey and Jordan they followed the Algerian story. The Algerians watched Latin America and Russia. The Syrians observed the destructive forces here in the 1990s with fascination. The Tunisian army wants to learn the Egyptian lesson, the Libyan army wants to establish itself like others. Arab armies are the Gordian knot of failed democracies in this universe; the dictators are merely the worst symptom of this nation-owning illness. The Arab armies have no profession, no calling, no real skill: no strategy for conquering the world, no widespread convictions. No pet issues, no trust, no love or mutual admiration. Just their routine as suspicious sentinels, their paranoia, agitating hymns, and flags. Can Arab armies be absorbed into a democracy? It requires great courage and significant guarantees. Can Islamists be absorbed into a democracy? You need an army to make it happen. And the people? Can they be absorbed into a democracy? No one knows that either. Especially after the Arab Spring and the massive vote for the bearded men, with a seal stamped across the front.

JUNE 24

SWIMMING INSIDE A WALL

Swimming on the inside of a wall. On the sand, facing the sea, Algeria is forced to confront its own body and the insides of the bodies of others. On the beach, without clothes, you can see nationality. The Algerian carries his body on his back. Sometimes, out of suspicion or shame, he keeps it at a distance. If he's an Islamist, conservative, or riddled with metaphysical guilt, the Algerian sees his body as a crime or a culprit. So he washes it, forbids its nakedness, its presence, beauty, visibility, and, finally, its existence. The body is also used to express superiority over other bodies: paunch isn't ungainly, but a sign of wealth. And for Algerian women? It's worse. There, the body is guilty of all the possible crimes of all other bodies. A woman's body is hunted, frisked, refused, rejected, and accused—not only of being the body of a woman, but also of being the cause of the male body's unhappiness. An Algerian man's body is a future crime; a woman's body is the evidence of this crime, even if it hasn't been committed yet.

On the beach, on the sand, between the sea and the sun, the Algerian body is at its worst—distrusting, animalistic in its suspicions, sullied by so many sick and violent ideas. Algerians are more aggressive when naked than armed. The Algerian body is uneasy between the parasol and the heavens: it doesn't know how to relax when bathing, to dress or undress, or approach another body without engaging in a game of submission and dominance; to float, or be

116

forgiven. These living bodies feel ashamed compared with the martyrs who unburdened themselves of their bodies.

In a country where death is a value, the body is a receptacle without meaning or sensuality on a path with no purpose.

So, Algerians make these impossible movements in the water, like figurines swimming inside a wall. Compared to us, the cave depictions of the Sahara seem like champions of relaxation and pleasure. The beach is treated like a body, too: paved over, stolen, assaulted, dirtied, trampled, and privatized. The Algerian beach is the naked Algerian body, seen from the inside. In old metaphysical texts the body is dressed according to the spirit. In this country the soul taints the body, keeps it from being naked, beautiful, lighthearted, and admired. You only have to walk along the Algerian beach to see what's happening inside the head.

SEPTEMBER 16

QUESTION OF THE CENTURY: WHAT DO WE DO WITH THE ISLAMISTS?

What do we do with the Islamists? The question is growing urgent for everyone—in the West, here at home, in daily life, and in the half-life of political ideas and theories. The proof is that you can't get around them with revolution: they're the only ones who will die for an idea, resort to martyrdom, and sacrifice the body. That makes them an armed force, belligerent for war. They are numerous, everywhere, so you can't form a political and social consensus without associating with them, inviting them in, listening to them and sharing with them. You also can't eliminate them, or not all of them—exterminate them, put them all in prison, torture them in a basement or in Guantánamo. You can't throw them all in the ocean like bin Laden, or usher them into the desert where they'll just reproduce.

The Arab dictatorships tried all that but succeeded only in turning them into absolute victims, which exacerbated their radicalism and their violence.

At the same time, the Arab Spring in certain countries is proving again and again that you can't trust the Islamists, let them in, democratize, delegate, or govern with them. Their project is exclusive, undemocratic, and seeks to establish a caliphate in one form or another. With one discourse or another. In one time frame or another.

After the atrocious murder of the American ambassador in Benghazi, and the horrifying photos, displayed like a gruesome memento, Hillary Clinton cried: How can a city that we've done so much to save from being massacred do this? It's the wrong question. Because it's an incorrect understanding. The West also believed that the Islamists were victims of the dictatorships, whereas they are the product, the delayed explosion, the remains. For decades the Arab regimes encouraged the bearded men while hunting down the progressives. And this happened everywhere, in manipulations at the national level and as deals between the conservative powers, zaouias, mosques, and sheikhs. In Algeria the deal is visible to the naked eye: in place of the biggest country in Africa you have the biggest mosque in Africa, propagating its projects. The Islamic Front couldn't have imagined better. And so the Islamists are there, reproducing, multiplying, becoming more numerous and more ambitious in imposing on Algerians their credo, their habits, ideas, rituals, and understandings. Their movement is becoming polarized between patient politicians and armed hysterics. So what do we do with them?

Duplicitously, the dictators said that the Islamists must be contained and killed. Then, by encouraging the movement to grow, they consolidated their argument that the dictatorship is necessary for stability.

The West believed in their power to integrate them or reeducate them through pragmatism—that if we help them, listen to them, associate with them, in the end they will join humanity.

Progressives, secular or otherwise, said that it was necessary to fight them: if you isolate them, dismantle their ideology, and expose them, people will lose confidence in them and they will be absorbed back into the sand.

But in the meantime these people of the everlasting advance, kill, conquer, and confiscate. How? It's obvious: in education, in the schools, in the womb. In the Arab world, while everyone believes they're being contained, there's an ideological womb that continues to grow Islamists from the cradle—at school, on TV, in advertisements, on the streets, and in the mosques. The world sees Islamists as the final product, rather than the origin of this century's evil: in the schools, books, and fatwas. The Arab world continues to grow Islamists from the roots, everywhere and with plenty of money. Wahhabi ideas and the other ancestors of these crimes are spreading, penetrating walls and heads. Everywhere in the Arab world there is a continuous drift from law toward fatwa, from officials elected in the voting booths to the imam elected in the sky, from constitution to Sharia, from school to recitation by heart. This source must be drained dry if we don't want a theological empire in a few decades. Without efforts in education, our ideas are no good and we will find ourselves facing the same question in fifty years.

While the world searches, the religious elite in Saudi Arabia and Iran continue to publish, explain, convert, and spread their opinions, ideologies, and conception of the world. It happens fast.

There's no time or space between a fatwa in Mecca and the head of an adolescent in the Sahel. We see it everywhere: this ideology has money, schools, and networks, and they're growing. Our children no longer believe in life, only in its gratuitousness. The Islamists are going back in time, faster and faster, and those who don't like it are killed, stoned, buried, or excommunicated. We must attack the cause, not the effect. But there, both the West and the Arab dictators are complicit: each Arab power has its own Islamists that it manages, avoids, encourages, or tries to hide. The United States too: one need only look at their blindness toward Saudi Arabia—a source of oil and suicide bombers.

NOTHING TIMES THREE

There's only one God in the desert, but they are three.

The Muslim says: "I'm the best, because we're the last living beings that God spoke to and to whom he gave a book." The Jew says: "That doesn't make sense. We're the best because God chose us and spoke to us first." The Christian laughs and says: "We're the best, because God came to us, he was among us, and he spoke to us one by one."

The desert says nothing, but moves ten meters toward the three travelers.

So the Muslim says: "Abraham is father to all of us, but it was for us and our mother that he left his Jewish wife to build a home in the desert." The Jew says: "Wrong. He is above all *our* father, because after going to the desert he returned home. Which is to say, our home." The Christian says: "Abraham is father for both of you, but he's only a man. Our father isn't in the desert or on a mountain, but in the sky and in our hearts." The Muslim starts to get angry: "No! His favorite son was Ismael, our ancestor. It was Ismael that God saved with a lamb on top of the mountain!" Same for the Jew: "No! It was *our* ancestor. Not yours. And since we're on the subject, today you slit the throats of both your sons and your sheep." The Muslim begins to gather stones, the Jew burning bushes. The Christian interrupts: "Calm down, brothers! Come to us. For us, God sacrificed himself, to avoid these problems."

And during this time, the desert comes even closer to the three pilgrims.

The sun was high in the sky, the wind gentle, humanity far away. A tension settled among the three companions, who were on the same journey toward the same destination, but wearing different shoes. "I'm not doing anything, it's Friday." The Jew jumps in: "But no! Today is Saturday." The Christian laughs: "My brothers, it's Sunday. I've known that since this morning."

For the desert it was the same day. Forever. The day when it would die and spread toward the sky to demand water.

"I like the desert, it's where our religion was born," says the first. "No, it's where *ours* was born," says the second. "No, you're really talking about mine," the third says. But they were all thinking: this might be where we all die.

And the desert moved another step in their direction, eyes squinting, throat open. A terrified lizard darted away.

After a long silence, the Jew dares to ask: "Why don't you want people to draw your prophet?" The Muslim retorts: "We'll allow it the day you agree to let others determine your borders!" The Christian bursts out laughing: "God formed man in his own image. We are God's design, and it's He who creates!" The Muslim and the Jew turn toward him: "Yes. And he's white, without a hooked nose or dark skin, armed, and likes colonies and ovens!"

Just then, the desert came even closer, arriving at the feet of the three travelers, who hadn't noticed anything while they were busy seeking the sky inside their eyelids. The silence was the highest minaret in the world, the most beautiful church, the oldest synagogue, but the three pilgrims hadn't noticed it. The beauty of that moment was spoiled by the pettiness of these three passengers to eternity. Their cries could be heard far away in the desert, which was advancing without stopping. The three argued about God, their ancestors, their sacred texts, the Holy City, Palestine, Andalusia, the meaning of the word "Amen/Amine," the origins of Islam and Israel and the Declaration of the Rights of Man. They accused each other of murdering the most men in the name of God (or the most pagan gods in the name of universal man), and said evil things to each other, accusing the others of copying passages from their own holy books. "You want to kill the entire world," the Jewish pilgrim cried to the Muslim, who shouted: "You want to take revenge on the whole planet!" Before the two had a chance to accuse the Christian of wanting to take over the world, the latter cried: "The entire earth asks me to save the both of you!" Then, as the desert came right up to their hips, and the sky covered its ears and the sun drank in the last waters, the three pilgrims came to blows.

One pulled a beard, then an ear, a rosary, then a cassock and a finger, and dug into quadriceps with the teeth. An eye tried to see a bleeding nose, just before a lip asked for help. One man shouted, another groaned. All three were monotheists, though their insults were polytheist. Fighting made them thirsty, and they fell into a stupor. The desert was now at their mouths, just below the lip, and was getting ready to swallow them. There was only one flask of water, a single one that had been placed on a small hill by an unknown hand. "It's a miracle!" the Christian cried. "Blessed water," he murmured, before making a dash for it. The Muslim knocked him down in the air. "No, it's the water of the zemzem well of Mecca," he shouted before throwing himself on top of the Christian. "No, it's the water of Moses and we are on my Sinai," the Jew said fiercely. The struggle started up again. And at the end, they all died. Murdered by one another. The desert ate them all, quickly, and then left.

Water flowed, and with it, time. A wind appeared and drew a thoughtful figure in the sand. A lizard seeking the sun settled itself in the reflection. And then, nothing. The world felt better.

OCTOBER 16 *

THE HEAVIEST TURBAN
IN THE WORLD

The day before yesterday, an Austrian completed the highest dive in the world—a free fall from the sky. He broke the sound barrier, and image barriers, too. Millions of people followed this giant winged leap for man, small step for a plane. And what did we do in the meantime? Talked about the Algeria-Libya match, as one clear-eyed blogger wrote. To each his own. Some want to break records, others want to break their neighbors. An Algerian scaled a mountain a few months ago: Nadir Dendoune, Everest. But in silence, and without accolades. Why is it that people elsewhere seek to vanquish the world, and here we seek only to vanquish the West, or our neighbors? It's about values. The West is the center of the world, the nest of human values, whether we like it or not. And so, their quest to be the embodiment of humanity inspires great desires: to walk on the moon, to walk on the air, invent the iPad, decode the human genome, send robots to Mars. Here, humanity hasn't even been born yet: only nationalities that subsume regions that subsume tribes that hide families that mask genealogical lines. We don't claim humanity, only nationality or religion or Arabness or any other label from

---

* On October 14, 2012, the Austrian skydiver Felix Baumgartner jumped from a helium balloon at a twenty-four-mile altitude, becoming the first person to break the sound barrier.

our ancestors. Where the West measures itself against the universe, we measure ourselves against the former colonists.

To each his own gods to fight and defy.

But it's a tragedy, to be confined to this decolonization without end, this perpetual jeremiad, this complex of the periphery. Everywhere you feel the weight of our secondary status: when our regimes seek the assent of the West, or an alliance, justice, knowledge, values, confirmation, and even when we go there to collect rejections, the better to justify our idiosyncrasies, our isolationism.

So, how do we recover the center of the world, measure ourselves against the world by challenging ourselves, with courage and mastery? How do we stop being indigenous, angry, envious, and sad? By accepting our humanity, and the human in oneself. And we can't do this so long as we claim religion as difference, culture as ghetto, keep our territory blocked off from others, see the other as a threat, and so long as women, half of humanity, are buried along with our desires for the world and the desires of our bodies, which are treated as a source of guilt.

You can see this difference in the tale of Prometheus: in the Greek version, he stole fire and paid for it as a martyr. In our version, he warms his hands with the fire, and pays for it with oil. Even worse—our Prometheus didn't steal anything from the gods in order to enlighten man; he's content just to grovel at their feet.

For those who know the myth, it's something to think about.

THE ISRAELI, THE ARAB,
AND THE ISLAMIST:
THE PALESTINIANS' THREE MURDERERS

What should an Islamist in power do about the Palestinian cause? Hard to say. In the past, when the Islamist was in the opposition, Palestine was a simple holy war; today the Islamist is in control, and Palestine is an impossible problem. How do you simultaneously help the "brothers" in Gaza, not contradict yourself on the tenets of your religion, keep international relations intact, not further erode your social capital, which has already been diminished by Salafists, and also secure aid from a West painted by religious propaganda as the great devil, the crusader, the enemy? How can you be at once religious and pragmatic? How can you free Palestine if you yourself are not free in your own country, but besieged, inexperienced, invisible?

The Tunisian and Egyptian governments made a swift gesture by sending their foreign ministers to Gaza. Top marks for marketing. But it won't end the war, only reinforce the fact that the Palestinians' misery will continue to legitimize their diplomatic policy. We all know the biggest flaw of a dead Palestinian: he's too Arab, too Islamic. They've tried to transform a tragic cause of colonization and decolonization into a "pan-Arab" and Islamic messianic one. This pleases the Israeli right and its ultra-Orthodox nationalists to the point of orgasm: extremists love extremists, and a religious or racist Palestine is an ideal target for extreme causes in Israel.

But the Palestinian tragedy will only enter into the preoccupations of humanity the day it gets rid of the Arabs and the Islamists. A dead Palestinian will be a murder victim only when he's no longer a bearded martyr or a bombed Arab. Arabness and religion exile the Palestinian to the margins of international attention; they empty him out, dehumanize him, turn him into a local issue. The Islamist takeover of governments in Tunis and Cairo may offer an ideological fraternity, and better positioning than on the Mubarak regime's shameful wall against the Gazans, but they do nothing for the future. This future is already blocked. Indeed it serves the image of the Islamist governments well, and they deal with their uncomfortable position by throwing fists of sand.

The century-old question is, what do we do for Palestine? The same thing we should do for colonized Tibet: tell humanity that it's everyone's cause, not just the Arabs' or the faithful. Palestine deserves the same as Tibet, like other stolen lands and souls.

The first battle, which will be difficult to win, is to show that the death of a Palestinian is the death of a human being, not a television clip, not an Arab or an Islamist. A colonized being, with a human death. A story of people, not beliefs. An issue of freedom, not a crusade. We must free Palestine: from Israelis who want to steal it, but also from Arabs and Islamists who want to sell it and buy it and throw it over their back and speak for it in its place.

DECEMBER 26 *

HOMAGE TO ALIAA MAGDA ELMAHDY AND THE ONLY NAKED TRUTH

The body isn't a stain. It isn't the crime of my parents. It's not a burden. It's my joy, my cosmos, my way in the world, and the only connection I have with God, or the rocky contours of the earth. It is my meaning, and the meaning of everything that I do, everything that obstructs me or enlightens me. I don't drag it behind me but carry it in front of me, it decodes my breath and my part of the world, its dust, odors, grain, and weight. My body is my pleasure, my truth. When they take my body they take my life, and life comes back to me when I meet the other's body, where I create life. It's a long story that I don't want to suffer through anymore: the history of religions in this world, which tell me repeatedly that my body is a blindness, a loss. My own truth is naked and clear when my body isn't darkness or shame. The body is the only thing that's divine, the only eternity that I can touch with my hands. I can give it a name, or take it away and share it. It's in the body that I find heaven or lose it, not in prayer. I dream of it, naked, proud, vigorous, praised for its performance, revered as a fortune, a conquest. I want it to be free: I don't want the body to apologize for itself, to hide, retreat, suffer, become

---

* On December 20, the Egyptian blogger Aliaa Magda Elmahdy demonstrated naked with other members of Femen in front of the Egyptian embassy in Stockholm, to protest against an Islamic constitution.

isolated, or want for anything other than itself. The body is not a nationality; it's my only source of humanity.

The body is not the site of your wars, it's the place of my encounters. It's an embrace. I'm not the child of a stolen fruit, but the fruit itself. I give it and I accept it. I want to live freely in my body. No longer hide it or impose it; accept it, not agree to get rid of it and betray it. Nakedness is sincerity. Sexuality is mine to share, not my shame. And I refuse the threat of hell and the promise of heaven only after being freed from my body, after betraying it. I don't want that. I am what I feel. With the sand beneath my feet I lift my eyes, not the palms of my hands, toward the sky. I am half the world, not its plunder, its anger, its blind spot, its dirty work or its waste. I want to feel close to the sun. To feel myself the husband or wife of plenitude. Why is there so much hatred for my body? Because it's my only source of wealth against the impoverished, disembodied gods. I am a body, they are only empires. I am the place, they are the history. The angels and the devils and the invisible rulers envy me for it. So I assert it with my skin: I'm against all religions that want to erase my birth so that they can live off my back. I won't hide it (me) anymore. Only death can kill me. Everything else casts a shadow over me. The body is a cry, not a crime or a creed: a jewel, not a cross or a stain. It's my joy and my faith. My resistance. I refuse everything else—what they told me about heaven, the Book, shame, sex, and eternity. I say no to everything they've always told me about my body, forever.

I dream of the day when the body isn't a source of shame—that's when life becomes a conquest, the country has flesh, the earth is maternal in a way that you can feel in your palms and your lungs and in the space inside yourself. I like ancient religions, those of the body and the sun, which were extinguished by guilt, abstinence, and mortal fear. Paradise is in my senses, not in death. And they need my body, not my soul, to populate hell! I'm not something to hide, but something to be revealed. Not something to insult, but to admire. The original written word. The mysterious, astonishing "pluriscrit." The true north of all bodies. The singular meaning of all meanings. God's design. The bridge between the world and my breath. And that's why they're against me: the hateful, the Salafists, the religious, the ashamed, the afflicted, the sad, the vanquished, the choleric, and those millions of people who are against themselves. I am unique. At each moment. A miracle. When women are trapped, men can never be free, and the body is an illness. Free me, and you will be more free...

AFTER THE REVOLUTION: SHOULD ARABS BE ALLOWED TO VOTE?

It's a quiet dilemma for elites: should they let people vote, in the name of democracy, or save democracy by keeping them from voting? It's an old calculation in Algeria, and now in Egypt, for example, too. There it's a total trap: free elections liberate the devil, not freedom. For the new constitution, the Muslim Brotherhood appealed to the piety of good people, and the "masses" voted yes for Sharia light. The economic and cultural elite, the middle classes, those who make money and values and surpluses, are against it. They're the minority. "What did you think would happen when you let illiterates decide on a constitution that they don't even know how to read?" an Egyptian woman cried into the cameras. When people vote, that's called democracy. Except that the vote of the CEO whose business employs thousands of workers is more important than those of an entire village that just chews and produces nothing.

But the majority opinion isn't necessarily right, and the minority opinion isn't wrong either. The elites of the world cry "Arab"—not aloud, but they think it more and more openly. Meaning, allowing people to vote who don't calculate the consequences of their actions, lack conscience and culture, who were born and remained long dead under dictatorships, people who are culturally checked out, fatalistic, trained in the religion of defeat and populism—letting these people vote is wrong. They can only choose ignorantly and elect the worst, who promise them paradise after death, but not before. The most important question, however, is more serious: what good is revolution against a dictatorship if it doesn't give voting rights to the people?

Others offer another idea: educate the people, reform schools and heads, secularize religion, reform Islam, pressure people to take responsibility for their actions and be conscious of the distinction between religion and managing the city and freedom, before giving them the right to vote. Except that that's exactly what the dictators said. In Algeria, Bouteflika repeated it often in his written correspondence: democracy must be learned; culturally we are not ready and we must give it time. In the end, we vote badly, or timidly, or not at all, and we have Belkhadems at the end of the assembly line, or former ministers' sons who own malls and deposit money in banks on faraway islands and secretly employ the Swiss from Algiers.

So in sum we have: (I) The right to vote must not be given to people who don't know how to vote (the position of regimes of supposedly authoritarian pedagogy). (II) We must get rid of dictators who don't allow people to choose their own destiny (position of revolutionaries: people, elites, and Islamists all mixed together). (III) The people have the right to vote against the elites because it's the law of the majority against the minority, and that's democracy (position of the Islamists, for whom democracy is like a camel—you can climb on top of it, milk it, eat it, use it as shelter, make clothing of it, raise it, but never hesitate to slaughter, sell, or buy it). (IV) We shouldn't let people vote who don't know how, vote against democracy (position of the postrevolution elites, or post—civil war in Algeria). (V) The regimes and dictators say, "But that's exactly what I was saying." (VI) The regimes continue: "Revolution does nothing if it just brings us back to what I was saying all along." (VII) There must be a revolution of mentality, culture, minds, and schools before the dictator gets thrown out, says part of the elite, trying to find a solution. The other part of the elite replies, "But that's no good, precisely because the regime controls the schools, religion, minds, and public spaces," adding, "That takes centuries, and we have only one life."

In the end we have to admit to ourselves that the principle is good, beautiful, but it puts into question the West's achievements since the end of the Middle Ages: direct vote by the masses. Is voting good for those who don't know how to vote? Should democracy be permitted for those who murder it democratically? Can you democratically choose a dictatorship, or its opposite? The answers to these types of questions are always bad. They lead to killing, massacring, stealing—or to liberation. It depends. And yet the solution is there: find a way for everyone to vote, but so that some vote more than others. But there too—who will be the big electors and who the small electors? Those who pray the most? Those who have guns? Business owners? Those who fought in the War of Independence? Those who've never committed a crime?

The other question is: when half the people abstain from an election, is the legitimate result in the ballot boxes or in the abstention?

2013

JIHADISTS ARE THE CHILDREN OF DICTATORSHIP, NOT REVOLUTION

"This is the result of the Arab Spring," an anonymous Algerian official told the *New York Times*, as recounted by the Algerian online journal *TSA*. It's the new equation of semantic shift in the words "democracy," "chaos," "revolution," "disorder," "Islamists," etc. In Algeria, the regime has played on the fear of chaos and the traumas of the 1990s to stop the demands for change cold, and to sell democracy as the enemy of well-being. Since the hostage crisis in Amenas, this equation is being repackaged for Western opinion: the jihadists are the consequence of the Arab Spring. Is it true? No. The revolutions in Tunisia, Egypt, and especially in Libya allowed Islamists to take power and jihadists to return to armed conflict. But the Islamists and the jihadists were not born of the revolutions. They were born well before, from the regimes, the dictatorships, the ideological emptiness of nationalism, the injustice. The Islamists are above all the first-born and rightful sons of the fallen regimes and the Wahhabism that's been globalized by books and satellites.

These days the only thing we seem to remember from the dictatorships is the "stability" and order that resulted from their talent for policing. We forget, with criminal ease, the torture, denial of rights, the plundering of wealth, the assault, fraud, corruption, evil, forced disappearances, theft, and assassinations. We forget the war on progress, the universities turned into vassals, the elites subjected to blackmail, the persecution of intellectuals and knowledge. We forget that these regimes cultivated the Islamists as an alibi ("If it's not me, it's them!"), fought off modernity, locked culture inside the mosque and the intelligence services. We also forget that, for lack of ideological alternatives to fake nationalism, people found refuge in Wahhabism and Islamism as a solution, because nothing else was allowed to emerge.

You don't create Islamists and jihadists by rebelling against a regime. You create jihadists when, instead of building the biggest country in Africa you build the biggest mosque, when you hound couples and freedoms, encourage bigotry and fatwas, and "Talibanize" schools and children rather than encouraging them to question themselves and the world and to create wealth and value. The modern equation is to "Afghanistanize" the people through the schools, and to "Pakistanize" the regimes through global war. It can only lead a country into a wall.

The Islamists are the direct descendants of the dictatorships. Qaddafi didn't have six children but thousands, from Benghazi to Gao. The same number as Mubarak. These aren't the children of revolution. You create them when you infantilize a population for decades, when you deculture them, reduce them to ignorance and take them back to the Middle Ages. The dictatorship may fall, but its effects are long-lasting: Islamists, abstention, disengagement, fatalism, violence as an institution, and intolerance. And if the Arab peoples rebelled, it's because of three major points of discontent: the political police, i.e., "Moukhabarats," which are a gangrene on the life of nations; the perversion of justice; and the dictators' sons. This is the crude reality, obvious to anyone unwilling to engage in illusions and lies.

To say now that the Arab Springs gave birth to jihadists is a manipulation, a lie, an oversimplification, and a trick. It's not true. In this "Arab" world, now at the center of the universe for its darkness rather than its avant-gardism or enlightenment, the Islamists and jihadists came about because for the last half-century we did everything to destroy anything that might lead to transcendence, reflection, freedom. We encouraged them, doped them up, kept track of them; anything that might offer an alternative to medieval times was put under surveillance and imprisoned. We destroyed any liberation or liberty that might have been attained after the colonists left.

Demanding democracy isn't a crime, and it's not the cause of the current turmoil. Chaos and violence are the crimes of regimes that know only how to create prisons, Islamists, and predators like the Tunisian president's wife. To say, now, that jihadists are a threat to the country is true, but we must also admit that you create jihadists when you refuse people freedom, knowledge, modern schools, free enterprise, creativity, and creation; when you encourage prayer instead of work, conservatism instead of citizenry, fatwas instead of the law. When you deprive people of their freedom, they get used to not having any—not in the name of a dictator, but in the name of God.

FEBRUARY 21

MILLIONS OF PEOPLE
WHO WRITE ONLY TWO WORDS

Like a country of thousands of idle fools, walking through the cosmos carrying labels and pencils with which to write on them. Write what? The two magic words from the binary of Islamism—this is haram, that's halal. For two decades this has been the preferred calculation in heads around here: categorize everything in creation with two concepts that derive from food and sex: halal or haram. Licit or illicit. It's a little like the favorite sport of the former colonists and their ancestors the explorers.

In the time of discovery, geographers, and silk roads, they sent the white man everywhere to affix his language, his vision, his names, and his numbers on new territories, primitive cultures, or those that were too weak to fight back. But while the colonist did this to appropriate the world for himself, the Islamist, or the bigot (the subsidiary product), does it in order to *not* eat—to rid himself of the world.

So almost all Algerians talk about it today, or a majority suppressed by itself and by heaven—spend the whole day, devote meetings, parties, and discussions to deciding what's haram and what's halal. According to the culture, the satellites, the old dog-eared books, or the decay of fatwa and deculturation. A product can pass from one category to the other depending on the mufti, the imam, geography, or money. They number millions, scribbling on stars or shells with their pencils, writing these two words. You can say over and over again that the items on the Koran's list of haram can be counted on one hand; it doesn't prevent the list from expanding to millions of things in everyday life. Which leads to the conclusion that this is not just about ritual and sacred space and dietary or sexual taboos, but a spiritual sickness that has taken off toward the sky, leaving its shoes behind. A kind of will to surpass laws, institutions, creation, and modernity with a simple game of binary numbers: zero and one. A neurosis for redefining the world into raw and cooked. It's a tragedy. To see wars of liberation, martyrs, sacrifices, elites, the millions of books read, education budgets, elections, fights for freedom and democracy, the universe of God or NASA, the efforts of geniuses and pioneers, all be reduced to an idiotic inventory of halal and haram. To see this mystical diversity of the universe transformed into an empty logic at the entrance to the human body.

And then you understand the tragedy: the Westerner, in his violent conquest, assigned names to things in order to appropriate the riches. Today's Islamists and Muslims lose this wealth by reducing the world to two concepts. Two words. Two colors. A lamentable undertaking of erasure, expunging, wiping out, with millions of pens in the hands of millions of imbeciles who, rather than explore the universe and try to take stock of infinity, prefer to shrink infinity to the size of their own pettiness.

And it only escalates: in heads, in families, on TV, in the mosques and on the streets. Instead of inventing objects and giving them names, we prefer to destroy things and take their names away. A Manichaeism that boils the world down to a great desert with a dividing line that cuts it in two: a halal desert against a haram desert. With, in fact, the same empty desert on both sides.

A dream of mine: to write the biography of a man who possesses thousands of words, and uses them to fight against the thousands of people who have only two.

WHY ARE ISLAMISTS
SO UNSETTLED BY WOMEN?

I wake up one morning and read a short item in an Arabic-language newspaper from London: the Saudi religious scholar Sheikh Abd Errahman Ben Nasser El Barek announced that giving women the right to drive would "open the doors of hell to the Kingdom," which pays his salary. It will lead to corruption, evil, misfortune, and disaster. I reread it, then turned to the real question: why are Islamists so uncomfortable with women? Where does this obsession come from? If you pry into it a bit, you could say that the troubled relationship with women is a byproduct of monotheistic religions in general: puritan religions born in empty deserts, in the time when abductions and rapes forced people to hide women, cover them, or bury them. You could also say that it's an idea that has persisted since prehistoric times: a woman can't serve the clan's needs for strength or war, she can't be a soldier, so she's a dead weight—an extra burden or another death. Even with the advent of monotheisms the idea endured, and it reentered heads when prehistoric dogmas reentered history. Today's Islamists are merely reviving ancient history, a time when having your women stolen was a sign of weakness, so for nomads or tribes woman was an incarnation of weakness.

But one might push even further into these problems: the Islamist dislikes life. For him life is a waste of time, blocking his way to eternity; it is temptation, a useless fertility, a distancing from God and from the sky, a delay on his appointment with the everlasting. Life is the consequence of a disobedience, and this disobedience is the consequence of a woman. The Islamist begrudges she who gives life, who prolongs the ordeal, who keeps him from heaven with a noxious murmur, who embodies the distance between himself and God. Woman is the source of life, and life is a waste of time, so woman incarnates the loss of the soul.

The Islamist is uncomfortable with a woman because she reminds him of her body, and therefore of his own body. The Islamist prefers to forget his body, to wash it until it dissolves, to reject it and sigh over it as one sighs over a shopping cart, to ignore it, despise it. But only in theory. Which is precisely what causes this violent emergence of instinct, and woman becomes guilty not only of having a body but of forcing the Islamist to have one, too; of forcing him to submit to it, or to compromise with its force and its desires. The Islamist is upset with woman because she is necessary, whereas he has declared that she is merely accessory.

The Islamist is uneasy in his body, and a woman reminds him of this. He has a troubled relationship with living beings, and woman, who gives life, reminds him that he brings death. The Islamist wants to veil woman to forget her, deny her, disembody her, escape her. And this is a trap, because he stumbles and falls back to earth, and then he holds this impossibility of surpassing life and attaining heaven against woman. She is thus his enemy, and, in order to kill her, he declares her the enemy of God, too.

The Islamist is unsettled by woman because he is also unsettled by difference. He dreams of a world that is uniform, unanimous; she embodies alterity, clear and unavoidable, the liberty not to be a man, and the ability to diversify the world.

And finally? Women remind the Islamist of his greatest, most profound weakness: desire. The desire to live, to touch, to endure in life. Desire that he wants to ignore but can't, is unable to vanquish inside himself without killing the woman in front of him. A murderous solution to an ancient judgment: Adam fell from paradise because of the woman who offered him fruit. To get back to heaven, according to the Islamist, you just have to kill/veil/ignore/ get rid of/stone women, which takes care of the fruit. That's where the Islamists' surreal obsession with the woman question comes from, their wars and their fatwas. In their sick world, women driving is the announcement of apocalypse, earthquakes, famine. And this idea is inculcated into them, and even female Islamists, who are the worst enemy of women.

Killing women is, therefore, to wish for the end of the world, the end of the struggle, to meet God and the everlasting, without punishment and with infinite comfort.

A naked woman is the Islamist uncovered.

A woman's body is the weakness he wants to erase.

Woman is not the Islamist's other half, but the entirety of his problems.

A LITTLE METAPHYSICS,
TO TAKE A BREAK FROM POLITICS

It's not my death that overwhelms me—no, that's mine. What knocks me over, makes me dizzy, fills me with rapture and disrupts my thoughts is my birth. My arrival in this world. How this immense void that preceded me ended with the completely chance consolidation and the extreme precision necessary to create me, my thoughts, and my identity out of infinity? What caused the emptiness to be filled with my presence? In what way am I a necessity, and how can a being of absolutely no expectation end by entering into the world as a person whom nothing else can replace? My tomb doesn't interest me, but the void that I stand on top of is fascinating. The vast cosmos that preceded my name is far more unsettling and inexplicable than the gravestone that will merely be trying to preserve a small piece of me. It's not death that's a big deal, but birth. That I should return to the void is a natural evolution, but that I should fill part of that void with my person, that's the great mystery that should occupy our thoughts, the deep anxiety that should make us all turn our heads toward our beginnings.

In the immense night, a fire alights. It's absurd to be surprised that it will go out, and we don't ask ourselves who's lit it in order to see what it is exactly, toward what end, whose hand is holding the fire, maintaining it, hoping to glean something from it. And in this night I sit reflecting on my predicament. Some tell me a hand lights the fire; others say it's an accident; others burn and turn their heads every which way; still others think it's useless to try to understand; others think there's a larger fire somewhere, and we're just the sparks. My only certainty is my own ardor. Everything else is stones thrown into black waters.

But my other certainty is that we travel through this night and illuminate ourselves for others. Some give their flame, others snuff it out on their way. That's the image I have of our condition. Of my condition. And that's all just to speak of this dizziness that seized me suddenly one night, when everyone was sleeping and I was alone. I closed my eyes and thought about my birth, and I almost fell from on top of a very high cliff, but I came to myself at the last second. Since then I find myself confronted more and more with something implausible that's hidden behind my name and my habits: the infinite being that I am, that I've always been without knowing it. Death will be merely a moment of déjà-vu.

THE DEADLIEST ISLAMIST TERROR ATTACK IS RIGHT BENEATH OUR EYES

When Mandela got out of prison, he was faced with a country that had been divided by skin color, class, and the toll of revenge, violence, and injustice. Yet he succeeded in creating the Rainbow Nation myth, unifying the country around his vision, truth, and reconciliation. When Morsi, the former president of Egypt, found himself with a country united in its desire for justice and freedom, he succeeded in dividing it, fragmenting it, cutting it up into two clans ready to go to war. Why? The answer lies in the stature of the two men, their ideas of justice and patriotism. Morsi comes from the Muslim Brotherhood movement: his vision is ideological, primal. His priorities are not bread, justice, and dignity, but rather they are "religious": women, haram and halal, sex, prayer, and fatwas. It's a profound misunderstanding between the Islamists and their voters, who elected them for justice, not to be re-Islamized. But in the religious vision of this group, an opposition figure is not simply an opposition figure, but an unbeliever, an enemy of truth, a devil. Morsi and his brothers couldn't even conceive of consensus, concession, dialogue, and negotiation: Allah doesn't do any of these things, so they, Allah's envoys, don't either. Morsi and his

---

* On July 3, 2013, Egyptian president Mohammed Morsi was deposed after massive protests.

brothers will forever have on their conscience this crime of dividing Egypt in two, and the rest of the Arab world as well—into them, and those who don't think like them. Them, and, facing them, Quraysh. Instead of being a man of reconciliation and reunification, Morsi will bequeath Egypt the most monstrous division. The tenth plague. That will be the Islamists' only achievement in power. Their inability to understand consensus because of the absolutist unanimity of religion is visible everywhere, and caused them to mistake 52 percent of the electorate for the vote of God—the absolute majority.

In Tunisia, for example, the Islamists and the Ghannouchi boys have delayed elections for two years because of their shopkeeping calculations; in order to gain time they've put off the constitution until later. It's the latest strategy: stall right up until the last judgment. Don't negotiate or cede ground, bury your adversary in fatwas and court rulings. Will the international "brotherhood" rethink their strategy, their duty to participate in dialogue, after the coup d'état in Egypt? The columnist has his doubts. It goes against these secret convictions. The brothers will simply slow down, try to win more time, play the victim.

But two images rise above the politics, the coups d'état, the ballot boxes, the paradoxes—two places: Tahrir and Rabiaa el-Adawiya. Those are the places where people defend the body, freedom of religious choice, the privacy of faith, liberty, and modernity amid the disorder and illusion of happiness. The other camp, which claims it saw the Prophet appoint Morsi to lead prayers, hides women like a crime, fears nakedness and truth, howls in its intolerance and embodies dead centuries and deadly beliefs. They believe Allah spoke to them and not to humanity, and want to impose their beliefs on everyone else. Eros and Thanatos—desire to live and desire to die. The rupture is total, profound, and it will travel across the rest of the Muslim world, leading one day to either war or suicide. This is not a simplistic image, but precisely what we are trying not to see, though it pierces our eyes and our screens. We don't yet have a country, but we already have two worlds.

AUGUST 3

YOU'RE AN ISLAMOPHOBE!
OR, THE FATWA
OF THE NEW INQUISITION

Day 5678. A month of sand that passes grain by grain. You're an Islamophobe! These days the word can be used for everything. It's the trendy ideological invention of this century, after the death of Communism and the moral decline of capitalism. So, in "Islamophobia" we put not just the dictionary definition but everything that the world is unable to define clearly. What is Islam? (A religion of duty, or a person's decision among family or before the god of his choice?) What is freedom? (Denounce your own for the sake of everyone else's, or defend your right to believe in things that others don't, or to believe in nothing and claim that it's your right?) What is a caricature? (A drawing, or a terrorist attack?) One could come up with other bad answers to good questions about tolerance, the separation of state and idiocy, about difference, culture, and defeat. "Islamophobe" in the world of Allah—that's like calling someone "capitalist" among Communists, or "Red" among Americans: you're an Islamophobe if you're different and you say so. It's what you are if you assert that a country has laws that must be respected, otherwise you should go live in Saudi Arabia. You're accused of Islamophobia if you attempt to think about Islam, at home, in your country, in your head, in your life. And you are even more so if you do it in a foreign language—for example, that of the former colonists. The accusation of "Islamophobe" is served up like a fatwa, with the same dosage of anger, rejection, exclusion, and intolerance: it's sort of a discreetly polite synonym for heretic, apostate, unbeliever. So if you're against the horrid invention of the burka as a living shroud, if you explain that there's a line between beliefs and rights, and that living beings have the right to live in this world and not in the afterlife, you're an Islamophobe.

You're also an Islamophobe if you denounce the behavior of Muslims who hide behind Islam (in the West, in the rest of the world, or in Algeria), or if you respond to the stupidities committed in the name of God. You're an Islamophobe if you say no to handing children's play space over to a mosque every ten meters in your neighborhood, or if you laugh at the cries of "Takbir!" during the theatrical conversions in the mosques, or if you talk about self-proclaimed "scholars," Allah's Googlers, who have opinions on everything and forbid you to have an opinion on anything. You're accused of Islamophobia when you resist that Islamization of the nation, of justice, culture, the meaning of the future, and the schools. You are also an Islamophobe if you try to think about Islam in terms of your hopes and questions, rather than according to dead books. You are, therefore, if you're different, free in your own home, in your own country, if you're critical or just sincere with people, or if you're a patriot. You are, what's more, if you reject Arab as an identity, even though religion has nothing to do with being Arab.

The accusation has become generic: it can be used against Westerners for being Western, against those who are just different, against those who don't think like you, against the visionaries of the future, against the objectors. It's practiced in cafés, newspapers, but also in the brains of a certain elite that feeds the obsessions about the West, who see a conspiracy beneath every arm, and who, with the swiftness of a beheading, label every difference in thinking as a submission to the West.

Is that to say that Islamophobia doesn't exist? Of course it does, like many of the other illnesses of this century. But this malicious accusation of being an Islamophobe is also a type of indirect fatwa—an insidious manipulation of meaning, and a torture instrument of the New Inquisition. The accusation of Islamophobia has bred a fear of being called an Islamophobe, and, from there, has expanded the space of things that are forbidden from criticism, reflection, disagreement. It's a threat, and so it paralyzes, breeds policing of ideas and creation of taboos.

One must not give in to it, nor withdraw. As long as those who call you Islamophobe are not named Allah or God, they have no right to make you be quiet. Being in the majority has never been an argument for being correct. And when you go back in time, you discover that the accusation of "Islamophobe" is as old as murder and ignorance: it was used in stoning Ibn Roch with shoes, and in the lynching of other enlightening thinkers. Today, it's used to hide the theft of shoes in mosques, the underdevelopment of our world, the denial. And elsewhere, in the world of others, the accusation is used to "victimize" those who want to impose their beliefs on others.

The conclusion? Accusing people of Islamophobia advances Islamism faster than the desert that this ideology offers up as a solution to the world.

SEPTEMBER 25

ALGERIA: A BRIEF INTRODUCTION FOR FOREIGNERS

So, let's summarize: Algeria is not a dictatorship. But it's not a democracy either. We have the Emir Abdelkader on some banknotes, and a plush version of Saidani on others. It's not exactly a fully Arab country, but it's also not fully its own Numidian and independent one. There is pluralism; but the single party always wins. It's a country that triumphed over Islamism, but where Islamism triumphed over the people. There are riots every day, and one revolution per half-century. It's a poor country, but an emerging one, but also a rich one that's sinking.

You can become a billionaire there, but the people there want money so they can leave it, flee it. We are nationalists, but we dislike our nationality.

We have a regime whose military is in the barracks, but the country is too, or something like it. The president is strong, but also sick, weak, and very old. A president who can appoint generals, one by one; but the generals, together as a group, can also appoint him.

Paradoxically, it's a country of youth who live like retirees, and elderly who govern with the audacity of the prime of youth. One person's career can end at twenty, and another's can begin at eighty. Wine sales increase 14 percent every year; same for the construction of mosques.

The consequence of this centralism is that ministers are weak, while *walis* are superpowers.

Oddly, it's a country that people died for, but they died so that those who followed them would die, too. It's a country that chased out France, but never really separated from France and sees it everywhere, dreams of going there.

Everyone there performs ablutions, but the country remains dirty.

In foreign policy, Algeria is neither for Western intervention nor against the West. We are with Bashar, but against his obstinacy. For a solution in Mali, all while saying it's not our problem. For dialogue with Morocco, but not if Morocco is the only partner in the dialogue. For France apologizing, but also for the free health care in France. For a new start, but only in between two de-escalations. For peace, but against love.

The Islamists are not making the policies; it's the policies that make them. We are for the global war on terror, but not on our own soil. Against jihadists, but for reconciliation.

In economics, Algeria is for a market economy, but statist. We encourage investment, but we don't like private enterprise and we distrust foreigners.

It's a country where the people don't rise up, but they are not entirely asleep, either. A kind of oblique position that defies foreign analysis and injects geometry into mathematics.

So it's a free country, but one that isn't liberated from its inner monsters. That defeated colonialism, but not degradation. A glorious history, told with bad breath. The country prefers nonalignment in foreign policy and zigzagging in domestic politics. It doesn't have a clear goal in the world, but each individual has one for himself inside his head or his wife's.

So it's a nondemocratic republic, but not a dictatorial one; a police state but not a military one; monarchist, but with two chiefs or a collegial royalty; liberal but an oil and gas regime; popular and populist; independent, but not always. And so on. It's called Algerian singularity, a black hole of meaning in the empire of clichés.

OCTOBER 14

TO BE A NATION IS TO DEVOUR

From martyr to mouth. Just for the rhyme. Tomorrow, we eat. Gaze steady, jaw slow like a grindstone, eyes wild to keep other predators at a distance, with a dull grunt that confines language inside a single syllable, neck bristling with anxiety. We've been colonized for a millennium, and our independence was, essentially, satisfaction. For centuries we've eaten poorly, little, or not at all, while the colonizers ate us. That's where the hundreds of synonyms for the verb "to eat" come from—to take, to clean out, to steal, to corrupt or to be corrupted, to chew, to fill up, to take a percentage on a contract or a bill, to colonize, to harass, to dominate, to irritate, to stress, to cannibalize, to pressure, to entrap, to win at a society game, to succeed in a checkmate, to beat, to vanquish. In short, "to eat" has the unclear, total, murky, and worrisome meaning of "to swallow": land, money, the adversary, the wallet, cash, a country, or history. To eat is to possess. To make something one's own. A lease is signed with the jaw, not by consensus or by institutions. Whoever chews, dines. Who dines owns a flag. Who has the flag has teeth. That's where the supposedly zany but secretly accurate synonym given to the national anthem comes from—"Kassaman." Meaning, "Let's share." Share the goods. A full stomach is a peaceful country, a serene regime, a people that goes with what comes. Sheep are prestige, a cow is excess. Hunger is ancient for us and goes back so far that we spoke of it even before we lived, so deeply is it planted in the collective memory. So its opposite assures fortune. A man who eats

154

well is a man who has attained the meaning of life in this country. Independence was a party, the vacated property is a full mouth; to eat is not to digest the salts and grains of the world, but to devour the world before it devours us. It's war not pleasure, a power struggle not a tasting menu. Look at us during Ramadan: you'd think it's the end of the world—panic, stampede, shortage. It's a secret fear of falling back into the weakness and scarcity that lasted a thousand years. Our entire history is a long war. Our meals have always been frugal, the bread dry. When at last we are able to eat, we do it not by tasting but devouring. In our universe, sheep aren't for sacrificing in place of a son, but to remind us of how our ancestors lived. And to eat in their place.

NOVEMBER 16

DOWN SOUTH: OIL KILLS STONE

Oil is killing the stone, the style, the architecture, the head and bones of this country. Along the expansive so-called National Route 1, the Trans-Saharan, which ties the South to the North, or vice versa: two days and two thousand kilometers, along with a dozen cities, hamlets, flatlands, dunes, and towns. It's the part of the desert that's not yet the Sahara, stretching up to the hard, blackened Tadmait plateau. The country's center of gravity, they say. We'll come back to it. The real subject of this column is that oil is killing the country's architecture. Everywhere, from north to south, you get the same aesthetic for the gendarmes, the post offices, the *daïras*, the city councils, company headquarters, and administrative offices. And you find the same monotony especially in the famous urban web—the residential buildings, the government housing—an architecture of mass relocation, launched in the context of the *Injazat*. That's the city of the aughts, a mixture of the bad taste of resettlement and a future performance report. The aesthetic result of a million apartment buildings is a Kazakh/petrol effect, in the form of five-story buildings painted beige and proliferated in suffocating density. They'll end up as dirty housing projects, strung with laundry and satellite antennas, fated to house tired couples, numerous children, leaky ceilings. Is there life after public housing, other than the national ritual? The Islamists say no. There's only a fourth term.

Oil is our wealth, and it has imposed a unilateral regime on us. It's the patron of projects, and a great displacer of people. And it has translated into this monotone aesthetic—projects, housing, rehousing. Algerians in general are housed by power, and the latter imposes its own taste. Outside the colonial nucleus, it creates these photocopied cities, with a Place des Martyrs, a Café Marhaba, a Khemisti Street, an El Wiam neighborhood (otherwise known as reconciliation), schools named for the companions of the Prophet, etc. It stretches from Algiers to Ain-Salah, then to the borders, then inside heads and into bids for contracts. The hearts of people are in their facades. Ours have been eaten by oil. Which hasn't made them into sculptures, but cinder blocks. When at last everyone has been displaced or resettled, what will Algeria become? A big housing project where people get bored, and where the first collective action will be to give donations for a funeral home and burials, as is happening everywhere. It's a sad, devastating vision of the country that arises along this highway, one that loses its heart of stone amid the hideous government housing.

NOVEMBER 17

DOWN SOUTH: THE DESERT ADVANCES, THE SAHARA RETREATS

There's emptiness, the desert, and the Sahara. The first is inhabited by the unemployed, who come from the North to the South—it's vast like the desert, uninhabitable, difficult to endure, to populate. Dreams of oil fill the empty space, though there isn't any. You see it in the cafés in the North, and in between the rare ones along the National Route 1 in the South. The desert is hard, rocky, blackened by the sun, dead, calm, and strangely serene below a sky that has murdered it for a million years. Then there is the Sahara, an old folktale, marked by curves and dunes, alluring to those who want to get out of their cities or their bodies, photogenic and generous despite its asceticism.

You might say, amidst all the disorder, that the Sahara was killed by the desert, and then again by the emptiness. These are just a few scattered thoughts, but what's fundamental is that after two days on the road you discover that this country is vast. Too vast to be governed by one regional division and the skills of a single official serving a lifelong term. We're going to lose it one day, because we're not able to defend it. In the meantime, the gorgeous Sahara retreats; you can still see magnificent instances of frozen time, between Ain-Salah and the few villages on the road to Tam, some of which bear the names of igloos from the North Pole: Arak, for example. We don't take care of the Sahara. We throw plastic wrappers along the

Trans-Saharan, bottles, blue things. It's a real national disease, there are carcasses of wrecked trucks, a garland of busted tires. The North is killing the Sahara with its pollution, with its plastics, and so are the terrorists of the deep South, who prevent travel, cosmopolitanism, tourism, exchange, and have extinguished a once vibrant sense of freedom. The Sahara is also besieged by multinationals, oil, global predators. In the end it's an old black-and-white postcard with a pure sky and hidden *walis* and fascinating names. In the immense desert, the Sahara comes and goes: islands, places, roads. It's an oasis.

The desert is vaster, stretching in every direction. It's a fantasy of the monotheists and the jihadists, who claim it as the patriarch of their caliphate, and shelter for their training camps. They rehash Arrissala, Lawrence of Arabia, and the founding of Islam. The desert is an unsettling feeling of loss, risk, checkpoints, roadblocks, pat-downs, baggage inspections, sentries. It is weighted with the daily issues and weekly wars of the Sahel and its nations. It deprives us of the Sahara with its giant rocks like gods sculpted by erosion and wind. One day, the Sahara will no longer exist. It will disappear. Only the emptiness will remain, with its kilometer markers. Facing it, beneath it, behind its back and behind ours, the desert advances, followed by the void, and the young travelers who inscribe their names and mysterious numbers on the stones that line the highway. Traveling through the South leaves one with the strange and sad impression of the end of an era.

NOVEMBER 18

DOWN SOUTH: THE NORTHERNER AND HIS UNEASY BODY

The farther south you go, the less people's bodies are constrained, contrite, cornered, or imbued with guilt. You can resist a tourist's reflex, but seeing the Touareg of Tamanrasset dance at night during the Ahagar International Festival of Arts is a pleasure. Here, the body is still uncontaminated by the idea that it's a burden or a crime or an obstacle between the self and heaven. Young people from around here dance with obvious joy, without the violence you find at festivals in the North; they are accustomed to music and desire, carefree. Ideas haven't killed their muscles or their lungs, or bent their spines into submission; the *kasmas* have done less harm, Arabization and the Islamists haven't ravaged everything along their reckless way. People have air inside their chests, they aren't suffocating as we Northerners are, they don't feel trapped or anxious, aren't shuffling through a dulled rush as in the North. They are themselves, and they resist the North's advances as much as they can. The southern body has suffered less from wind and sand than people elsewhere have from encroaching murderous ideologies: Islamism, Arabism, nationalism, chauvinism. The southern body is still filled with itself, and not with others' ideas about it. It *can* dance.

And so when you come from the North, you discover what you've been carrying on your back since the first years of school: the dead weight of your own body. The nation's history reproaches you for not having sacrificed it in the war—no matter that you weren't born yet. Faced with the martyr who has no body, you are guilty for having one that's well nourished and doesn't deserve to live, you have to justify it. The rampant Islamism of beards and in brains cries at you that your body is dirty: you must wash it, hide it, avoid it to get to God, kill those of others, despise it to attain purity, look down on it and malign its genesis, its desires, its pleasures. The Islamists ask you to betray it and hide it, or to punish it, distrust it, be ashamed of it. So you can't dance, share it, offer it, love it or the other's without wanting to possess and dominate it, in order to deny it.

Plunged suddenly into sand that stretches all the way to the bare stars, the Northerner discovers what's making him suffer: the body, and the idea we've created of it. Northern celebrations become moments of violence and restriction, have the sense of a shameful release, regulated by police batons; weddings are drudgery, dancing an unwholesome exhibition, singing is grief or rage, joy an evil sensation to be hunted down.

You discover what ambient Islamism, the *kasmas*, the politics, the Arabization, the theft of your history, the textbooks, and the self-denial have done to you. You've been indoctrinated with shame for your self and your body, you're not well. All of Ahagar tells you this, without saying a word.

NOVEMBER 24

DOWN SOUTH: THOSE WHO'VE COME FROM THE NORTH

The Northerners of the South: they're a separate people, an Algeria taking a break from itself. You find them there, living their lives with their backs to the sea. Managers who came down for a day and stayed forever, transfixed former soldiers, married women, single women, children with mixed geographical roots, cultured men and men who've turned to the great dunes, to the sky, and to cultivating a small vegetable garden. Ochre-colored homes and stress-free careers, they say. Generally affable, like people from the South, they've discovered humanity and generosity and have more or less recovered. It's how the South rests from the North and the weight of the country. You'll find simple human relations and contacts, meaning that in the North those things have been destroyed by colonization, Arabization, resettlement, exodus, and profit. In the South people still work their land, smile, chat with each other; they don't appear to be the children of neurosis, but of the fathers of other times. Perhaps this is the impression of a tourist, a cliché, but it's also an immediate truth—the South is sufficiently interesting to keep you there for life, because it's the last memory we have of our country prior to its slow destruction. An impression can be misleading, but there's also evidence: the Northerners who've moved to the South seeking healing and calm. In general, they've found it. "The desert is a hard place for those with no interior life," a new friend and her companion told the columnist. It's true: many people buy homes, come here, and then sell them and leave because they can't tolerate the blowing sand and the perspective they find when faced with themselves. But many others stay, because they've finally found the meaning they were missing, a taste for planting and waiting, watering and picking, smiling and sharing. It's an idyllic image but it's not a false one. To live in the South is to be confronted with the self, but it's possible. So people come from the North, decide it's their home, and build. It creates strong connections, though sometimes misunderstandings, too, along with property speculation bubbles. You can come here as an asylum seeker or a hidden colonist or as a simple traveler. But you don't forget the South after you've left: you take it with you, it follows you, you return. You move away, or you reimagine it, or it haunts you, and you advance toward it, step by step.

This fascination grows slowly, privately, secretly. It reveals the North's afflictions, its dead weight, the suffocation it breeds, and the Algerian's quest to find a healthy proximity to nature, the self, and others. It's often said that people seek peace in the South. That's precisely right, because in the North there's war—a terrible loss of meaning where we kill time, as opposed to the South where time accompanies you. Here's a writerly pastiche: the nonsensical North sometimes leaves an immense desert in the soul, which the South, curiously, doesn't reflect but rather cures, slowly, without saying a word.

IT'S TOO BAD WE DIDN'T HAVE
A MANDELA IN 1962

Nelson Mandela is dead. The world will salute his life, his work, his smile, his death, and his philosophy. And we Algerians? We'll do the same, amid the long processional of homage. But beyond that? A secret regret, a bitterness. One day, the columnist wrote: What if, in 1962, we'd had Mandela instead of Benbella? What if we'd had truth before reconciliation rather than reconciliation without truth, as with Bouteflika? What if…

We might dare to broach the taboo because it's a great dream that's been awakened: rather than an Algeria that kicked out the Algerian French, an Algeria that had a reckoning with its own development, economy, and the cultivation of its human resources. A rainbow-colored Algeria. Mandela's South Africa had its OAS, its *pieds-noirs*, its colonists, its white farmers, its black radicals, its traitors, its torture victims, and its Aussarresses and Larbi Ben M'hidi. Except that Mandela made the decision to bypass the trials and revenge, choosing instead to build with open arms. Mandela's slogan wasn't "suitcase or death," despite the painful history of those who were killed, tortured, and murdered. The man had a vision that we didn't have; he saved his country from civil war and slaughter and grandiose nationalist vanities. Thanks to this man, South Africa's 1962 had no summer crisis, no fraternal wars between clans, no Oued Sly massacres or cyclical coups d'état, and avoided the stranglehold of the barracks and the political police on the country. Because Mandela saw far, the whites weren't kicked out and massacred, nor excluded in the name of Allah or identity. The tanks wouldn't have rolled toward the capital of this country and violated its legitimacy; we wouldn't have given ourselves over to the illusion of socialism, only to end up sick with plunder and vacant property. We would have avoided the futile agrarian revolutions that destroyed property and the value of work, and our patriotism wouldn't have been degraded by propaganda and persecution. An Algerian Mandela would have avoided the second war of the 1990s, its false conclusion through laughable referendum, and a president for life (unique in the world) because an Algerian Mandela would have had the dignity to impose a term limit of two, no more.

We would've made good choices, thrown our weapons and machetes into the ocean, decided to smile at our adversaries rather than murder them, and every day from then on we would have conjoined the words "liberty" and "liberation." An Algerian Mandela would have taught us that experiencing violence doesn't necessarily mean you must perpetrate it; he would've broken the cycle.

An Algerian Mandela would have allowed us to avoid the country we have at present, its bad convictions, bad days, soft dictatorships, its muddling. We would have lost fewer lives and less time, and we would've been a great country. Because this man is one of the very few who was able to give meaning to decolonization. All the other epics ended badly: the glory of decolonization led to horrendous or insidious dictatorship; to massacres, sanguine caricatures, and underdevelopment. Which is to say, you don't decolonize with weapons, but with the soul. Decolonization isn't triumphing over the colonist, but over the demons inside yourself. Goodbye to the man with the dismantling smile.

DECEMBER 9

STABILITY, THE NEW INTERNATIONAL RELIGION

It's the new international religion, intended for Arabs, among others—for the restless, the antiglobalists, the rebels, the revolutionaries, the people who are uneasy, the people who dream of better and are threatened with worse. Stability. What does it mean? That depends. For a forty-something Algerian who gets up in the morning to accompany his pants all day, stability is the opposite of what's on *Al-Jazeera*. On TV, it's clear, nothing moves, not even the images. There are people marching without killing, breathing without dying, having children without fear, and lowering their heads so as not to lose all that. Algerians have been inculcated with the idea that stability is the best thing that can happen to them, compared to their neighbors. They've been sold a soft dictatorship disguised as collective security.

Stability is thus indoctrinated into people as the least dangerous path for those who wish to live without moving. Stability can be eaten, bought, paid for, exchanged. In sum, it's been a strong currency for many years.

For the West, stability is something different. It's calm, serene silence around the oil wells and the gas reserves, with dates and palm trees if possible. It's the security of the supply line, control over migration flow and terrorist threats. A poor country in the South is deemed stable when it doesn't send over any lifeboats, sells its oil without interruption, and hunts down its terrorists, killing them conscientiously and systematically.

For a white tourist, stability is being able to take photos without being taken hostage; to go on vacation without finding yourself on YouTube, gun to the temple; it's losing your breath, not your head. Stability comes before beauty when you decide to see the world or travel across it.

What is stability for a rebel on our side? It's a scam. It's the sheepskin that conceals the wolf. It's the fable of Little Red Riding Hood. It's growing old without hope, with no accidents, no skydiving. It's stagnation, and tea. It's doing nothing, moving nothing, changing nothing, eating, not bothering, not dreaming, diving calmly into the water and then floating, waiting for death. That's how it is. It's a new religion that offers calm as a new god, immobility as ritual, and lack of hope as being better than hopelessness.

Can this last? No. Stability can't be decreed. Stability is, rather, a profound equilibrium that isn't attained through the politics of burying your head in the sand and turning your back in denial. In fact, stability has a clear, precise, and incontrovertible synonym: democracy. This old, proven system in which each watches over the excesses of the other without making an attempt on anyone else's liberties. That's what produces a system that stands up on its own, defends itself, is resistant to shock, and doesn't swing back and forth between repression in the name of stability and stability to the detriment of freedom. Because some of the Arab Springs have crashed, it is explained to us that democracy is not for us—not today, and not in a hundred years. They sell us stability coupled with infirmity and senility.

But no one wants democracy for us, and we don't even want it for ourselves. Not the West, which wants the oil wells; nor the regimes, which want to last; nor the people, who don't know how to unite. That's become a widespread conviction.

Stability is the faraway avatar of a very old proverb that says, "The fearful always have a very meager fortune."

A PRISON CELL HAS BARS AND A ROOF

What can I say? In the cafés, no one understands anything anymore. People drink and look at the ground turning around the coffee cup, the waiter circling around the ground. The guy in my head is old, the land is dry, rain is rare, and we head toward tomorrow with no baggage and no address. We don't know any of our great-grandchildren. We do know almost all our ancestors, who knocked themselves over for us in order to give us their first and last names. And after that? Nothing. We don't know whom to elect, whom to vote for. And, moreover, who's going to vote? We don't know that either, it's such a new activity that we don't know how to manage it. Slipping someone's name into a box isn't voting, it's ballot stuffing. Now I'm old. Not because of my age, but because of the immense waiting room inside my head. I read a single sentence in a book once, and after that I didn't need any more books. The phrase said: "In a prison, there are bars and there is a roof." The prisoners are, therefore, of two types—those who see the bars say we lack freedom. So they ram their heads against the walls, shouting, wailing, or rebelling by refusing to eat, so long as the wall isn't the horizon and the lock isn't a pigeon (a white one). I know them, they're behind my back and they force me to dig holes in the wall and shout the things they shout. They're right, but I don't feel right with them. I fear the cliff that awaits us a few meters beyond liberty. I'm afraid that after I'm set free I'll fall.

And the others? They're those who see the prison's roof. It protects from rain, cold, the sky, and from exposure. They don't see the bars, only the protection. The prison is their coat, the lack of freedom comforts them. What do you want me to say about them? They believe the prison protects them from freedom. They don't dream of leaving, nor even going outside, but just staying. They'll vote for their prison guard because he guards over their fears. He doesn't prevent them from going out, he blocks the monster from getting in to where they are, inside of them. There, that's what everyone thinks at the café of your ancestors, everyone, right up to the emir Abd el Kader, who no longer even knows what to do with his horse after he dies. Everyone knows that freedom isn't easy, and it's not everyone's goal. So it depends, my friend—the roof or the bars. It doesn't mean that one is right and the other wrong. It's a question of choice. Behind the bars, people are killing each other. Outside the bars, people are dying of boredom. It's hard being Arab, especially when you're not really Arab. I think you understand what I'm saying.

Good night. It'll be a long one, without stars pointing the way toward sunrise. *Wallah*, I don't know what else to do—between a dead man who wants to be president, and a president who refuses to die.

2014

THE TUNISIAN DREAM
AMID THE ARAB NIGHTMARE

The Arab Spring has given birth to a civil war, a coup d'état, a transition that goes on and on though ever more slowly, two hundred militias, an apartheid, and one success. In order, that's Syria, Egypt, Yemen, Libya, Bahrain, and Tunisia. And this Tunisian success is fragile, so rare and so recent that one is afraid to speak of it, to comment on the latest developments. But as to the question of whether Arabs are capable of anything beyond violence, dictatorship, and theocracy, the answer is still no. This one time that a so-called Arab country has succeeded in establishing an accord with its Islamists, its secularists, its progressives, and its former regime members, the fear is still that it's just an illusion. It's an old fear, one that's existed forever on the planet of Allah, where there has always been only sand and mirage. Andalusia was nothing more than a myth and nostalgia; democracy was never our fate, nor lasting peace, consensus, reason, justice, or dreams.

So, very quietly, we salute our neighbors' success: three years after kicking Ben Ali out, they've created a fundamental new law that, precisely because it took so long to write, proves it's a text that people believe in and care about. On one side, the Islamists didn't cede everything to utopianism and jihad; they seem to have admitted to the existence of others and the need for consensus to survive, even if their fetishized *hadith* say that all war is a stratagem; and on the other side, the upper middle class, Tunisian civil society, the elites, don't seem entirely anesthetized, annihilated, enslaved, checked out, or fatalistic and ready to abandon the project, as is our case. And so their peace is different from ours—theirs is the result of effort, ours is the peace of cemeteries. Ours is the consensus of cadavers laid out; theirs, so laborious, seems to be one of living beings.

In this sacred text, written on paper made by monks, a woman—rather than being an obsession of man, amounting to one-quarter of him, one-half, or just a dead weight—is a man's equal. That's an achievement. The text sanctifies justice and the institutions that watch over it, the separation of powers, and other important details. You could read it as a work of poetry, so much does it make one dream.

Tunisia is in its inaugural stage. It gave birth to the Arab Spring, and it can save the cries that have turned into wails and crimes. It can prove that there's hope after revolution, that revolution is not always infertile chaos. Our neighbor may be the unrealized and overlooked point of embarkation into the modern world, an isthmus of hope, where the solution to the terrible malaise of being Arab (even when you aren't really) is being designed. And for nothing other than the cost of the time and blood that's been lost. To our esteemed neighbors: onward!

THE SAD FLAW OF
THE ALGERIAN CONSTITUTION

The Algerian constitution is strange: like Algerian law, it's procedural and without philosophical foundation. It deals always, first and foremost, with the question of power. Who takes it, who keeps it, for how long? It doesn't establish the purpose of life in Algeria, the meaning of the country's existence, its collective destiny. The great constitutions are renowned for their concern for the ideals of existence of a nation and its people; they build a national myth on top of a quest, and propose a model of meaning and vision to the rest of humanity. Our constitution seems dull, limited to questions of power and mandates. For three decades it's been under revision, always to address the president's mandate, the relationship of the president with other centers of power, the president's prerogatives and the prerogatives of those around him—judges, and history. The Algerian constitutions are the traumatized texts of 1962, the Congress of Soummam, and Boumédiène's coup; they continue to turn in circles around supremacy, power, precedence, and prerogative.

You won't find anything in there that indicates what Algerians are pursuing in their existence, in their death, or in their future. Nothing about what this country is beyond the default definition of land freed at last from colonization (at least officially). Nothing about why we should defend it, stay here, have children here. Any philosophy to be found is brief—in the preamble there are a few generalities about religious identity and Islam as the religion of the state. But that's a profound contradiction between the concepts of patrimony and *ummah*, universal religion and declaration of sovereignty. Someone put it well when he said, "Does a state need to have a religion? No, only people, individuals." Adding that a state doesn't go to heaven (nor hell). But moving on—back to this anomaly of our country's foundation: our constitution is a neurosis of power, not a fundamental legal text defining our origins, our plans, our duties, and our great ideas for humanity and for our children. At each cycle there is always the same constitution: procedural, resembling the codes that governed the sharing of slaughtered cattle among ancient Arab tribes. It's a document of mistrust, not consensus. A notary's text, to govern factions.

So I dream.

I dream of a constitution that sets happiness as its goal. That consecrates the individual as the capital of the nation. That defines power and its counterweights. That announces to humanity that Algeria is a land of all religions, but above all of the religion of tolerance, wealth, and asylum. A nation that asserts its history and its identity through its own versions of these things, through its own languages, and not the Arabias of elsewhere. A text announcing that Arab identity belongs to us, but we don't belong to it. That Islam is a choice, not something to submit to. That democracy comes before self-enrichment, and power lies in merit, not in inheritance or spilled blood. That justice is free because it rests on the transcendent principles of virtue, truth, and responsibility. That wealth accumulation is legitimate, money is a reward, effort is the religion of the state, and to be Algerian is to have a capital and a vision that we bring to the marketplace of humanity. I dream of it.

A constitution without a philosophical foundation that gives meaning to the individual and to the nation is, in other words, just a dictator's manual.

The value of a people is built through what it proposes to the rest of humanity, and that starts with its philosophy and its constitution.

THE FAR RIGHT IS JUST AS SALAFIST AS THE SALAFISTS

Satellites bring us together; gods and ancestors divide us.

I wake up to the news of a Europe and a France that, with the most recent numbers from the European Parliamentary elections, are slipping more and more toward the far right. What is the far right? Beyond its long explanations and speeches, it is above all a cult of soil, of racial purity, of the ancestors of Gaul, who are not brunette, black, or undocumented. It's a matter of asserting racial supremacy by seeing alterity as a threat, a pollution of territory and identity, and believing and making others believe that the solution lies in restoring the past, its men, its bloodlines.

The far right is, quite simply, a cult of Salafists, if you just translate their ancestors into another version. Which is to say, it's a form of Salafism.

Because apart from the identity of their gods, there's no difference between the far right in Europe and the Salafism in our lands. Both lay claim to soil and purity. Both dream of restored kingdoms and an uncontaminated past. These two Salafisms complete each other—they are mutually necessary. Both feel threatened by difference and want to turn back the clock to the time of isolation. Marine bin Laden and Osama Le Pen. They divvy up the world map, thrust it toward war, aggravation, and a return to the utopias of genetic purity. And these two sicknesses, which are really one, affect all countries. They fascinate people with their false promise of resurrection. "Islam is the solution," say those in the lands of theocracy. "The first party of France," cry the others, in the lands of genetocracy. Both have a tendency to rave to form moral vigilance brigades, to cloak themselves in fluorescent colors, to publish utopic screeds, to issue decrees, encourage despair and wanderers. Strangely twin evils: some use Islamophobia as a propaganda instrument, others are fervent haters of Christianity, which they present as a threat, a foreign power, a fifth column, a conspiracy, an attack. The former have a habit of holding on to the futile and the halal butcher shops, where Salafist brothers speak of Christmas as an impiety, of Christianization, and who are haram when they talk of women, flesh, and joy. They share these roles on the back of a humanity that's lost, doubts itself.

Because the French far right speaks of Islam as a danger for the nation. And for the Salafists, and their devout Islamists, Christianophobia is part of their nature. They don't even have to pronounce the words, it's obvious and normalized. You see the perils of Christianity everywhere, you suspect it in others, denounce it as evangelism.

This is the world of Salafists; those of Allah and those of Marine. Those who kill men in the name of their ancestors. And this country of Salafists is expanding. Winning elections and souls. Plunging the so-called Arab world into halal/haram purgatories, and the Western world into one of origin/impurity. This movement promises to upend, offers a violent return to ancient beliefs. It will bring war in a century or two. It's a dangerous cycle. Somewhere in between the Gaullist emirate and our ancestors from Medina, the human being sits with his head between his hands.

WHY I'M NOT IN "SOLIDARITY" WITH PALESTINE

No, the columnist is not in "solidarity" with Palestine. The word "solidarity" is in scare quotes because it has two meanings. First—no to selective solidarity, stirred up over the Palestinian tragedy because it's the Israelis who are bombing them. And which is, therefore, a reaction to ethnicity, race, and religion, not pain. A solidarity unmoved by the plight of M'zab, Tibet, or Kabylie a few years ago, nor by Sudan, Syria, or other suffering in the world—only Palestine. So, no to "solidarity" that is conditional on religion and nationalism. This solidarity blackens the victims and their supporters because it entraps Palestine as an "Arab and Muslim" cause, freeing the rest of the world from responsibility. This solidarity perches atop the history of an abused people, who are practically without land in the name of hatred for the other. A duplicitous solidarity that the columnist ingested in school, textbooks, Arabic songs, and through religious unanimity.

The Palestinians' tragedy has been outrageously Arabized and Islamized to the point that the rest of humanity may now feel relieved of the weight of their suffering. It's an Arab affair, a Muslim one. This solidarity transformed a story of colonization into a religious clash, hatred, and ancient mythologies of exclusion. Rather than thinking about how to build strong countries, powerful nations that would be in a position to help others, which would carry weight in the world and in decision making. This VIP solidarity the columnist does not wish to accept, to become part of. This "solidarity" which chooses indignation over Palestine, while preferring not to acknowledge the "Palestinization" of M'zab or the South or other territories in the world. This solidarity in the name of Islam and hatred of Jews or the other. This easy solidarity, a public good in our region. This whiny, sentimental solidarity that chastises you for watching the World Cup in Brazil instead of *Al Jazeera*. This facile solidarity that turns a blind eye on Hamas and its true nature and on internal divisions within Palestine, their inabilities and their weaknesses in the name of the respect "due" to the combatants. In the name of the pro-Palestinian orthodoxy that one must not think about too carefully or interrogate.

So, no, the columnist is not in solidarity with this solidarity that peddles the end of the world and not the beginning of a world; that sees the solution in extermination, not humanity; that speaks of religion, not dignity; of a heavenly kingdom, rather than sowing a land that's alive.

If the columnist feels any solidarity at all, it's of a different type—one that doesn't distinguish among misfortune and suffering according to the labels of race and faith. No pain deserves solidarity more than another. And solidarity isn't a choice, but an encompassing energy toward all. Solidarity with people, everywhere, against those who would kill them, steal from them, dispossess them, everywhere. Solidarity with the victim against the executioner, because he is executioner, not because he's Israeli, Chinese, American, Catholic, or Muslim. A solidarity that's lucid: we must stop with the jeremiad. The so-called Arab world is dead weight for the rest of humanity. How can we, countries who are weak, corrupt, ignorant, without knowledge or power, ineffective in the world, uninventive and unfree, pretend to help Palestine? How do we allow ourselves the vanity of "solidarity" when we're unable to play the game of democracy; unable to elect Jews ourselves, as Arabs are elected in Israel; offer condolences for their dead, as Israel does for the young

Palestinian who was burned alive; say that we are sensitive to dead children, when we're insensitive to humanity. The columnist is in favor of this other kind of solidarity: total, entire, undivided. The kind that, by the force of one's own dignity, obligates the rest of the world to accept its responsibility toward matters of colonization, not beliefs. The kind that raises you up as interlocutor, negotiator, partner; which illuminates your means and your weight, forces you to distinguish between your emotions and your actions. The kind that begins with you, your own people, in order to better help others, everywhere—those who are different just as much as those who are part of your own community. Solidarity with the Christians persecuted in Iraq and Syria, Muslims in Burma, the inhabitants of the Amazon, or the youth still in prison in Oum El Bouaghi for snacking during Ramadan.

The images coming out of Gaza are terrible. But they've been that way for half a century. And our indignation is still just as futile, myopic, rotten; our lucidity and our humanity are just as rare and hard to find. Something needs to be changed, accepted, and confessed to.

"Solidarity" isn't solidarity at all.

What Israel is doing in Gaza is an abject crime. But our solidarities are another crime, one that's killing Palestinians from the back.

May amateurs who throw stones rise up: it's the proof that, without their stones, they don't know how to do anything else.

JULY 14 *

WANT TO BECOME A ROLEX CALIPH?

It's unprecedented: the hunt for a caliph. And one forgotten detail this week, between Gazan blood and Brazilian mourning at the World Cup: the French and Spanish intelligence services are on the trail of a jihadist of Algerian origin, coming from Syria and headed toward Allah, passing through Europe, according to available information. Most interesting is the aesthetic of this chase: they're no longer looking for a suicide bomber, a hostage taker, or a simple terrorist, but a candidate for caliph, sent to create the caliphate of Europe. That's the current jihadi trend: restore the empire of the past, the ancestral utopia, the golden age, from before time and decadence. The caliphate. So there must be caliphs among the Islamists, like a new position to fill.

This concerns all humanity, not just the police and their investigations: the presumed caliph is ancient history in the "Arab" world, in the "Arab" family. It's integral to Arab history—a caliph is a representative, God's delegated regent, the center of Islam and his political papacy. His resurrection is the first step toward ancient times. The lost caliph is a loss for Islam—for jihadists, but also in the mechanics of "Arab" politics. The caliphate crisis is a recurring one—with a deficit of state institutions, the Arab countries live

---

* In early July 2014, the first photos appeared on the Internet of Abu Bakr al-Baghdadi, the head of ISIS, in which his face was uncovered. He also wore a watch on his wrist that strongly resembled a Rolex.

under the reign of regimes, which are themselves discreet euphemisms for the notion of a caliphate. Just like an "Arab" dictator, a caliph is not elected but chosen by the army and by the powerful; like every "Arab" dictator, the caliph keeps his position for life; like the "Arab" dictators, he dies violently; like the "Arab" dictators, he retains absolute power. Each dictator is designated and is lived and suffered under like a caliph. You can be a caliph in the name of Allah, of a war for decolonization, or with the army at your back. Caliphs die, sometimes as blind and miserable beggars in the street, like Al-Qahir l'Abasside in 951. Sometimes they die bathed in blood, or betrayed, or murdered by their own mother, brother, or father. There's a long line of caliphs assassinated in the history of the Muslim empires, and it's extraordinary. From Omar to Muammar (Qaddafi)—only blood and glory.

So, the job is not a pleasant one—the long line of caliphs of the Muslim empires is a catalogue of violent death. Of the first four, Abubakr, Omar, Othman, and Ali, three were horribly murdered. The other Omeyades and Abbassides? The same: some were stoned, eyes scraped out, slaughtered in the bath, during orgasm or war, from behind. A tradition emerged, but also modes of governance: from "elected" caliphs, they passed on to hereditary caliphs, then to caliphs under the tutelage of powerful financier families. And that's how it's been in the "Arab" world for a century. Nothing has changed. We've moved from caliph to dictator father of the people to putschist colonels, then, in reverse, from putschist colonels to dictator and family reign, and then to the caliph. The only new detail? Contrary to ancient times, the caliph of the Islamic army of Iraq has a Rolex on his wrist. He's stuck in between ancient time and Swiss time.

THIS HIDEOUS FUNDAMENTALISM
IN THE NAME OF PALESTINE

Is there such thing as a fundamentalism of the "Palestinian cause"? Yes. It's distinct from Palestine and its tragedies. The latter is a stolen country. The former is a kind of religion, a posse of lobbyists, backlogs of insults, myopia, and cowardly behavior, all in the guise of leftism or engagement or Islamism or solidarity. The fundamentalism of the Palestinian cause, what's more, resembles Zionist ideology—it functions through lobbying, exclusion, violence, insidiousness, monopoly, and propaganda. The Zionist accuses you of being anti-Israel as soon as you say something against him. The fundamentalist of the Palestinian cause accuses you, as soon as you think anything other than the orthodoxy and its posse, of being bought off by the Jews, of being an attention seeker, or just naive.

Like all fundamentalisms, this one is blind. It has its hierarchy. At the bottom are the insulters—those who want to "liberate" Palestine with their tongues, and who, from their locations in Lille or London, insult the "traitors." They collect emotions, photos of children in Gaza, and are unmoved, like worms in a jar, by burning flags or spitting on Jews. In the middle are the "religious"—the casual students of schoolhouse Baathism, bigoted Islamism, or violent imams. The kind of person who generally doesn't understand the wish to present the Palestinian tragedy as a human one: "It's the Jews!" he cries. "If you think differently than us, you're with them. If you're not anti-Jew, you're not Muslim, you're a collaborator, one of Allah's *harkis*, or a swindler who wants to please the West." At the top are the intellectuals—the former Arab progressives who've soured a bit, are disappointed, and profoundly hesitant. Shut up inside their good intentions, they confuse faith and analysis. Support for Palestine must be unconditional, no analysis or criticism allowed, and it must be packaged together with a kind of condescending birthright. To think differently is to think wrongly and to be mistaken, always. There are others along with them: the intellectuals of affect. Those who think clearly except on this one point, darkened by their reaction to the Palestinian cause. They have remarkable analytical abilities with regard to matters of the rest of the world, but they cede to this kind of sacred halal obligation that's revived and expanded with each bombing of the territories; and then falls away again, like sprigs of tea in an "Arab" café.

In short, like any kind of fundamentalism, the Palestinian "cause" is above all an affect. It's blinding, terrible, monstrous, empty, powerless, bad—and comfortable. If you say that you refuse armchair "solidarity," one that's selective and myopic, and that you prefer the solution of strong countries and powerful economies capable of weighing in on international decisions, you'll be insulted. If you say that the Palestinian cause is not an identity or religious monopoly, you'll be insulted. If you say it's a tragedy that all of humanity is responsible for, not a group of Baathists or Islamists, you'll be insulted. And if you add that it's not a holy war but a matter of decolonization, and that hating Jews degrades those who wear this solidarity and dirties the Palestinian cause, everyone goes haywire—you're nominated for prizes, they pay your way to Tel Aviv, you're a dirty Jew, a mercenary, you understand nothing. When this lobby is unleashed, it's just as virulent as that of the Zionists, and puts into question their ideology in the name of Israeli interests. They have the same methods—exclusion, embargo, attack dogs.

This fundamentalism, like its elder siblings, doesn't read what you write, doesn't think, doesn't see, doesn't ask itself questions: it is the truth. Everything else is treachery. It sees only what it wants to believe, in order to satisfy its violence. What's more, the Palestinian cause can be used for anything in the so-called Arab world except helping the Palestinians. People take out photos of mutilated children in Gaza, they scream in your face, cry betrayal: it's the "solidarity" vacation package, secular suntan/crouching Islamist option. Then you go home and wait for the next bombing. You find yourself alone, on top of your humility, trying to understand, to think, to analyze the reasons for this powerlessness to help people or awaken reason. Alone in wanting to look beyond the affect, and put together the right words to explain to fair-weather friends that it's not about being moved, throwing stones, and screaming, but a need to revive, think, get out of the Middle Ages.

"An empty bag doesn't stand up," an American president said about the necessity of being a rich and powerful country. Here, in this pitiful Arab world, the bag throws insults, burns flags, screams, prays, whines, and then fades away. They want to put it over your head to kill you, suffocate you, and prevent you from speaking.

A terrible time we're in: fundamentalism has become a religion, one common to all religions.

PALESTINE: ON THE QUESTION OF "DENOUNCING"

The massacre in Gaza continues. What is there to do? A friend called the columnist one afternoon during the first three days of the murderous attack against the Palestinians. "Write a column denouncing Israel." A moment of anger about our anger: are we still at the point of denouncing? Do we still believe that that's what the duty of each of us is? Can't we see that the crime is obvious, the dead are dead, murdered every time; that it's no longer a question of denouncing but of understanding, even amidst the emotion, how we got here? You denounce a crime at the beginning—in 1948, perhaps one or two more times, you become indignant. But after that you have to realize that what's necessary is to find a way to stop it. Denouncing has become a useless gesture.

It pushes the limits of a trend, and a quest for a peaceful conscience. Even if emotion is understandable, it must not blind people anymore. So, this afternoon, the columnist decided he would indeed denounce: not the crime, because it's being committed over the world's rooftops, before the eyes of all, but denounce our perfect powerlessness. Denounce what has made it so that the oppressed are so alone. Denounce our blindness, our ill-conceived solidarities, our weaknesses, our unhelpful anger. A choice not to denounce the crime, but that which enabled the murderer to be able to accomplish it in broad daylight, without backing off.

The columnist tried to come up with something beyond emotions, the ones that have already been so convenient: in Palestine, as elsewhere in this "Arab" world, which has been dying for four centuries. These are failures that have never been acknowledged. We prefer to accuse the "regime," the lobbyists, the conspiracies, the other, the West, its media or its power, the Arab League, or women who go around with their heads uncovered. We don't want to see in this powerlessness an act perpetuated by all of us. Denounce, sure: but denounce weakness, failure, and blindness.

We must seek peace for Palestine, but also to have the power to negotiate it. And this power has to be constructed over generations by everyone. What can this Arab world, which gives nothing to the planet, has no high-performing economies that can apply pressure, few armies, little means, do? Can't we see that, if the killer is killing in Palestine, it's because he has made an accurate appraisal of the power structures? Can't we see the direct connection between Arab dictatorships and the underdevelopment and obtuseness of the people? Why do we refuse to see the link between the daily compromises that each of us makes—the cowardly choices, the theft, the civic absences, the failure to be engaged—with our countries' weaknesses, and consequently the Palestinians' isolation? Why do we refuse to connect the meaning of our actions with our powerlessness? Why do we refuse to understand that power comes from creativity and that creativity comes from freedom as a religion and a value? How can we secure Palestine's freedom when we are unable to conceive of freedom at home?

And so, on the third day of the massacre, the columnist refused to denounce the obvious in order to write about the hidden: the trend effect, the lack of conscience, the calls for war delivered from armchairs, the easy emotion that will evaporate when the war is in remission, the selective solidarity, the damaging calls for hatred. The images of the crimes in Gaza are horrifying, and the crimes continue; they will be stopped only on the day when the great powers decide to do so. So that's the path: become powerful. In the long term. And, faced with all this suffering, what about the immediate? Indignation, yes, but without letting yourself off the hook. Be angry, but also with yourself. Denounce, but don't make yourself out to be innocent.

Now's not the right moment? On the contrary, it's exactly the right moment. We have this criminal habit of forgetting afterward. Of not thinking about it and getting caught up in our routines. It is exactly at the moment of the crime that we must lift the veil on the reasons for the crime. It's right now that we must begin to understand. Indignation is legitimate and helps to humanize the cause and the inhumanity of war. But it's not enough. The murder of the oppressed is our action, too, discreet as it may be.

The columnist chooses not to denounce a crime committed in broad daylight. Such words become meaningless. Everyone can see who is killing whom. He dreams, instead, of lucidity, of people becoming conscious of their responsibility. Peace, like power, must be constructed—with knowledge, when we push our children to go further than we did in mastering the world, when we invest in the world rather than turning our backs on it, and when we create countries, not exiles. In the meantime, the crimes are there, and they will continue.

SEPTEMBER 6

FIREWORKS WITHOUT CELEBRATION: A MYSTERY

Algerian nights. The trend of the moment is setting off fireworks. In Oran, in Algiers, elsewhere. For no reason. A bursting sound, followed by immense flowers of colored light that die gracefully. They've been exploding everywhere, for several days now. Without explanation. It's bizarre. A sign of this confused national calendar: there's nothing to celebrate, no dates, nothing. And yet there are fireworks. The foreigner accustomed to ritual fasting during holidays wonders why? Because. Rumor has it they're goods seized during import and then resold. Uselessly. Other chatter suggests a businessman who became a khalifa and handed them out for free. Altogether it's true, it's false, as inexplicable as the fireworks themselves. But there's a fascinating question: why do Algerians launch explosives when there's no celebration? It's a scene of people who are bored, outside of time and the dates that register it. No road markings or speed limits. You don't see this in other places in the world, where they have clocks. We are unique, alone in confronting time. The reason? Boredom. The Algerian night was murdered by the war of the 1990s. It fell into the domain of the desert. Outside the field of vision of the state. It's a space of cries, flashing lights, patrols, everything that's forbidden, and the homeless.

The war is over, but the curfew is still in place.

Today, maybe it's another people who roam and light the fires of their tribes. Or maybe it's because of young Algerians. Stuck between ages. Boredom reinvents fire. All pyromaniacs know it. Or maybe this people has moved into the stage of eternity: we don't celebrate time, but the moment. We celebrate ourselves with nothing else but our names. We're without calculation. We don't count anymore. Celebration is what there is between celebrations. Nighttime is a country without history that flows toward its ending. Strange. Remember: the victory party was invented before the match. Out of fear of defeat, which is assuaged through celebration. Soccer fans say that if they win, they'll celebrate more, and if they lose, well, the essential thing is that they'll have already celebrated. Because there's nothing to celebrate, we celebrate. We celebrate the emptiness, the night, the time to spare, idleness, eternity. A friend explained to me that fireworks are a kind of distress signal. A national island in the black night of a volatile sea. Land seeks land. The country seeks its feet on the ground.

Idleness is the essence of this gesture. The impossibility of truly celebrating ends up celebrating the emptiness inside oneself. Showing your presence with the two oldest methods: fire and noise, in the face of the darkness of the newborn world. Faced with the night. We are in a prehistoric time, the one before time. An endless analysis of this act that exists nowhere else: launching fire into the sky, watching it die, doing it again and then waiting for the night to tire. Sleep a little and wake up in a country lit crudely by the sun like a worn-out traveler, seated on the side of a road that isn't his.

SEPTEMBER 27 *

A BEHEADING THAT SPEAKS FOR US

In Algeria, fear is a memory that grabs you by the hand, the stomach, the head, the lungs, the whole body. A Frenchman had his throat slit in this country, and it's the people who are afraid of disappearing. Murder is horrifying: it reminds you that death is not reconciliation, that everything can come back. Be killed, beheaded, outlawed, isolated, evicted, turned away. The idea of Algeria is such a fragile thing, so tenuous in the world, so costly: a small incident and we fall back into a country to be avoided by tourists, by birds in migration, by endangered species. It kills you while you're still alive: why are we forsaken from the beginning? We've only just returned to life, and already we're pursued by the odor of death that we carry with us. Why this sad fate of being an invisible country, or visible only for the worst reasons? Why, of all the "Arab" countries, did it have to be in ours that these men responded to the call of ISIS and other barbarians?

Paris. The streets are illuminated by a clear sky. Trees bend over their own shadows. The green foliage is like a river scattering upward. Pedestrians in a hurry. And then there is this story of beheading. It fills discussions, mouths, heads, newspapers, the media, and the words of the taxi driver. The whole of Algeria is coming back to them, but through the wrong door: its war, its decolonization, the

---

* On September 23, 2014, Hervé Gourdel, a French hiking guide, was beheaded by jihadists in the Jurjura Mountains in Algeria.

1990s, its exiles, red hands and black feet and tired faces, the images and the strange invisibility of Algeria in France, because of the proximity that creates distance between them, the history that hides it, pretending to give voice to the dead in order to raise those of the living. What is there to do? Explain. But it will be hard. Their country sweeps you up and carries you off, it has no need to say anything else to others. The streets of Paris are lit by the early autumn sun. The beheaded man speaks everywhere about his death, shouts it endlessly from the rooftops. It's destructive, because it kills the only country that you possess and that possesses you. The affair brings to the surface all the prejudice, the trials, the mistrust, the anger of others. Almost to the point of reviving the image of the *fellagha* who slits throats. It spreads like a bad odor.

This story has made Algeria retreat into the shadows and into the past. It hurts us in images. It tells everything, and at the same time nothing. It's the times. Algeria, living land where death is the sun and blood is a last wave of the hand before silence. It's causing everything, total nonsense, to be said about the country. And there's mostly nothing we can do. We didn't decapitate a Frenchman, but a human being, and all the rest of us along with him. He lost his life, we are unable to find ours. It's sad for us, terrible for the man's loved ones.

OCTOBER 7

THE COSMOS IS A SELFIE
WITHOUT A FACE

The selfie: a subject that is, according to some, very controversial in the domain of God. Can you take a photo of yourself smiling, amused, or ecstatic in Mecca? Yes, because it doesn't harm anyone. No, because pilgrimage is a solemn act in which one is supposed to efface oneself before God, not strike a pose at His side. There's no answer, as for all the other questions Muslims ask themselves when confronted with modern times. At the deepest level, the columnist finds the subject intriguing. Memories of reading the great mystics who weighed their lives so carefully: El Junayd, Al Jili and his great metaphysics of the totality of man. And the Muslim Gnostics, who explained the world as a message from God: I am a hidden treasure destined to be discovered. A theory of life as a search, and the world as a labyrinth. The cosmos could be then, according to these ancient traditions, a faceless selfie snapped by God, who leaves no trace except in hearts, in blood, or in books. To create is to reflect. The world is an untarnished mirror. Fire and darkness, according to Zoroastrians. For the great Persian Suhrawardi, the cosmos is a nearly infinite gesture of reflection that has deteriorated a little from the time of the first living being. It's a niche carved out by light, which leads to the face of human beauty, delicate as a woman's eyelid. The great architecture of angels as a kind of selfie that stretches down from one reign to another, from the ultimate Source right up to the fire of Lucifer.

Furthermore, the subject is fascinating even outside the context of philosophy. The human face and the body are forbidden in the world of Islam. Or at least that's what they want to believe, and impose. To sculpt is to "imitate," to design is blasphemy. The One does not multiply. It's absolute. And a selfie? It's an open field, a bug in the halal/haram system. Mecca is a holy place, but also, for the Sauds, a fruitful one. It brings money. Faith tourism. Experienced by the pilgrim as a journey, and by the royalty as a good deal.

So you can pray there, but also take pictures. A selfie is a neutral gesture. Neither halal nor haram. You can take a photo of yourself, say that you wanted to share a special moment. Or you can prohibit it, because the space is meant for effacing the self for the sake of a proclamation or a vertical prayer, freed from the flesh. Can you photograph prayer? Is it possible to see ecstasy?

An older possibility: the selfie is the first artistic act of man. Beginning in prehistoric times, deep inside the caves right up to the grand statues of ancient emperors. From cave painting to digital. The Sphinx is a broken selfie. The cloud is the selfie of an idle man. For Christians, man is a selfie of God in his lapse of mortality and suffering. Satan, in our tradition, is a selfie of fire. Narcissus was the first recorded selfie, and astrology is a selfie of everyone projected into the sky of no one.

Without end. Everything is a reflection or an echo. Except death, which can't take a selfie without dying forever.

THE REVOLUTION IS TUNISIAN, AND SO IS THE SOLUTION

Made in Tunisia. It's the trend of the moment. Why? Because a strange way forward has opened in this country. People seem to want to be able to stop the flight of time after Ben Ali's departure. The secularists, as they like to call them, won a majority (even if it's relative) against the Islamists of Ennahdha. This has aroused a kind of feverish enthusiasm, an almost crazy sense of hope. At last, a people, standing for everyone, who have understood that Islamism is not the solution and that religion is neither a buffet nor an engine. It thrills the dormant orientalism of foreign observers, the political exoticism and internecine illusions of local elites. It's the only case where an Arab Spring seems to be having a good harvest. Is it true? Yes, with caveats. First—turnout for the Tunisian vote was not high. Disillusion tired out the electoral body; voting is not eating for someone with an empty stomach and a mind turned off. The vote wasn't huge, but it was intelligent. Second—the winners are obligated to form a coalition with the Islamists. That means political calculation and concession. The integration of the Islamists into the political game is going to cause an overradicalization of terrorists, if you can say it that way. With their former outlet compromised by the demands of coalition, they will opt for sound and fury.

But? It's a victory. The first in the so-called Arab world where a solution has been found outside the army-mosque binary. A path has opened. It will offer ideas—good ones—to Islamists of good faith, who perhaps will begin to understand that participating is more profitable than imposing. It will give hope to pessimists who, after a century, had concluded that nothing is good for anything, and everything serves either the Islamists or the army. It will bring light into the darkness that fills our spirits. The Tunisian approach offers a chance. We should appreciate it enthusiastically and lucidly. We're not going to spit on the dawn because of the light it brings. Tunisia invented the "made in" brand of the revolution. It has invented the brand for the solution, too. And we will admire this country, which has been saved, or is in the process of it, by their own. By Bourguiba. By this small, hopeful detail that he doesn't have an army at his back. It provides arguments against blackened souls, against our pessimism, and against our regimes, who sell immobility as stability and fear as threat. It shows, above all, that the progressives, the secularists, and the others are not all lying down and watching the sun set on their hopes while endlessly analyzing their defeat or its inevitability. A so-called Arab country is alive. There again, I dream of being Tunisian. Despite a few serious concerns.

NOVEMBER 24

A WAYWARD KITE IN A COFFEE CUP

Gray sky. With a kind of hot wind that suffocates like wool. A vagabond summer, forgotten by time. Emptied-out autumn. No winter for the moment. Only clouds that resemble angry sheep eating in the depths of the sky. Far away, a road. Cars scale its forearm like glinting, determined ants. Then, farther away still, fog, then the sky, and behind it a bazaar of our beliefs. In the abyss: the heavens are the most overpopulated country in the world. Barely a free square meter for a man who wishes to go there alone, without the company of a self-proclaimed guide harassing him as if he were a tourist arriving at an airport. How much does the sky weigh? A lot. As much as land on the backs of decolonized peoples. Altogether, in the divvying up of territory, the "historians" steal the land and the religious steal heaven and camp out there like parking attendants with their cudgels and their taboos. The sidewalks of heaven. A philosophic dream of the columnist: uncouple religion and spiritual quest. Demonopolize the spirit; give it its freedom, follow it in its ancient search, which is no longer possible with all the dogma. How do you find God and meaning without walking on the bodies of the dead? How do you invent a philosophy that's dignified rather than a prologue to submission? How can you feel the world as a vivid mystery without inviting the chatter of worn-out beliefs and the screeching of preachers? A dream of acceptance as religion, calm, peace, and equilibrium. A dream of talking with heaven rather than praying to it. Because what's most bothersome in the hereafter is the overpopulation and the noise. Negotiate with heaven, speak to it. Contest its eternity with this right given to you by your mortality: you're the one who will die, so you're the right one to ask the question, to rebel, to revolt, to refuse.

Just poetry? No. It's the most pressing issue for the columnist—how do you question the world and heaven without abdication, submission, lying, self-defeat? How do you move toward God, or come back from him, without denying the humanity in yourself and around you? How do you bind (the word has the same etymology as the word "religious") heaven and earth without binding your hands behind your back? How do you get out of the dogma without landing in a dead end, a dried-up swamp, or the crepuscular dandyism of the banlieues in the West? How do you question heaven without losing your voice?

Gray sky. The earth is a story, the sky its essence. Since ancient times we've loved reading the future in the stars. But the stars—what do they read in us, watching us live and die? That's what interests me.

DECEMBER 2

CAN YOU BE MUSLIM WITHOUT UPSETTING THE WORLD?

A creed in the cranial republic of the columnist's head: When women are confined, men are prisoners. This can be confirmed in Senegal, in the streets of Dakar, among the dust, the light, the hum of motors, and the women, who are so elegant as to take your breath away and leave you paralyzed, gaze fixated. Colorful like giving fruit to the wind. Smiling. Bodies betraying desire, precise in their movement. Free. The columnist asks: "Do the women go out at night?" and, later, finding himself alone at night without friends, scrutinizes the darkness. "Of course. Why would you ask that?" a colleague responds, shocked at the question. Because for Algerians, night is a kind of empty end of the world filled with cries and plastic wrappers. It is desertion. Evacuation. A prehistory, where the immense trees resume their nighttime stroll and monsters surprise you from open cellars. Women in the Algerian night are an impossibility. This impossibility turns our country into a kind of cliff for the suicidal each evening. So let's get back to Senegal—the women are dressed like works of art. Their refinement is striking, in the dusty streets, dirty and littered with plastic packaging. Headscarves are rare. "But you see it sometimes," a teacher says. Among the students encountered, one or two have their faces surrounded by a length of fabric. "It's recent. We didn't see this before," another says with some regret. Like a skin disease. It advances with money from Qatar and their sectarian satellites. It threatens to transform the colorful fabrics into tools of separation.

This advancing disease kills like a fire of ashes and progresses everywhere in the world like a tumor, snatching children, walls, minarets, and people to suck out their blood and replace it with the murmurs of an ancient millennium. In the meantime, a question: can one be a Muslim without disturbing others, without killing them or incriminating them, without begrudging them and seeking to insult them? Yes—the Senegalese prove it.

A man who is discreet in his religious practice—he talks for a long time, then walks away, isolates himself, prays, without seeming to want to create a spectacle. Belief is not an ostentatious ritual, it's not howling about what is forbidden or taboo. It doesn't leave traces of water on your pants, plastic sandals in your desk, a carpet on the back of your chair. It doesn't lower the curtains or fetishize beards as our ancestors did, hovering over the land or the sky to pray. You can be Muslim without murdering the world, and respect the lives of others, their own cycles. It is possible. But, more and more, it's an idea that's reduced to embers.

DECEMBER 11

A BRIEF CATALOGUE
OF ALGERIAN *HARGA*

The news is rich, the head impoverished. No lightbulbs lit up this morning beneath the scalp. Emptiness, and a clock staring at it. Return to the old subject, the only one in Algerian metaphysics: the *harga*. The word translates into burning, fleeing, leaving, refusing, denying, crossing, arriving, turning your back, your tongue, your hands, your eyes, or your body toward the inside. According to social class and the elements of ancient alchemy. The *harga* of the sea are well known—it's the water element. The Algerian takes to the sea, walks across it, wanting to change territory, his life, his birthdate. Lifeboat, life vest, Spain, fear. There are statistics for the water version, legal proceedings, smugglers, laws, coast guards, drowning victims, but also those who were saved. The sea is scalding.

Harga by fire is something else. The candidate for this igneous type of immigration burns the country that he can't change—so he changes its weight with fire, turns the fire into ash. He feels purified, that he has attained another place, newness. Fire is a *harga*. His body burns, or his country, or both. A way of escaping while also making those around you flee. Refusal and burning. Set fire in order to change. Shout and alight. The element of fire is at once light and darkness; it purifies and destroys. It transforms into air. You need only a match, flesh, a country, an impasse, a request for housing or happiness. A joint, too. Burn the lungs to burn the days.

The third element—air. The *harga* by air is also well known: pray to the point of dissolving. Point your index finger without knowing why. Look at heaven like a threshold and the land like the sole of a shoe. Ask a verse for wings and a minaret for the moon. Let your beard grow, shorten your pants, draw in your shoulder blades and then take off—as high as possible, far from the Quraysh and from gravity. Change the land into sky. Sublimate the body in prayer. Depart vertically, by way of Mecca. Deincarnate yourself. Go back in time. This *harga* is an internal one, a refusal to carry the world and its weight. Negation of one's condition. The candidate transforms land into air, and air into recitation.

That leaves the fourth element: earth. How do you leave the territory while staying at home? By digging. Close off the perimeter. Heighten the wall and the enclosing structure. Change languages, change your circle. Shut yourself up at home, recruit security agents for the entrance, dig a well for water, set up four satellite antennas, multiply the number of televisions like aquariums of the outside world, engage only with your reflections, purchase a generator. The *harga* by land is already a familiar recluse among the Algerian middle class. Self-sufficiency, retreat, exile by way of Chinese walls, confinement, negation, sighs. To leave you shut yourself away, stretch yourself out, fold yourself up—depending on your means, and desires of the body.

For alchemists, the other elements are the puzzle of the cosmos; its deterioration, in numbers. Its roots, quadrupled. The goal is always gold—for the alchemist, the voyager, the one who prays, the smoker, the voluntary recluse, or the one who dreams of Spain. To each his own.

DECEMBER 14 *

FIFTY SHADES OF HATRED

A fascinating question: where does this come from, that some people feel that their identity, their religious convictions, their understanding of history, or their memory are threatened as soon as there's someone who thinks differently than they do? Is it a fear of being wrong that pushes them to impose unanimity and fight against difference? The fragility of personal convictions? Self-hatred that runs through hatred of the other? A long history of failures, frustrations, love without release? Is it because of the fall of Grenada? Colonization? It's a maze. But it's strange—those who defend Islam as the only thought system often do so with hatred and violence. Those who feel and claim themselves to be Arab by origin have this tendency to turn it into a fanaticism, rather than a positive identity or a choice of roots, capable of bearing fruit. Those who speak of the essentials of the nation, nationalism, and religion are often aggressive, violent, hateful, dull, unsociable, and myopic: they see the world as attacks, conspiracies, manipulations, Western tricks. With their gaze turned toward this North that crushes them, fascinates them, makes them green with envy. Back turned on Africa, where we die when they aren't concerned. God created the West and these people as a couple, the rest of the world is just flotsam. There are sheikhs and fatwas for each woman who wears a

---

* On December 16, 2014, the Salafist imam Hamadache called for a fatwa against Kamel Daoud on his Facebook account, for "apostasy."

skirt, but not a single one to feed the hungry in Somalia. The Abbé Pierre Foundation can't help Muslims.

Let it go. Keep your eye on what's underneath—what is the meaning? Why is identity pathology? Why is memory an aggressive cry rather than a peaceful tale? Why is faith mistrust? These people who attack you each time you think differently about your nationality, the present, or your religious convictions—what are they defending? Why do they react like scorned owners, like pimps? Why do they feel so threatened by other people's voices? Bizarre. It's like the fanatic isn't even capable of seeing what he has before his eyes: a weak country, a poor and ruined "Arab" world, a religion reduced to rituals, necrophage fatwas, and an identity cult like jaundice, after having given birth, a long time ago, to Ibn Arabi.

It's not even a question of ideological, linguistic, or religious distinction: the identity-obsessed imbecile may just as well be francophone, arabophone, a believer, or a bystander. A friend explained to the columnist that there's a secular version as well: with the same stupidity, the same shrillness, the same idiocy, and the same ridicule. One speaks in the name of God, the other in the name of the 1970s and the suffering of his political consciousness, and still another in the name of an outdated imperialist fight or the exclusiveness of Berberism. But back to the mechanics—what is this a sign of? Of denial—dirty streets, hideous buildings, worthless currency, an ailing president, a dozen migrants killed in a bus on their way back to their country, dependency on oil and preaching, miserable educational results, feeble armies from the Gulf to the ocean, delinquency and increasing surveillance committees, corruption, assault, riots. Nothing in there is especially comforting. Except women's knees, the opinions of Kamel Daoud, the film *The Man from Oran*, denunciation of armchair solidarity in bed with Palestine, the West in general, the bikini in particular, the assertion "I am Algerian," or an analysis of Israel as a structure created by sick imaginations.

Why does this exist? Why is the Algerian soul surrounded by a pack of shrill dogs and ravenous monsters?

THE NEW QURAYSH: MOHAMMED WILL BE KILLED IN THE NAME OF MOHAMMED

Cold sky, swollen, filled with the coming rain. Gray like a bad mood. Beyond the glass is the world with its miniatures, its roads, a car crawling along the forearm of the horizon. The trees are old and stubborn; their greenness seems like luggage that's been left behind in this season, clothing from another time, hung on the coatrack of dead branches.

The birds are black specks that roam. Many things no longer have names. Just traces of them, their frozen nakedness. The land is a brushstroke. Above it, the sky, in a firm line. The weather version of the *I-Ching*. All of creation is a giant hexagram.

A question hangs in my head like a beam of light in an empty mosque: should I continue to write? This practice that resembles a little boy with a matchstick is perhaps an illusion when the world is a willful blackout. Things are going badly. The world is becoming unhinged. Wobbly like a rusted door between a silent god and a man who prays in the wrong way. A transition between two times.

Visions of scattered angels who no longer know what to do with their wings or our solitary prayers. A thought for oneself, one's body, one's children, and for this young Mauritanian that the Internet tries to keep floating above our line of attention: Mohamed

Cheik Ould M'khaitir. Twenty-eight years old. Sentenced to death for insulting a prophet.

In Morocco, a film has been banned for falsifying "the real," which is to say a myth, a fiction, a representation. It's a sign of the monstrous infringement of fiction on reality. Here, a columnist is blamed for all evils in his country since its creation: Judaism, Zionism, Harkism, apostasy, impiety, treason, Francophilia, conspiracy, etc. In a few days, several years, the earth will no longer be round, the wheel will be uninvented, the sky will turn back into an arena of the gods; already monsters are being reborn and unknown animals are emerging out of stomachs. The end of the world isn't a breakdown but a countdown.

My world is sick. It wants nothing of the world. It wants the end of the world. It's a geography of hysteria that my matches can no longer illuminate.

Lower the curtains over the balcony, with a thought for Mohamed Cheikh Ould M'khaitir. What can I do for him? With the announcement of the verdict, a terrible detail: sounds of car horns honking, dinghies to celebrate this crime committed in the name of an imaginary justice. The poor young man is, therefore, alone. If you don't protest you are complicit. Everyone kills Mohammed, in one way or another.

The Muslim world today is an unanticipated version of *Arrissala*, the film by Mustapha Akkad: it's the Quraysh who win, and a prophet who dies in a cave with a single verse and one friend. Hard world, painful to live in or to leave, a kind of crazy Noah's ark constructed by fools to kill the species. A monstrosity. Haunting, the photo of this young Mauritanian. He is each of us. Sitting inside my head. He is me. Better than me. Faced with worse.

Why does ISIS attract more recruits than light, books, reason, humanity? Is God a property? Is a prophet illumination or a condemnation to die? A sad, monstrous blade cuts through the world of Islam, killing, taking, transforming man into an animal, dismembering, stoning, beheading. A wave that kidnaps women and sells them, climbs imaginary trees, wants to appropriate fables, stories, reason, films, aesthetics, creativity and faith and questioning and dignity. It is frightening. It is dark, nocturnal, suffocating.

Mohamed Cheikh Ould M'khaitir is sentenced to die in the name of Mohammed Ibn Abdellah. From Mohammed to Mohammed, in the name of Mohammed. We turn round and round. In a vicious circle. The trap shuts once again.

Mohammed is alone in his cave, in his cell.

2015

MOURNING AND THE WHIP:

ABDALLAH AND HIS SLAVE BADAWI

Mourning, and the lash of a whip. On Friday a sky of enormous clouds; a giant's brain, made of air. Hypnotic colors. The news of the day: three days of mourning in Algeria, for one of the tottering kings of this Saudi Arabia that weighs on our souls and our roots. One king is dead, another will inherit the throne for a few years in the name of Allah. These lifelong terms in the kingdom of eternity are curiously brief. Three days of mourning for us. It's dietary, political, you can tell. But what about the other one? Thoughts, indeed, should go to the one that a fellow columnist honored in between *Je suis Charlie* and *Je suis Mohamed*: Raif Badawi. The blogger sentenced to a thousand lashes of a whip and ten years in prison for a blog post on the Internet. According to reports, he's already received fifty lashes—that's 950 to go. And ten years in prison. That's how it is: the so-called Arab world has its raging, inhuman obsessions: whipping and condemning bloggers, dissidents, people who are unique or different, rebels, those with dignity, those who tell the truth. Insulting Islam and attacking the king's person or the president are more serious crimes than dirtiness, underdevelopment, international cowardice, poverty, or national corruption.

So, this Friday, it's simple: ten years of mourning for Raif Badawi, the slave who's far more valuable than a king or his kingdom. It's the fashion of the moment? Too facile? Predictable? Of course. And we should continue to see indignation as a trend, and the duty to expose injustice as a public good. It allows us to clear our names, go back to being sheep without feeling too much guilt. The young blogger is alive, in prison, he has two children and a family, and all the rest is just blah-blah. It's not a question of Islam or insults or salvation or anything else. We can gripe about it for centuries, and it won't change the facts: a young Saudi is in prison for ten years and will receive 950 lashings. It's an injustice. And to those who, today, want to come and defend Islam, it's useful to remember that justice is a value that rises above faith, even in the sacred texts. So, ten years of mourning. Each for his preferred recipient. Before God I choose to support the powerless, not the king. We must remind people right now, in this moment, those who forget or try to drown out the scandal, and those who present themselves as defenders of Mohammed, and forget this injustice. To the gigolos of the mosques who will go "study" and come back to this country as agitators, to the prostrate admirers of this kingdom. You can say it's nothing, it's easy, but it's just a reminder not to forget, and to make clear that *Je suis Mohamed* means nothing and does nothing if you're not also Raif Badawi. Just a reminder. So we don't forget amidst our prayers and the fatwa against building snowmen, as was recently decreed in the kingdom by a "savant."

NEITHER EXILED NOR PROSTRATE

Is it possible to get out of the French-Algerian neurosis? Because that's what it is, a neurosis. You see it in the colorless faces on both sides—the emotion is strong, the truth tense, with this monstrous tale between us and a future of dead leaves in photocopies. The neurosis can be diagnosed by the footsteps in your head: they turn in circles, while you run on empty. You want to write the world, expand the window to the size of the ocean.

What does a Japanese person bent over an ancient rhyme or a new motor think of me? What does the Land of Fire say about my name? Am I known to the slick snow at the North Pole, or by the woman with voluptuous hips in Dakar? What is the image of Algerian identity amid the noise of all these varied dimensions? How do you escape this long war that fills my mouth with ash and the chatter of ancient symbols? I dream of new lungs, new verbs that come to me like instincts. To walk on a world of pebbles with bare feet. How? I could talk about my book wherever I go: my words would be heard, digested, or pushed away like foliage on a path through the jungle.

But to speak as an Algerian in France, or as a Frenchman in Algeria, is like tugging at a continent with your teeth. Everything is heavy, even humor. Every word has a triple meaning, and four cemeteries lying beneath it. It's all troublesome, slow, pregnant with meaning, laughable, and carries an odor of must. It's a dead world that won't stop talking. A rotten relationship. I don't want to refight the war, nor go into exile. Only to talk without digging up graves.

Speak of leaves when they fall. Like a dawn with no one who will listen to it, so it goes away, or a sky seeking its reflection in every possible land. Tell the story of the world by beginning with a name. Stories of love and laughter. Tales of neighborhoods and neighbors. Liberate myself.

Because the colonists leave us every time and we are left prisoners of ourselves: Arabs, French, Spanish, Vandals, Ottomans. They go away but won't leave us alone, and we shut ourselves up among our dead. We carry them around with us, then send them away. I am waiting for the liberation of language, and an Algerian dream. Serenity that smiles with benevolence. A profound self-confidence. The possibility of regarding the sea as a threshold, not a closed door. I dream of desiring the world—not war, revenge, a wall, imprisonment, collapse, or a conversion with ablutions. I dream of a country whose present is more imposing than its memories; of escaping this prison whose structure is an endless confrontation. A country. A woman. Descendants who are both close by and scattered wide.

Troubling. How do we rid ourselves of this lethal relationship? Recount the world in a different language than that of forced memories? I want to be a Japanese writer while also being an Algerian who is sure of himself and his country. It's hard to make these nuances of my dream of liberation understood.

I don't want any more history. It wants my words and my death. It can't tolerate me alive. I don't want to prostrate myself. I just want to live in my land.

MY MONA LISA, MY GUERNICA, MY LOVE

Shaimaa al-Sabbagh. Mona Lisa of this couple, Guernica of femininity, crucified. The man holds her in his arms, his face buried in her stomach, gaze distant. As though he wished to give her his life, find her womb, turn back time with his bare hands, to childhood so that she comes back to life, so that he can be pardoned for not protecting her.

She is standing up, carried more by wings than legs. There's blood on her face, already turned toward her wound, which surprises her like an unknown galaxy. You feel her life has become so poignant that she will die of it. The moment in the photo is eternal, and paradoxically it will immortalize her death. The brief apparition of a god. In the background there are passersby, a friend, some people, you, me, others so far away, all of creation, the history of this country and of all countries.

The couple falls but stays frozen, united, stuck together, he crying for her, for the mother, the sister, the woman, the daughter, the womb, her destroyed maternity, a woman being ripped away from him by having her own skin torn out. He refuses, tries again, cries

---

* On January 25, the Egyptian activist Shaimaa al-Sabbagh was killed by a bullet while celebrating the fourth anniversary of the revolution with other demonstrators in Tahrir Square. The photos of her death were seen around the world.

out the most immense "no" possible; his eyes give you pain, make you want to cry and beg the gods who are passing by. The man is cleaved apart, tearful, lost to time, fighting with his muscles against the obvious.

She has already become a martyr, with that gaze they have when they're looking at something immense, desired, mortal, capable of giving eternal life with a simple brush against it. Shaimaa murdered in the back. Living forever in this captured instant, offered up, held back, shut away and open to all.

Then time arrives. It dissolves the couple into a thousand pieces: the woman slumps, then rises up. The man tries to catch her because he knows death is a deep well where the water gives no reflection. He lifts her, along with the world and its trees, skies, friends, children, and stars, and carries her. But already she's no longer there where he's fighting hurriedly. In the third photo they are separated, her body has already lost its name, gone out, forgotten. The woman returns to the immensity. Time restarts, flows, people shout, run; and then comes history.

Back to the first photo. The one of the embrace. Where you see the woman in profile. The gaze of a woman wounded in the back, an expression of betrayal. And the man who holds her as though begging her, shouting, asking forgiveness. Haunting. A naked moment in our history. Murdered revolutions. Plundered springs. Dictatorships that fall and rise again.

Shaimaa falls, and doesn't rise again. Not yet. A devastating image. Mona Lisa of this couple, Guernica of our revolutions. My respect for you, Shaimaa. Because I don't have your courage, I won't have your death.

ALLAH IS GREAT, SAUDI ARABIA IS TINY, MICHELLE EST BELLE

The hair versus the kingdom. A title for a poem, one that's possibly already been used. Or for the news of the day.

The entire world was at the burial of another Saudi king. Among others, Michelle Obama and her husband. A moment of uncertainty about protocol: would she come with her head bare or veiled? The first lady of the world opted not to cover her hair for these monarchs with hidden heads and interred women. The message was clear, because she took care to cover her head when she was in Indonesia. So it was indeed a message, and not just a hairstyle. A reminder that in this kingdom—which has claimed Mecca, Islam, and the sunrise as its own—women are veiled, hidden, buried, whipped, banned from driving, deciding, going for a walk in the universe alone, and traveling (unless accompanied, or with an electronic bracelet like branded cattle). Some amateurs in the art of denial on the Internet insisted that the new king will be a Muslim hero (he left the American couple to go pray). But that doesn't change anything: Michelle Obama came with her head bare and was received. They didn't dare cover her up, as they do with Saudi women, whom they stash away in black packaging. Rather they smiled at her, she spoke, and reminded us that this country is absurd—it kills, criminalizes snowmen, stones people, beheads them in the streets. Allah is great, but Saudi Arabia can make itself very small for the sake of its protectors. It was good. It reminded us that, despite the cover the West provides for this freedom-killing country, it is the womb of this century's afflictions, manufacturer of suicide attacks, and the birthplace of fatwas, perversions, and this Wahhabi Islam that wants to expand the desert with its Bedouins across the rest of the world. In this sense, Michelle accomplished more than America itself.

Because the West has spoken to Saudi Arabia with two female voices. On one side, Michelle Obama's hair; on the other side, the enabler Christine Lagarde. "In a very discreet way, he was a fervent defender of women," is what she said after the Saudi King Abdallah's death last Friday. A beat-up Saudi in the throes of torture couldn't have put it any better. A Scheherazade who says nothing to avoid being beheaded. *One Thousand and One Nights*, the inaudible version. Grounded carpets, oil lamps without magic, Forty Thieves who are invited everywhere, honored by all. That's how it is. From this burial, let's keep the memory of Michelle's hair, Christine's prostration, Aisha's silence, and Raif Badawi's back.

FEBRUARY 4

ZABOR

Writing is the only effective way to fool death. Others have tried prayer, medicine, magic, and stubbornness, but I think I'm alone in having found the solution: writing. But you have to write always, without stopping, hardly even to take the time to eat or do your business, to chew properly. There are too many notebooks to fill. I used to buy them according to the number of people I met: often ten per day, though sometimes only two (when I didn't leave my grandparents' house), or even more; once, after attending a neighbor's wedding, I bought seventy-eight notebooks in one shot. The nearest bookseller knew me and never asked me questions about my purchases; in the village people referred to me as the postal worker's son, the one who read endlessly. And they more or less understood that I darkened notebooks like a possessed person. People sent me old books they found, yellowed pages from the colonists, torn reviews and manuals for extinct machines. At school I was silent but brilliant, and I had a handsome penmanship. So I bought notebooks and, with my eyes closed, my body stretched out beneath the twisting vines of our courtyard, during the hour when everyone else was napping, I'd recount the people I'd met the day before. It was a bit tiresome, hard always to have a number associated with a face. Sometimes the faces of people I knew blocked out the faces of those I didn't know, or stole some of their features. Which made this inventory kind of random, its magic fragile. I replayed the film in my head, scrutinizing the details and the features, recited the names to separate them out of the crush. Why do all this? Because if I didn't, one of the people I'd forgotten would die the next day. When I forget, death remembers. It was confusing. I couldn't explain it exactly, but I felt myself tied to the reaper (as they used to say, in the time of harvests): its memory and mine were connected, like two vases—when one emptied, the other would fill up. Well, actually, the equation wasn't perfect. It must be said that when my memory is empty, death empties the world. When I remembered, death became blind and didn't know what to do. So it killed an animal in the village, took hold of a tree or some foliage, or gathered insects in the fields to crunch while waiting for its sight to come back. What about when I slept? God watched over. All I knew was that I had better count out the people I'd met during the day, buy notebooks for however many there were, and then write when evening came, or at dusk, or even the next day, these stories with so many names. Between the time when I last saw someone close and then forgot them, I had a grace period of three days; I could delay writing about this person for three days, but no longer.

I just mean to say that when I write, death steps back a few meters, like a dog that bears its teeth but hesitates. The village and its few hundred-year-olds remained well (thanks to me), and no graves were dug in the western flank of our hamlet. It was a miracle that went on for a long time. But I kept it secret—not out of modesty or fear, but because (I think) if I told anyone this story, the writing would be interrupted, which would cause deaths and I would be responsible. The only way to avoid this was to speak to the notebooks with my pen. In the village there were few people who knew how to read, so the secret was safe. Of course it would be hard to explain, certainly a little dubious. A man telling you that he writes in order to save lives is a bit off, megalomaniac, someone distraught with his own futility. I'll never make that claim, but I can tell you how I finally became convinced. I know I'm the reason for the increase in the number of people who've lived past a hundred in our village, that I've warded off their demise by describing the trees at length, that my notebooks are a counterweight, and that I'm tied to this work of God like a solitary scribe with an inkwell who creates portraits of the ocean. It's the puzzle of my life, being born to create, and, in the black workshop of my head, to hold off the oldest force in the world. What else can I tell you? My name is Zabor. It was by writing it, for the first time, that I heard this noise in my head. So that's it, that's how it happened.

ASSIA DJEBAR CAN CONTINUE TO LIVE IF WE WANT HER TO

Savants against writers. Imams against books. Fatwas against fiction. The end of the world against the world. Death against stories.

The country has made its choice, sort of, sometimes, for the most part. On one side, the writers, who are chased away, who die so many times over, are exiled, forced out, reduced or transformed into caricatures of themselves. On the other side, the triumphant and giddy rise of these armies of "scholars" who murder the world with language, tarnish life, and transform religion into a sexual pathology.

On one side, writing that seeks meaning without killing anyone, wants to restore dignity, mystery, gravity; on the other, those who want to kill women, freedom, the right to take a walk, the body, and meaning. The country lies between the abyss and the novel, between ritual and imagination, between a book and all other books. So the essential question is: does the country need its writers? Not really.

What's the purpose of a writer in a country where fiction isn't tolerated? Where it's subpoenaed for suspicious activity? Where imagination is not a right but the devil?

What's the use of writing when it's repeated to us that everything there is to say has been said in one single and unique book? What good is dreaming, when we claim that everything happens

---

* Assia Djebar died on February 7, 2015.

after death and the end of the world, but not before? What's the purpose of the novel, when faced with the monologue of history and the inquisition of religious men? What does it mean to tell the stories of people, when the only hero is a god or a caliph? Who is Assia Djebar? There are so few traces of her in schoolbooks, or other books, in life, in the streets, in children's heads, and in our schools and cities and our feelings of pride that arise from things other than hydrocarbons. Like so many Algerian writers. It's enough to flip through a textbook to be convinced. She's been dead a long time. She's not the Algerian-Egyptian singer that she would have to be in order for Bouteflika to deign to pay homage to her. She's part of this organized forgetting and disdain. She was elected to the Académie Française, in France she's immortal, but in Algeria she's long dead. Like so many others. She doesn't suit the national myth, nor the caliphate that has settled into the streets of this country. She has three fatal flaws: she's a woman liberated by the language of the Other, she discovered life in France and in the rest of the world, and she is deeply Algerian. Thus, she has been dead for a long time in Algeria, and we've done everything possible to make it so that she is not a model, an icon, a voice, or a path in her own country.

Assia Djebar is a writer. Rather than the hymn to life that she offers, we prefer rituals for unlocking the everlasting. Instead of the questioning that she defends, we prefer submission. In place of the glory that she brings to the country, we prefer indifference or insult. To the liberty that she exercises, we offer suspicion about her beliefs, her loyalties, her hidden motivations.

To the necessity for imagination that she seeks to uphold, we respond by shrugging our shoulders, or with vulgarisms. We must not pretend otherwise: the homage will be brief, the volumes won't be read, the book burning will continue. And between the streets named after martyrs, and the mosques named after the heroes of Saudi Arabia, Assia Djebar's name will be given only to her tombstone in Algeria. Apart from those who wish to continue to give her life by reopening her books, the country will close up behind her.

Algerian writers were already poorly considered by an uncultivated and contemptuous regime; and they are, from here on out, useless to the caliphate being constructed before our eyes.

Defend writers' lives, their work, their memories. They are the possibility of salvation. A source of pride and a place to discover oneself and the rest of the world.

THE WAY WOMEN ARE TREATED
REVEALS WHO ARE
THE WRETCHED PEOPLES

Farkhunda. It could be the name of a land. Or a kingdom? A legend? No, it's the name of the Afghan woman who was lynched last week by a crowd, filmed, and then thrown into the Kabul River, cut into pieces and lit on fire.

You have to look at these images on the Internet: police officers with their arms crossed, an Afghan filming, a pack tearing into a dark mass. The woman was accused of burning a Koran. At one moment, a man arrives and starts hitting her with a bucket. Then another joins him with a board. There's dust. Atrocity. A feeling of terror and shame.

Later, when the dirt settles, the Afghan minister of the interior explains that in fact she was guilty of nothing—she didn't burn, throw away, or tear a Koran. She was guilty only of being a woman. Farkhunda. One tries to imagine her last moments, her pain beneath the stomping feet, her cries, her dark solitude.

Then you recoil: it's atrocious, and also impossible to represent the internal horror. Rage inside the heart. Something approaching hatred for these people. You had to see these images, the horde of animals attacking her in the name of a book or a god.

Savagery that makes you vomit. Inhuman. One must imagine this woman's life in this emptied-out country, where women are treated as shameful organs and lives without meaning, freedom, or desire, which ends, in the name of a book, under the feet of this herd.

The world skims past it. In Egypt, General-President El-Sisi welcomes a woman who had to disguise herself for forty-three years to escape the "social" ban on working. Sisa Abou Daooh, sixty-five years old, admirable, nourishing children and the disabled. An entire life in secret beneath her own skin, in her country, amongst her people.

That's the state of our world: women live under the laws of live burial. Everywhere among us, women are guilty—of their bodies, their femininity, their condition. Debased, chased down, hunted, harassed, accused, despised, or alienated to the point that they themselves hate other women, in the name of men or God.

And it doesn't change: between the fate of Sisa Abu Daooh, and Farkhunda thrown flaming into the Kabul River, and those of so many others, there are only degrees of dispossession and lynching. Women are guilty and their trials are initiated by the mobs that lynch them, the men who ban them from working, or these rats who, at the Algerian parliament, flinched at the proposed amendment to the law on sexual harassment (since women are guilty of their immodesty). Same fate, death, and body. Everywhere where people talk about heaven, they start by trampling on women. And it's terrible.

Because *never* will a people walk on the moon, be powerful, honored, and respected so long as they treat women—the half of life who give life, their source of desire and imagination, their place of love and acceptance—as shameful. *Never* will a people know peace or strength so long as they treat women as animals or slaves or an immodesty to be hidden. *Never* will a people that speaks of women as a living condom know serenity, community, and tranquillity.

A people that wants to hide women like something shameful buries half its economic force, holds half its strength in contempt, cannot claim to be a people or a real country.

Living is shame and misery is to be endured. That's the law of life. The fate of Afghanistan is in the fate of Farkhunda. The misery of Egypt is in the destiny allotted to Sisa abu Daooh. The sadness and failure in Algeria can be read in the mouths of the Islamist deputies who accuse women of being guilty of immodesty. You want to read the future of these peoples? Look at the present that they subject their women to.

APRIL 1

ONLY SECULARISTS
CAN SAVE RELIGION

In the so-called Arab world, heaven determines the earth's borders, transforms nations into ephemeral clouds. It's a new century, and the countries in this corner of the world are imprints in the sand, a caravan with a hymen and a flag, a prayer or colonists. Heaven plays around and kills people who pass through or linger there. That's what happens when you don't separate religion and state, sin and crime. "Separating state from religion saves the state, of course, but it especially saves religion," a friend told me in the streets of Brussels last night. It's strange that we don't think about this in our country, even the most open-minded. The genuinely religious should, in reality, be the first ones to defend secularism: it allows religion to stay far away from political parties, to remain in the purity of the heart and a question of personal choice. Shielding religion from politics means shielding it from ambition, calculation, violence, corruption, and the manipulators who come to it out of greed and hatred, not because they're seeking the right path. Those who come to prayer or guidance do so out of choice, love, compassion, spiritual quest, desire to find meaning. We would thus get rid of these evil beings who, in the name of religion, kill faith, man, bystanders, women, laughter, and the world.

Except that the word gets bad press, tarnished by those same people who say that secularism is a crime against God and a Western conspiracy. It's understandable: the murderer defends his mask. If he says that separating politics and religion is a sin, it's because he is involved in politics in the name of religion. He doesn't want to lose this mask. He does good business with it, doesn't worry about turning belief into his workhorse or the sole of his shoe. To separate religion from politics is to separate career from belief. It also reveals the ambition of the man who wants to take power in the name of God's power. He'll tell you he wants what God wants, that Islam is the solution, and that we must apply the law of God. Except that that's not what it is. It's not about guiding hearts toward heaven, but rather people toward submission. Separating state and religion saves religion from those who tarnish it and manipulate it. It allows us to see the best hearts coming to faith. It liberates religion from being hostage to violence. Religion is when we speak about man, love of a god, meaning, vision, conviction, community, giving, and sacrifice, rather than fatwas, prohibitions, taboos, haram/halal, conspiracy, sex, women, and nudity. The first letter of the alphabet will be a smile. To separate politics from religion is to unite man around the desire for a god. The world map will thus be drawn by pilgrims, by killers, and by the dead. And this so-called Arab world will never know peace so long as it confuses verse and sword, religion and politics, caliphate and calculation.

APRIL 6 *

THE POSSIBILITY OF TUNISIA

The Tunisians are hard on their revolution: it's going badly, causing harm, is being poorly executed. The country is in trouble, doesn't have much money, and mini—Ben Alis are quietly growing in the shadows of indecision. It makes the Algerian onlooker smile just a bit, because there has been disillusion in our country for nearly fifty-three years. In Tunisia, disillusion is so young (three years only) that it seems more like caprice. What should we say to them? Everything—that they don't realize how valuable their still-strong revolution is, symbolically, amid the disaster of the so-called Arabs, that they're the only country that still offers hope. We can't say it enough, because the Tunisians have little consciousness of how their reflection looks in our deserts. We must say it to them again and again, that they must succeed, because it gives us the possibility of an island. Otherwise, the dictators will be right. Already in Algeria, the Libyan, Syrian, and Egyptian examples will ensure the miraculous survival of a regime as long-lived as Mubarak, as insane as Qaddafi, as violent as Bashar, engaged in as much subterfuge as Ali Salah.

Tunisia has little idea of the weight it carries, accustomed as it is to its discreet geography, and the modesty of its regional ambitions. "A small country with small problems," a friend said in the

---

* On March 18, 2015, the Bardo museum in Tunis was the target of a terrorist attack, leaving twenty-four dead and forty-five injured.

illuminated streets of his country. Wrong—because this country has also invented the great solution. You can feel it, in the streets and in spirits. A discussion with a brilliant young man who, in between his business and his recreational time, is reinventing solidarity in the Tunisian hinterlands: initiatives for high school students, women, forgotten villages, etc. A feeling of astonishment, and maybe even a little jealousy, to hear these people speak of these initiatives in total freedom: "Here, the ministries have little money or means; when someone starts an initiative, they're glad to have it." It sends you into a reverie about the country behind you—your own. There, you can't even move without accreditation, authorization, bureaucracy. Everything is in the shadows of police suspicion. I can't go into Algerian schools, talk about literature without the wet stamp of Bouteflika himself. If you start a subsidized internship program, sustainable energy, recycling, or food programs for high schools, you need two containers' worth of authorizations, which require a century's worth of processes. You can't do anything for your tied-up country except whine, curse, and watch the radios in the thousand hills (Echourouk and Ennahar) reinvent the Islamic Front beneath your nose, and craft the coming civil war.

What's striking in Tunisia is this enlightening, liberating, essential concept: the possibility of starting something, of doing something. Activism doesn't have this sense of competition with power, but rather solidarity and engagement with the people around you. Which is to say that you can do something, do it without distrust, doubt, the decay of suspicion, or inquisition. Why? Because Ben Ali has fled, there's no "gift of God," a.k.a. oil, that transforms the people into a demographic misfortune, there's no pressure from the army, no former mujahedeen, no revolutionary family that spoils the spoils of war. Tunisia also has problems with Islamists, terrorism, and crisis, but it still expects something from itself, it tries and tries again, and doesn't shut down. Many Tunisians know intuitively, even if they try to forget it in their chatter, that their Tunisia depends on them—on each of them, and that they don't have anything else beneath their arms in their journey through this world except their country.

Revolution is hard, costly, but initiative, enterprise, and action are possible. Tunisia is the possibility of an island, Algeria is a lost continent. It's striking. Of course the grimaces in Algeria are legion when we speak of hope in our neighboring country. We don't like to see others succeed. We feel solidarity with failure. That's our metaphysics: in this country that shined in its war for liberation, we are pained to see others remember freedom or live it better than we do.

The attack at the museum is still being talked about here. But Tunisia is not a museum frozen in time. It's a vivacious country that lives in the present.

IMPRESSIONS FROM BUCHAREST

The Romanian sky has the purity of a precocious summer. On earth, the traces of Communism and its aesthetic: drab buildings in tight clusters, sad facades, gigantic public edifices (a temptation for all dictators, right up to our "biggest mosque in Africa"). Strange how socialism imposed its rituals: the doors marked "official," the inevitable "Palace of the People," the memory (which makes Romanians smile) of shortages and slippery customs officers—the Axa deodorant, Fa soap, and cigarettes required for "Western" publications or rationed products to get through. In a restaurant in the city of Ploesti (forty minutes away), the Algerian columnist talks to Romanians about this "socialist" country: rationed hours of TV, the speeches of the single party, the secret services and their terrorism in the name of security, sadness, fear, the chicanery required to survive the bureaucracy, denunciation, authorization to leave, etc. It makes you laugh. But one of the differences between Romania and post-Algeria is that the Nicolae Ceauşescu episode is taught in textbooks, while in Algeria there is still denial of October 1988. After their dictator's fall this country liberalized, chaotically but without disaster. We brought back dictatorship, reinstated it, and it works even better now sitting down. With one more detail: we've moved from group think, as a friend said, to group nonthink.

Back to Bucharest: you see the architecture of the old regime, its pretty houses, and the hideous socialist ones, with the gray memory of glory that ended badly. The country is calm, doesn't feel resentment, and has moved gently since the regime's fall toward restoring the facades and the beautiful buildings. Is there nostalgia? "For the elderly, yes," one academic says. A curious ailment of the present: Romanians sometimes miss the dictator because of the things that, in Algeria, cause problems—"free" goods, "union" solidarity, housing "assistance," fake jobs, unanimity of thought.

The French writer Michel Tournier said that in a prison, some see the bars, and others admire the roof.

Romanians speak to their children of an imagined golden age when the father-dictator assured a secure and free world.

This fantasy image is passed down through the family and by the old confronted with the hardships of the present. It divides time into before and after. But in Algeria, this calendar is confused—the "before" has come back and is blocking the "after"; from October 1988 we lurched into the Algeria of 1990 so that the current president could take us back to the Algeria of 1970. Time is a twisted rope, a snake without teeth, water without a source. Algeria is a spiral, Romania a straight line—it curves slightly, but corrects itself. The country is beautiful, it doesn't have this aggressiveness of nations that are sad and angry with themselves. It welcomes, but with a kind of pleasant apathy. The city is clean, the "single party" has become the chamber of commerce. Why hasn't this path, the end of a regime and a transition without major catastrophe, worked for us? It's the big question that one is forbidden to dig into.

Romanians talk about revolution, but with a crooked smile. The theory that their revolution was provoked or manipulated—in other words that it was a false revolution—has its followers: the dictator's fall was prepared, people say, and there are clues to prove it. It's part of the folklore, speculation. The essence lies elsewhere. A strange sensation of being a prehistoric man in a posthistorical world: Romania, which was once like us, has done something. In Algeria, no: we came out of socialism and fell into war, then the ambient Islamism of today, and an economy of plunder. Turning in circles, then losing shape: neither democracy, nor dictatorship, nor caliphate, nor socialism, nor liberalism, nor anything. A repulsive mix, headless, incapable of formulating an ideology of the state or a strong regime. An absent president, and a minister for higher education who is a fervent believer in long skirts and Taliban-style security. These are just details? No, they're a major indication. In Romania, short skirts don't cause earthquakes, controversy, a shameful obsession with the nation's legs. This story about a minister against short skirts in Algeria says it all.

Lovely city, Bucharest, in a country without resentment toward its past or its present.

JUNE 8

IN HANOI, AN ALGERIAN
IN RUBBER SANDALS

Eleven hours of flight in a powerful iron horse, fighting in the sky against the night and the end of the earth, to arrive in Vietnam at this exact moment in life: feet in the rainwater of Hanoi, hot, clothes soaked, the body finally freed, calm, serene, open to the world like the palm of a hand, soles of the feet in rubber sandals, gaze relaxed. The city is stunning: a thousand motorbikes per minute cross through the streets and through your head.

An insane chaos that doesn't end in collision: here, motorbikes are the descendants of the Communist bicycle, and the people riding them achieve, amidst the disorder, an art of fluidity. Motorbikes can circulate among pedestrians, in tiny narrow streets, and they aren't expensive. So you get implausible scenes like entire families stacked on a bike, the children absolutely calm, as though with their faces pressed against a car window.

There are still rickshaws, but the kind with drivers who pedal. In between the noise of engines, the country is serene. A terrible, suffocating heat that's intolerable, especially with jetlag. Altogether you need about three days to adapt. The first day's visit is to the temple of literature, sanctuary of the patron prince of letters, founded in the eleventh century. An ancient site of Confucianism, replaced by Buddhism, then Communism, then consumerism. One has the impression of walking through a film, between silent lotuses

and trees so big they're practically genealogical. Then, a surprise—
a Coca-Cola machine behind one of the temples, surrounded by
stone tortoises that students in the feudal age rubbed with their
hands for blessings or courage on their exams. It's symbolic of this
country: a country that's still Communist, but only formally. In
reality the Party is invisible—there's no ostentatious propaganda,
and a discreet compromise between the apparent ideology and the
liberal reality. Colonel Mao in an American jacket. Confucius and
Coca-Cola.

Another immediate impression: the women. Their bodies are
free, they aren't blamed for earthquakes. In Hanoi, people have this
strange way of living in public spaces as though they were private
spaces. Dinner is prepared outside, people eat on the sidewalks
between the thousand and one motorbikes (with parking as in Algeria). There are images of the offerings on the menu, you devour the
food on a plastic stool, the service is smooth, impeccable, smiling,
efficient. Late-night scenes resemble those inside our homes: they
wash restaurant dishes outside, squatting, laughing about the day or
telling stories.

A minor investigation by the columnist, who judges people
based on how they treat women: the women here can have bare legs,
they are elegant, and not harassed. No gazing, no hatred, no neurosis, harassment, or salivating. Women are equal to men. The body
isn't a misfortune: it's carried well, experienced, cared for atten-
tively. Tourists walk around the famous neighborhood of Thirty-Six
Streets where the columnist is staying.

Central Hanoi and its tourist attractions: there are many, because
Vietnam has an image in the world. Visitors eat in the streets, seated
among the Vietnamese, a dish with a fruity flavor. Concern for the
appearance of food goes so far that they make a salad into a painting, a portrait with flavors. Women drive motorbikes, often in high
heels!

Pleasant impressions of this country with single-party rule and
a liberal life; land of the boat people only a few years ago, today it's

booming, a major exporter of coffee, tea, and rice. The nation was murdered by two or three colonizations but won its wars, including the one against the fatal vocation of war veterans who kill their own country. On the way from the airport, a first question for the guide: do you have a minister for war veterans? Answer: no. An association.

The minister for work takes care of the disabled. Words that you never see together in our country—work and the war-wounded. And what about the wars? Some irritation, and then a response: we're thinking about the present and the future, is what most say. Is it taught in the schools? Yes, but not excessively. Freedom of the press? Uncomfortable silence from the journalists encountered. The Party still controls the media here.

That signals something troublesome in politics, perhaps: corruption, lack of transparency, etc. Another question: effort, or in other words, work. Here, people have a culture of double employment because "full employment" doesn't exist: everyone sells, buys, eats, or moves, as they say. There's no oil, only hands.

The columnist's arrival coincides with the visit of a Vietnamese delegation in Algeria, the country that buys everything and sells the "gift of God," otherwise known as oil. A revival of the old relationship, from the days of colonization, and then of socialism. Is it possible? We'll see. Hanoi is luminous, energized, filled with coordinated chaos, commerce, the religion of ancestors and turtles, liberalism and caution. It rains abundantly today. The tiny streets are protected by giant trees. Electric poles resemble a monstrous maze of wires and cables. Mist rises from the earth and pedestrians cover themselves with plastic for protection; a CD vendor sees the columnist shelter himself from the dense rain. She brings him a bench and offers him a place to sit.

The world is open like a hand. The terrible monologue that haunts the head of each Algerian as he carries it with him through the world suddenly stops. There's no more anger, no more words. To belong becomes a gift. The rainfall lightens, washing the trees and my body. An ablution.

Beneath my feet, the street and the sandals. A memory of an Algerian who traveled through Hanoi in 1967, perhaps on these same little streets. He wrote "The Man in the Rubber Sandals," a play about the utopianisms of the era. He died in a place of equidistance between worship and indifference. In the evening I return to my room. In order to write you have to open this book of sand that is the Internet, come back to your country: all of a sudden, the Salafists, the short skirts, the return of the single party, Bouteflika and his offspring, the malaise reappears in your head.

The country's chatter comes back to me, stains me. You discover that the social program for new former mujahedeen is back. The single party is back. Pricing, shortages, provisions, the life and times of a country turned into an intestine. Behind the windows, the streets of Hanoi remind you that the world is a possibility. That it isn't made of our malaise or our face-off with the West. Beyond our mental limits the world is also this vast Asia(s). Vietnam leaves you with the impression that there are other possible outcomes of decolonization besides ruin, dictatorship, the cult of veterans, and a deflating, unyielding hypernationalism.

Headed for the imperial city of Hue. Vietnam's tomorrow is Algeria's yesterday.

Because of the time lag, and the mental lag.

JUNE 18

ULTRA-SELFIE SOLITUDE

Solitude is a baton. You run thousands of kilometers to meet the Other, their culture, their land, but right at the moment of encounter you take out a baton and snap a photo of yourself, consecrating your solitude, your rupture with the world, your isolation, indifference to the Other, and renunciation of him. You end up abstaining from what you were seeking in the first place: the Other and everything about him. A selfie is solitude. One finds a fascinating spectacle in the streets of Brussels, or by the Perfume River in Hue, Vietnam: a man has come from far away to see the world, but only experiences it as though in the back seat of a car. The world is a pretext. The face of a screen. In the past, tourists asked others for directions like pilgrims, provoking at once an encounter, a misunderstanding, an exchange of language, and a connection, which ended in a space of understanding and an opportunity for a story. The selfie has insidiously allowed us to retreat from the world, from the Other, from the need for the Other. It's a solitude, but also a global affliction. A kind of Ionescan rhinoceros: it's a contamination, and after a short time can be found everywhere. It leads you to believe in the worst of the old gnosis: the cosmos itself is perhaps nothing other than the faceless selfie of a god who has turned his back on us but bounds through our myths nevertheless.

It's a ritual act: the tourist or individual finds a place, a moment, takes out a long baton that will help him to freeze his own reflection and keep the universe at a distance. This isn't the ancient tradition of self-portraiture—that was interested in man and didn't need the pretext of the rest of creation as an armrest for the face. The selfie turns the cosmos into a utensil, and the individual who takes the selfie into an ego. A portrait is a displaying of the self, a gift, a presence; whereas a selfie is solitude. Portrait by selfie is an absence from the world, a refusal, a withdrawal from the place of encounter as mere decoration, nihilism. The Quebecois are right to use the word *égoportrait* to refer to a selfie. The Japanese tourist who has an opportunity to speak with a passerby in Brussels misses it; he takes out his selfie stick, cutting off the possibility of an encounter, and carries with him only his mental image in order to freeze it, tie it up, and bring it back home like plunder, only the skin from game-hunting the world, a taxidermy of appearance. Tourism becomes an extension of your feelings of belonging to your country of origin. You don't move toward the world, but rather go around in the same neighborhood, with the same people, whom you bring with you as spectators on your closed-off itinerary. The selfie stick is a shepherd whose only concern is the psychology of its flock, not humanity.

Because selfies are a sickness in the world. Members of ISIS were recently identified by their selfies (they couldn't resist this globalized temptation), then killed and destroyed. It even provoked a big debate in Saudi Arabia among scholars, who refused to allow pilgrims to take selfies in Mecca. They were suspicious about the real implications of the gesture: the pilgrim wasn't coming to meet God, but to get a photo with him to take back home and show everyone. It's the act of a pagan.

A fascinating image found on the Internet: a young person is running, pursued by a bull. The most curious thing is that in his hand he's holding a phone, taking a photo of himself while being chased by this gruff animal. So he's concerned about immortalizing this moment, conscious of being in a permanent spectacle, thinking, from inside the mechanics of fear, about what he will show, say, and recount to others. Even deep, primordial emotions are affected by this powerful need for the selfie! The stick is the immutable gap between civilization and image, between man and the encounter of others. The distance between Crusoe and Friday can be measured: fifty centimeters. Tragically, it's expandable. The stick is no longer of use in pilgrimage but in its refusal, it doesn't sustain the journeyer but isolates him, doesn't open up the land but folds it away beneath his arm.

The end of the world lies at the opposite edge of a selfie stick.

SEPTEMBER 17 *

A THOUSAND WORDS
IN ONE IMAGE

The universe is a hologram, the news an image. For once we are still dealing with a twentieth-century protocol: a satellite image can start a war, a picture of a child can stop one. Everyone remembers the little girl and the vulture in Sudan, the little girl running from napalm in Vietnam, and so on. And it grows. To the cast list of collective feelings add another international impasse that will unlock a strong emotion: the photo of Aylan, the Kurdish child rejected by the sea, summons something profound but also something superficial. Certain images have the force of the *imago mundi* "end of the world" version. A kind of archetype that can be reactivated. In this case, with Aylan, a child of three, we have first of all the Child: a state of innocence before the reality of the present took him over. A moment of union with what was before. The son of man, but the ancestor of humanity. The child is innocent and the image of his death stirs guilt and shame, but also a memory of what was before time fell. His death is a closed door, a sentencing. It requires us to relive the descent, the trajectory from the apple to the shovel. The dead child is dead from drowning, but also murdered by us. This

---

* On September 2, 2015, a Syrian Kurdish child, Aylan Kurdi, age three, drowned in an accident at sea of refugees trying to escape the Syrian civil war. The photograph of his body on a Turkish beach shocked the world.

transcends our nationalities. It's a common root, which has been cut and destroyed. Aylan is therefore a crime.

Then there's the child's posture: he isn't turned toward the sky but tossed down, not buried but rejected. He's a revelation. A final and paramount insult: he seems to bury his face where he can't see us. He doesn't want to see us. His face hidden in the sand is terrible, a choice of solitude that's unbearable for the witnesses. Finally, the clothes. Those of a Sunday, a holiday, a regular weekday, for going out to a neighborhood park. It's both banal and a tragedy of unimaginable depths. The child is childhood itself. His death seems possible in the families of each of us: the child lost in a crowd, that the world swallows, chews, devours, erases. It activates that ancient and terrifying fear of being abandoned, lost, separated. The photo of Aylan is an unbearable collusion between the news of the day and a tragedy that exists outside time. It's not just a dead child but also the dead child.

And are we guilty? Yes, each of us, on some level. Is the West guilty? Not by itself: the universal language of the jeremiad likes to accuse the West, who invented the morality of universal responsibility, of being alone in this. That's false: the so-called Arab world is responsible above all. The butcher of Damascus wanted the presidency for life at the cost of millions of lives; the Mediterranean is a cemetery because of fortress Europe and the dictators of the South. Who killed Aylan? The smugglers, ISIS, Assad and his father, the Russians, Bush, and the Iranian regime: it's a chain reaction. To say that the West is reaping the rewards of its interventionism in our caliphates is horrifying: it's our dictators who are chasing our children into the sea and the sky. Aylan was murdered before he was even born. Insisting that the West must engage in humanitarianism shouldn't make us forget the terrible hypocrisies of the Arab world: Saudi Arabia likes to welcome pilgrims but not refugees. The Fatwa Valley has a fatwa for every woman, but not a single dollar for the refugee. The raft is each of ours. When Aylan drowns, it's the world that's in shipwreck. So, should we not have supported the uprisings in the Arab world? That's a joke, like trying to invent a machine to polish time. But it isn't possible—history is on the move in this area of the world, and the dictatorships, sooner or later, were going to provoke revolutions, immolations, exodus, and drowning.

The evil isn't the revolution; the evil is what makes revolution inevitable. Our revolutions are failing? No. That's confusing revolution and Jack's magic beans; that's believing that a tree grows in one day, a giant can die from stumbling, and the future is a golden goose. We should have supported Assad and his cronies because it's better than seeing drowned bodies ejected by the sea? No, that's myopia: you don't avoid evil when you support the cause of the evil. The solution is to shut yourself up at home? Impossible: we are all connected. The earth doesn't have a nationality.

SEPTEMBER 21

THE MEDITERRANEAN:
BETWEEN RED SEA AND DEAD SEA

The news is terribly mythological: how should one cross the sea? If you do it alone, you're an illegal, an immigrant, a drowning victim, a swimmer, a sinner. If you do it with people, it's called an exodus, a biblical tale, which can be the founding of a religion and a people. As a group, you're a flux, a boat people, an escape. The sea, but not the whole sea: it has to be red or white. The Mediterranean: cradle and tomb. Throne of the gods or perfect afternoons. Site of man or superhero. I recall a conference in Avignon on reimagining the Mediterranean, and the strange sensation of listening to others speak about their own memories (of the Mediterranean of the Greeks), whereas I was thinking about the present (the sea of refugees or migrants). The experience of this sea as a tourist or as an inhabitant of the South is not the same. For the one, it's an opening up of infinity, exoticism, first steps and first signs, a prologue to pleasure, the possibility of an island, the suspension of time. For the other, it's a wall, an obstacle with teeth, not a suspension of time but a countdown.

For the one, it's flat like the earth. For the other, it's vertical, something to be scaled. In the North, the elites speak of it with nostalgia; in the South, with anger. It's a memory of ancient Greek times for some, proof that the earth is a cliff for the others. It was an untethered moment, this day of meeting around the theme of the Mediterranean in Avignon: I didn't know what to say about the sea between us because I haven't experienced it as a limitation, a border, an epic. And so I said: in order for the sea to become alive as the Mediterranean, as a presence and a nation, it needs a narrative, a myth, something of men and gods that shares the horizon equitably. Then, while the others were speaking, I had an odd realization: in Muslim cartography, the sea isn't considered territory but an interruption. The pure-blooded mythical "Arab" is stopped by waves. The Koran says very little about the sea. ISIS, furthermore, drew up a new map, *imago mundi* of disaster, reproducing the place names from the eleventh and twelfth centuries: Khorasan, Abyssinia, land of Cham, Andalusia, etc. Curiously, the map doesn't give a name to the sea. Because the sea is always called "sea of darknesses": it's the place where divinity is interrupted by its opposite. The land shies away from the sword. The opposite of the desert and its monstrous infinity, its excesses, its even more terrifying side where there are neither palm trees nor oasis. Seen from the South, the sea is the opposite of conquest. Terrorists hijack planes, countries, or revolutions, but never boats, at least for now. There is holy war, holy land, but not holy sea, and in the South the Mediterranean has never been holy.

Today the sea is the news: a child has drowned in it, countries are throwing themselves into it. The sea is at once a space to fill, to cross, and to ignore. It is the world's back, as well as its awful face. Its limit but also purgatory. The Mediterranean is a space of disaster. It is body for some, soul for others. It's the Iron Curtain of our time. It separates by cutting the top of the body from its trunk, or from language. So the question is, how do we restore the Mediterranean as a site of encounter of the body, home to men who are dispensed by gods and dream of harmony between the self and the sky?

We can dream. But for the moment, the sea is a wall. On the north side, it's a nostalgia for the body; on the south side, an affliction of the body. We have to see, from the south, the sickness of the swimmer and this bikini hysteria. The coastline is also the limits of shame, guilt, and crime. The beach is immensely troublesome in the religious man's cartography. A place of tension and constraint. Of immobilization and indecision. The sea reveals the body that one prefers to hide. The sea and the everlasting are adversaries, even if they resemble each other.

And so the sea is today's news: to drown in it, swim in it, cross it, or be crossed by it, in dreams, in fantasies. Anger and submersion.

SEPTEMBER 29

AUTUMN IS THE OLDEST BOOK
IN THE WORLD

A thin rain, like the talons of birds. The kind that reminds you of leaving school as a child. Plain bread. The strong smell of the earth awakening. A hesitant, sparse rain that arouses something sensual in the soil. Sitting and looking at the sky, you plumb the depths, like throwing stones into a bottomless well. The gray clouds aren't sad but gently melancholic. The whole sky seems like a head resting on a shoulder. A moment of remembrance. And then the main subject: purpose. What exactly is the purpose of being here, sitting, with this language, this nationality, this memory, this history? What are we supposed to do with them? Maybe my ancestors knew: the country is vaguely conceivable when you don't possess it, when you are waiting for it or dreaming of it. But as soon as it falls into your hands, it turns back into a cloud. It must be rebuilt. What ties me to this land? A love at the deepest level. A kind of tortured passion that has nothing to do with hymns or vanity, but rather with sensuality and will. I loved this land as a child to the point of drawing it, thousands of times, as a rocket. I hated when people spoke to me instead of the earth; I was in love with the tastes that I discovered alone, seized by intriguing family tales, the village borders, and by the blood of my grandfather who lived so long that he turned into sky.

I talk and I write about this country with a violence that comes from my passion, the radical act of a laborer, the man who brutally shakes the olive tree to gather its fruit. I am tied to it. With words and fists. It's hard to understand. People think that the demands I make of it are an expression of hatred. And it hurts me that my passion should be perceived this way in the eyes of men who are seated, paddling along the river of time with the tips of their fingers. This land is a union between my birth and my steps.

And I love it. Bare, silent, offered up with no brokers, nothing between it and me; the flame of its presence sets fire to me, and I move between its stories at night. I love this land, half divine like a metaphysical force, or physically inside me like my body. Other verbs tire me out; I hate that this love requires me to sit down and explain it.

I don't like having to give an account of how I perceive things. I dream of them at the center of the earth, the navel, elevated, dominating, achieving power and victory. I want to spend time with this land's trees, not its cemeteries, listen by myself in the rain and not the formulaic, archaic cries of patriotism. I don't like it when others decide for me in my place. I claim total sovereignty in the palace of my language. Heritage is not a museum for me, but seasons, harvests that come in cycles. I despise intermediaries in every circumstance, and especially between myself and the scents of the earth after the first rain, when the land softens from its tough exterior into its feminine pistils.

A light rain, accompanied by eternal questions. I want to understand the purpose, the intent of my presence, explain to children what it is to be Algerian, instill passion, release perspective. Pry, collide, question, push, and hold each word by the throat until I find inside it the rationale of another way of living, find what's been missing for us, what makes a place a nation, not just a giant intersection.

I dream of a land that's released, bare, virginal. Without the misleading hymns nor the leaders of the inquisition. A land that puts language at ease, mends its presence in the world, offers a harvest and courage, welcomes but creates laws, gives without killing. That

I love this country in my own way doesn't mean that I don't love this country. I'm not attacking anyone, but I like to question. Who has the right to judge my way of loving because it doesn't resemble theirs? The same person who doesn't respect all the children of this earth, believes himself to be a spoiled only child.

The rain falls on the earth, scattering across the gray sky.

Yes, judging by the leaves, autumn is the oldest and the longest book in the world.

SEPTEMBER 30 *

THE FAMILY OF SAUD
WILL NEVER APOLOGIZE

The image of the year: tangled corpses in Mecca, in the home of the family of Saud. One week after the tragedy, in which more than two thousand pilgrims were trampled, this country, this hardened regime, has neither apologized, nor admitted responsibility, nor ousted any of its serfs. Nothing. The regime doesn't feel responsible. What's more, they seem to be saying, it's a privilege to die in this country, the first step toward Paradise. The taboo on how they manage this rite is total: you never question this strange privilege of a guaranteed profit for the regime and the family, you don't question life over ritual, nor the absurdity of the expense, when you go there only to expire in a stampede, with no apologies or penitence from the crime's authors. We are in total denial of the value of life. The image of these bodies piled up is itself a revelation of a sinister metaphysics—in which death is a destiny that exempts everyone from responsibility, the body is a rag we seek to rid ourselves of, the sacred is an excuse. There is, in this mountain of flesh, the reflection of a holocaust, an image of butchery, and proof that the regime's ideology is built on a negation of life. We barely have the courage to admit the unthinkable, and yet it's true: the king of this regime

---

* On September 24, 2015, more than two thousand pilgrims died in a stampede in Mecca.

received condolences from others, from Bouteflika, but he has not offered a single one himself, to seek pardon for his responsibility in the affair. The trial has already been concluded for decades: Allah is God, the Sauds are his representatives, and the Holy Sites are a gift to this dictatorship from God. It is glory unto Him if you die there.

And yet someday we will have to admit the reasons: this ritual remains strong and attracts lives, hearts, and people, but it's a matter of business, money, and complicity in crimes. God is at the heart of it, but not for the Sauds. Why is stone more noble than life? Why is a temple worth more than a heart? Why give your money to a place rather than to a life? Why does sacred land give a regime absolute immunity? The image of this piled-up flesh is a horror, a deeply intimate violation. It is intolerable, inhuman degradation. The failure of this caste with regard to its duty to apologize and accept responsibility is proof, yet again, of a contemptuous regard for life, a certitude of immunity toward human beings, an insidious dictatorship. In the Holy Lands, life is not holy. It's a deep insult. The public criers who wail in the name of Allah and Islam are not as indignant as they would be over a female knee or a woman in jeans.

For many preachers, Saudi Arabia pays the best salary. You don't bite the hand that feeds you; you excuse it in the name of God and destiny when it tramples pilgrims and the dignity of those who died in their land.

THE WORN-OUT METAPHOR OF ARAB WINE

You know, friend, you asked me what I think of these wines. It's hard for me to say when our two lands have such different topographies. For you, a glass of wine is taste, flavor, color, and palate. For me, it's dissidence, disobedience, infraction, exile, and shame. Look— the body of bacchanal poetry in my corner of the world has always been vast and in fuller supply than wine itself. There are more sensitive poems about wine than there are varieties of wine. So there are more poets who sang about wine than there is wine to drink. I mean in the past, in the time when the sun circled around us and our empires, according to legend. What beautiful poetry. You must read it! The lives of these people (Omar Khayyam, Abu Nuwas) were so entwined with the goblet that the substance had a mouth and a tongue and offered to explain the sky and the earth.

But during this same period you had to be clever: use the game of metaphor to make the glasses and the euphoria disappear. Speak of intoxication as though it were a meeting with the divine. Hide drunkenness in a song. It was the only way to have the poetry of wine be read and heard without getting your head or your words cut off. Still, it's strange that the greatest mystics of my land drew their images not from the holy book but from the bottle! Wine expressed heaven better than verse?

Today I don't even have that anymore: wine no longer sings, it's mute. You drink it in the shadows, inside the walls of the bars, when you don't want to go find God or your wife. It's not particularly good, sometimes poorly made like stones, sour like a refusal, but we drink it: its taste comes from our disobedience. Sometimes it's strong and bright, a success just by chance. The winemaking profession disappeared from this place along with the dead. Those who made wine for a living died one after the other, and the caves are now in ruins. That's history. In addition to its banishment by the sky, the wine in this country is affected by our history: God and colonization gave it a bad reputation.

I drank uneasily at the beginning of my life. I didn't appreciate wine for its taste, but for the disgust it brought. My face always revealed my worry. It took me some time to let it mature in my head, to accept it, tolerate it like the taste of wild boar, to feel it, choose it. To drink it without feeling guilty like a fugitive or a liar. To appreciate it and buy it without hiding it. An entire life to learn to drink wine in the sun and not behind walls. And still! I remain prudish, I hide my bottles and, before throwing them in the trash in the morning, I wrap them up heavily to hide them from the garbage collectors. Odd isn't it?

You see, my friend, writing about wine leads to writing about an entire life. It's curious that here we have to wait for death to drink, because wine is permitted only in the everlasting. And what does that do for me, exactly, drinking wine in heaven? They say it flows in the rivers. But where do these rivers lead to? Maybe after death you have to drink to relieve the boredom. But I wanted to write about wine. It's an entire life; and where you taste and choose, I resist. In wine bars here we drinkers have an air of the survivor. And that's how you get these old scenes from these enclaves: some men cry messily for a woman, others fight with an incomprehensible god, others play crossword puzzles, the rest arm-wrestle with wrinkles or memories. Come and see how we drink wine. You'll understand, Nathanaël, why, despite its sometimes unpleasant taste, we drink it here: the roiling hereafter of the cursed. We go home with the tint of a sunset, or the vigor of men who stood up to the gods, at the risk of having our livers devoured by birds...

OCTOBER 21

THOUGHTS ON POLAND
AND EUROPE: REFUGEES ARE
DECIDING ELECTIONS

Krakow. The Polish sky is gray, as it should be. The city is beautiful because it's one of the few that were spared from bombing during the Second World War. A thin rain that inspires the lost art of the pedestrian. Why lost art? Because in Algeria (you remember) there is an art of leaning against things, rather than moving around. If our roads are bad, the sidewalks are even worse: crowded, invaded, falling apart, poorly made, impossible to walk down. Between bad paving and the prayer schedule, the art of being a pedestrian gets lost. To go for a walk you need a country and shoes, and a quiet philosophy that mixes waiting, contemplation, and internal peace. Rarities. Back to Krakow: the facades are beautiful and the elections are soon. Elections for a new parliament. And, as everywhere in Europe, the far right and populism are on the rise. The campaign is centered on the migrants who arrive each day: what to do with them? How to deal with them? Depending on your response, you're either on the right, on the left, on the far right, or terrorized. The Polish have not escaped the consequences of hyper-mediatization. "Sometimes I'm ashamed to be Polish," one colleague said at a festival I was invited to. Why? "Because of how we deal with the migrant question." The Polish experienced this themselves barely fifty years ago, and today they've forgotten: like the Italians, the French, the Portuguese, etc. And the conversation rests on the same themes as Echourouk (in our country) faced with the Sub-Saharans: migrants bring illness, crime, and violence. The anti-refugee propaganda is vicious, and has touched public opinion at its core sensitivity: fear. Especially in countries without much cross-border cultural exchange with the Other, who may be subject to hysterical media and geographically far from the so-called Arab world. In Cologne, Germany, a mayor was stabbed for her pro-migrant activities. Refugees are accused of bringing disease, of being terrorists, Islamists, of coming to hide themselves in Europe while cravenly abandoning their wives and children, and so on. On the other side, in place of trying to dismantle this inhuman portrait of the Other there is mostly silence and discomfort. The question has divided the European left, and paralyzed souls practically everywhere: between this fear of invasion and a moral obligation to welcome, they don't know what to do. A dilemma far from the South, where the question is sometimes poorly weighed: in the sacred lands of Allah (i.e., the states of the southern Gulf and Saudi Arabia) they welcome no one, and in the streets of Algiers or Cairo they offer a bit of bread because the regimes don't know what to do with the migrants—chasing them out is impossible, but helping them goes against the ideological solidarity among the regimes. Letting them loiter in the streets is good for scaring those who may be tempted to demand democracy or threaten an uprising.

The West has the misfortune of wanting to embody universal morality: now it's being judged in the name of that morality. The trial will be hard, there will be truths and falsehoods that will give life to Islamism and recruitment to populism. Geography is an affect, and the world map is a shoe: structured to flee, or thrown to strike. The refugee is the contradiction of the moral West, but also the embodiment of our own deep contradiction: we spit on the West in the name of Islam, but it's toward the West, not Mecca, that everyone flees to save their lives.

So in a week Poland will vote for its parliament. The Law and Justice party is favored to win. The "migrant terror" will play a big role, as everywhere on the continent. A memory from last night of a slogan painted in fluorescent orange on the road to the Charles de Gaulle airport: Marine, fast! Do we need to build a wall made of grievances? No, exactly because the West is afraid it would be legitimate. They are subject to massive propaganda, that's the reality. The migrant question is about humanism, politics, and elections, but also about slow and constant explanation. We're not doing any better in the South with the Sub-Saharans. And if the Syrians are throwing themselves into the sea, it's not because the revolution is an evil. Evil is what makes it inevitable.

Krakow. Warsaw tomorrow. In the restaurants people look at you with indifference, good faith, or apprehension: your skin is a flag. Maybe you're this refugee that everyone's talking about everywhere. And yet the city remains beautiful. They sell angels everywhere, because the church is part of the culture and the sky is a kite for the city's many cathedrals. Solidarność? The word was Polish not so very long ago.

NOVEMBER 9

MANHATTAN: RANDOM IMPRESSIONS THROUGH THE HAZE OF JET LAG

Central Park, beneath the sky of an intense Indian summer. This giant lung of New York makes you forget the city, the dense island of Manhattan. Enormous trees with their dead-leaf tones that make the world seem like a cold fire, or the yellowed page of a poem. Children play. People pass by, running—the big American cities have a cult of deep breathing and the body. Every morning I see the joggers there at dawn through the windows of the hotel. The paths in the park lead to even bigger trees, a sky with the colors of water. It makes you want to just stay put, to listen to November, tidying up the classifications in your mind that arrange nationality, skin, names, impressions. Relax. Let the sediments of tea fall to the bottom of your soul. You could spend hours in Central Park, despite the noise of nearby Fifth Avenue: a long window into the chic and the pace of the city.

The sounds of New York are celebrated by residents. "If I don't hear the ambulances and the police sirens, I feel uneasy," said M. last night at the wheel of his enormous car, beneath the violent lights of Times Square. It can be funny to listen to Algerians in exile talk about their foreign cities: their sangfroid ties to the place, by accident or through a slow-developing love. There's a time-honored tradition of comparing the lost country with one found at the end of a road. Disappointments and ambitions track the time like a clock. The most intellectually amusing point is this "third way of exile" in a land that, for us, is far away. Explanation: the Algerians in New York are conscious of at least one thing—having escaped the geography of French Algeria and Algerian France. Here, there's no history weighing on them except their own. You encounter new souls. New possibilities. It has its own particularities. A few brilliant successes, and they make the pilgrimage each year back to the source, these clever Algerians who want to give something to their country but aren't welcomed, and are instead ignored. It's the bitter narrative of brilliant exiles in America; there is also the narrative of those who don't know if staying is dying and if exile is betrayal. The youth of the present generation ask the question with anxiety. There is, additionally, the narrative of those who chose decisively, live well, have children and new names. There are those who stayed by accident, discovered America inadvertently like Christopher Columbus. And then the epic narrative without an end of those who can't forgive the homeland for wanting to finish them off, those who don't forgive Algeria for what it is or what it did to them. It's a long catalogue of soliloquies for the Algerian who carries his land with him.

Dinner with everyone that evening at Nomad. Welcoming faces. Life stories. Proud eyes. One of them shows me stills from the shooting of the film *The Battle of Algiers*. An anecdote about the confusion, for the Algerians at the time, between the tanks of Boumédiène's coup d'état and the mock demonstrations of the military extras on the set. Laughter.

What's unsettling when you arrive in New York is its gigantism, which finds relief only in the reflections of the illuminated apartment buildings in the water at night, from Brooklyn. A short jaunt through the body of an urban giant that flattens you. And in the lectures, what do you say about your little invisible country? Because that's the traveler's worry: how do you make your country be seen by those who don't know it exists? What does Friday, faced with

Crusoe, do when he's not only black but invisible? Today, Friday is a man without color, but also the center of the world as well as the end of the world (especially). It's a paradox. History is being rewritten because Friday is digging up the island; he can pull it apart, cause it to sink. Meaning shifts. You have to speak to your audience with clarity, explain an unknown color to the visually impaired. Algerianness doesn't go down smoothly (it eats you), can't be visited (the chronic impossibility for foreigners of getting a visa to Algiers), doesn't have a global narrative other than the Battle of Algiers. It's hard to describe a country with just a scrap of paper. Even the desert seems more inhabited, easier to recount. But these things can be built. A country can be a book.

Through the window of the sixteenth floor, the city is infinite and stretches to the ends of the earth. You create images in your head of New York. Snapshots and fragments of films. The hotel has a certain vintage luxury that resembles the movie *The Grand Budapest Hotel*. Excess and compunction. The warmth is heavy. People are in a rush.

An insistent sentence inside your head: "New York is a giant smartphone." Absurd. This city is, above all, an empire. It has buildings that grab the sky by the neck. People who work in the clouds, and then come back down at the end of the day.

NOVEMBER 19 *

WHAT IS THERE TO SAY? THINK? DO?

What can I say? The news dropped at night, on my head, in Brooklyn. A black fear, suffocating, dry. Because I'm Algerian, and I know that this means war, human ruin, rupture, the triumph of blindness. Something I've seen building up inside the world for years with the intent to destroy it. So I feel hunted, cornered, plagued because of my position: I was between the world that kills and the world that's being murdered. What good can people like me possibly do in a time of open warfare?

My first anxiety, after the shock of the dead, was about the nationality of the killers. Because today the murderer murders his victim but also his country of origin.

The hardest thing to do was offer some kind of reaction. There's nothing left to say. Condolences have been used up, shouting your indignation is insufficient, banal, like shaking the hand of a dead man. Humanity doesn't have my skin; the barbarians have my face. A tragedy of being held hostage. I was a brown man between two sides, trying to sell a vision of the world that was unmasked by the explosion. This cry that I had heard so often terrorized me: *Allahu akhbar!* God is great. And there it was again, in the mouths of the murderers, to shrink the world and with it bring accusations, racism, mistrust, insult, and corpses. "God is great" makes you feel

---

* On the evening of November 13, 2015, Paris was struck by a series of terrorist attacks that left 130 dead and 413 injured.

small, it anticipates not ecstasy before divinity, but death. What is there to say to this country that it hasn't already heard, and struggles to believe the words despite those who mean well—that Islam isn't Islamism? That terrorists kill me just as much as they kill you? That they kill more Muslims than Westerners (as though it's a consolation to compare numbers in our cemeteries)? That you must not be like the killers by killing tolerance and goodness? That Muslims must go out in the streets? But how do you speak to people who've lost their reason amid fear and pain? What value do these words, just a fistful of sand, have?

So I took two days to react. Because I don't see how a few words can restore reason. The universal September 11 has lasted for a decade now, and has moved from a hijacked plane to open war. Among journalists in New York, where I've been for several weeks, I was struck by the dull routine of reaction after the attacks in Paris. They threw themselves into it, wrote and commented, but hollowly, with the inarticulateness of fatigue—as though indignation or lament could no longer capture the facts. As though there was nothing to add to the end of the world, or the end of the sentence. Everything has been said. War has become routine.

What to think? First of all, there's fear. There's nothing worse or more all-encompassing than the butterfly effect of an attack. You think of your own skin, and those whose skin is the same color as yours and who are going to "pay for" the crimes in France and the West: immigrants, refugees, expats...ISIS struck France because of what it represents: its secularism and its diversity. ISIS knew it had to strike there, precisely in order to provoke the subsequent rejections, racism, hysteria, and rise of extremes. A godsend for future recruitment: this monster feeds on rupture and old messianic texts. It needs only a book, a desert, and a goal. This series of attacks only makes sense if it strikes the country that's home to the biggest Muslim community in Europe. It leads to the worst possible outcome. France is rich and fragile because of its diversity. And this diversity is going to suffer. The world will close up even further. And ISIS will claim that it was right.

Next, the attacks carry the attributes, the organization and patience, of a state. An Islamic state or some other thuggish state responding to international pressures that it considers intolerable. They've moved from "Assad must leave" to "Hollande must leave," as the cynics say. This attack is the godsend of the world's evils. France will be forced to launch an internal war against its own people, in the name of its own people, in order to make believe that it's defending itself. The attacks killed 130 people, but will kill more, elsewhere, when Europe closes its doors to refugees, cloisters itself away, and simply listens to the echoes of footsteps around the exterior of its continent. This cycle will feed the excluded of the world, the rampant Islamisms in my world, and bring war. Because war is already here, more or less inevitable: in the North, people struggle to understand the crumbling of the South into ISIS's morbid utopia. It's no longer a fantasy of just a state, but a fantasy of power and vengeance that will consume generations to come. To say it so brutally like this will upset those of good conscience in my region who fight against the monster, but it's a battle that we're losing. We're just avoiding admitting it.

You already have corpses in this open war, and vultures circling around them: extremisms, manipulators of grief, peddlers of racism and the "kill them all!" philosophy.

What to do? That's the real question. Because there's not yet an answer. Some pick up weapons; others cry revenge. What about the Islamists, what do we do with them? It's already an old question in a too-young century. Islamism is a kind of fascism. Its vision is built on global ambition, a kind of muffled totalitarianism, and a stratagem of war: it can't be moderated. It is patient. It erodes humanity in the name of a religion, but the religion is only the means. It doesn't defend God, but wants to replace him. So what do we do? Killing the ideology only proves it to be right. It functions like a martyr:

the more you kill it, the more it becomes eternal, and the more it's right. The war against terrorism can be a kind of terrorism itself. It's necessary but insufficient. The idea is to eradicate terrorism today, but it can only be a victory if you prevent it from being reborn tomorrow. Because one is not born a jihadist, one becomes it: with books, TV channels, mosques, hopelessness, frustration. All of that comes from a womb, a country, a kingdom. We accomplish nothing by fighting a poorly dressed ISIS in Syria, while shaking hands with a well-dressed ISIS in Saudi Arabia. It's postponing the attack, not avoiding it; idealism is an ideology that has money and it spreads. We must understand it in order to respond better, and not only with airplanes that drop bombs or by electing the extreme right.

The key is not to play the game of the Islamists, abstain from feeding them, but above all not to let them come into the world in the first place. The idea of shutting up France to its own people and to the rest of the world is a predictable reflex, but it's not a good one. There is no offshore zone for this fascism, and closing your eyes doesn't put out the fire. There is only engagement, human and firm. ISIS kills, divides, excludes, terrorizes, lies, profits, recruits despair, separates and dehumanizes. It must be eradicated everywhere, without imitating it, in France and elsewhere. Can we do it? I have my doubts. But I also have children, so it's an obligation. I'm afraid for France, but also afraid that France will react badly and hurt its own people. The killers came from elsewhere, but also from France's own womb.

NOVEMBER 20

SAUDI ARABIA, AN ISIS THAT HAS MADE IT

Black Daesh, white Daesh. The former slits throats, kills, stones, cuts off hands, destroys humanity's common heritage and despises archaeology, women, and non-Muslims. The latter is better dressed and neater but does the same things. The Islamic State; Saudi Arabia. In its struggle against terrorism, the West wages war on one, but shakes hands with the other. This is a mechanism of denial, and denial has a price: preserving the famous strategic alliance with Saudi Arabia at the risk of forgetting that the kingdom also relies on an alliance with a religious clergy that produces, legitimizes, spreads, preaches, and defends Wahhabism, the ultra-puritanical form of Islam that Daesh feeds on.

Wahhabism, a messianic radicalism that arose in the eighteenth century, hopes to restore a fantasized caliphate centered on a desert, a sacred book, and two holy sites, Mecca and Medina. Born in massacre and blood, it manifests itself in a surreal relationship with women, a prohibition against non-Muslims treading on sacred territory, and ferocious religious laws. That translates into an obsessive hatred of imagery and representation and therefore art, but also of the body, nakedness, and freedom. Saudi Arabia is a Daesh that has made it.

---

translated by John Cullen

The West's denial regarding Saudi Arabia is striking: it salutes the theocracy as its ally but pretends not to notice that it is the world's chief ideological sponsor of Islamist culture. The younger generations of radicals in the so-called Arab world were not born jihadists. They were suckled in the bosom of Fatwa Valley, a kind of Islamist Vatican with a vast industry that produces theologians, religious laws, books, and aggressive editorial policies and media campaigns.

One might counter: Isn't Saudi Arabia itself a possible target of Daesh? Yes, but to focus on that would be to overlook the strength of the ties between the reigning family and the clergy that accounts for its stability—and also, increasingly, for its precariousness. The Saudi royals are caught in a perfect trap: weakened by succession laws that encourage turnover, they cling to ancestral ties between king and preacher. The Saudi clergy produces Islamism, which both threatens the country and gives legitimacy to the regime.

One has to live in the Muslim world to understand the immense transformative influence of religious television channels on society by accessing its weak links: households, women, rural areas. Islamist culture is widespread in many countries—Algeria, Morocco, Tunisia, Libya, Egypt, Mali, Mauritania. There are thousands of Islamist newspapers and clergies that impose a unitary vision of the world, tradition, and clothing on the public space, on the wording of the government's laws, and on the rituals of a society they deem to be contaminated.

It is worth reading certain Islamist newspapers to see their reactions to the attacks in Paris. The West is cast as a land of "infidels." The attacks were the result of the onslaught against Islam. Muslims and Arabs have become the enemies of the secular and the Jews. The Palestinian question is invoked along with the rape of Iraq and the memory of colonial trauma, and packaged into a messianic discourse meant to seduce the masses. Such talk spreads in the social spaces below, while up above, political leaders send their condolences to France and denounce a crime against humanity. This totally schizophrenic situation parallels the West's denial regarding Saudi Arabia.

All of which leaves one skeptical of Western democracies' thunderous declarations regarding the necessity of fighting terrorism. Their war can only be myopic, for it targets the effect rather than the cause. Since ISIS is first and foremost a culture, not a militia, how do you prevent future generations from turning to jihadism when the influence of Fatwa Valley and its clerics and its culture and its immense editorial industry remains intact?

Is curing the disease therefore a simple matter? Hardly. Saudi Arabia remains an ally of the West in the many chess games playing out in the Middle East. It is preferred to Iran, that gray Daesh. And there's the trap. Denial creates the illusion of equilibrium. Jihadism is denounced as the scourge of the century but no consideration is given to what created it or supports it. This may allow saving face, but not saving lives.

Daesh has a mother: the invasion of Iraq. But it also has a father: Saudi Arabia and its religious-industrial complex. Until that point is understood, battles may be won, but the war will be lost. Jihadists will be killed, only to be reborn again in future generations and raised on the same books.

The attacks in Paris have exposed this contradiction again, but as happened after 9/11, it risks being erased from our analyses and our consciences.

NOVEMBER 23

MONTREAL

Montreal. Beneath the gray sky of a late winter. Normally, people tell me, there's already snow, but not this time. Quebec might be the third country of Algerians, for those who live there, for those who dream of it. It has the French language without the French malaise for Algerian travelers. They can speak French here without feeling the history in it. A country that's naked and new. With giant trees, snow that stops time, diversity that calms the fear of being a foreigner, and beautiful cities with familiar names. So people live well here, in this France Jr. that was spared the process of colonization and decolonization. We are in France without the weight of France, and we're in Algeria without the wars of Algeria. We're even in America.

Happiness? Yes, a lot of Algerians will say they are at peace here. It's strange to be colonized for three thousand years, fight for seven, be liberated, and still feel that you are living in war: at home, inside oneself, with your own people, in the streets. At the most profound level it was an error to set independence as our goal in the November declaration, without at the same time aiming for happiness. Why does the declaration talk only about justice, and not happiness, too? It may be that we've dreamt of freedom forever, but as for happiness, in our cultures it's promised only by death. Here the Algerians always tell you their first reason for exile: to save their children or their future children. To give them a land they can tread on. A tree to rest under, a wall to protect their bare skin, a face for tomorrow. It's simple: you can't restart Algeria in Algeria. So you have to restart it elsewhere. A parting slogan. Are they without guilt? Sometimes: it's hard to leave a land and the people there, its years, its smells and tastes. Exile is uprooting—it's been that way since Ovid. Faces become hazy when you pose this question to many Algerians here about living far away by choice: they defend peace as a life goal, but there's a painful regret about what pushed them to leave. An age-old reaction of the instincts against the horizon.

Winter here is like drought elsewhere: everyone is talking about it always, it chants the time, and divides the year in two. People wait. By the river the sky is so clear, the air so pure that it sets fire to the lungs. The stone of the houses is ancient. Children pass by, entertained by fake deer horns on their heads. They're getting ready to celebrate.

There is such a thing as a country of starting over.

NOVEMBER 25

AFTER SO MANY ATTACKS, WHO AM I?

The creation of the enemy. A fine method laid out in a lecture at a round table in Montreal. Its source is Gilles Bibeau, author of *The Genealogy of Violence*. It's a powerful image because in it you realize that the enemy is not a person but a construction, one that can come about slowly or suddenly. As part of a culture, or after an attack. An enemy comes into the world through blindness, rumbling, from a distance. It's the entity where people project their fears, and the opposite of their own skin. It is cultured versus uncultured, a process that reactivates the bestiary, the idiotic, reductive narrative, and mythology. A mix of clichés with the effect of a magnifying glass. But the enemy isn't just an optical illusion, it's also an embodiment. It's a co-construction: foreigners participate in it too.

Why these questions? Because at the moment the West is obsessed with the barbarian. According to another specialist, encountered at a radio broadcast session, the word "barbarian" derives from sounds for stuttering, murmuring, rumbling. For the Greeks, a barbarian was someone with an incomprehensible language. The West can't understand this permanent attack against its body, its solitude, its humanity, nor its attack against the rest of humanity: for example, it truly doesn't understand what ISIS wants from it and fumbles for the right word to clarify things for itself. "Barbarian" sticks to the tongue when you can't come up with an

271

explanation for this unmitigated violence. We know how this monster recruits, how it operates, how it writes and films its horrors, but we don't know what it wants: al-Qaeda wanted revenge, the Islamists wanted rebirth by reselling the ashes of our golden age, the jihadists wanted a caliphate. But ISIS goes further: it wants nothingness, emptiness, ground zero. It doesn't want. Its goal is the end of the world, the end altogether. The irruption of the hereafter in the present. The world conceals the divine, and the end of time will reveal it. It's this abyss of messianic thought that inspires these attacks, like an accelerant of time and the end of time. Back on earth, the West has chosen the word "barbarian" to designate the enemy, and it's right: for us it's no longer a question of enemies of war, but rather a sickness, a black irruption of something profound that has come to the surface. So the word "barbarian" is the only one that can describe this black hole, this murderous riddle.

But the idea of an enemy has reactivated the worst instincts: rejection, cultural prejudice, a hateful orientalism, a yearning for crusade. Moments of crisis have this terrible habit of bringing us back to a revival of something we've all seen before.

So the enemy has been constructed and reconstructed: the Islamic State dreams of a Christian State, fashions it with its desires and its bombs. Fear has infiltrated the media and the culture, and has patiently sewn together this enemy figure.

A few further thoughts: history forges war and enemies; literature promotes encounter and embrace.

The idea of "the enemy" is a fascinating one: it is self-portrait and scrutiny, both individual and national, a mirror effect and also its rejected shadow.

Of course, this parenthesis is seductive, but we are far from World War III. Today it's Tunisia that's struck, after Paris, Bamako, Lebanon, etc. The worst part of these attacks is the fear they inject into routine. ISIS hit, war is here, it banalizes life and also itself. "I am Charlie" becomes "I am Tunis," then "I am Bamako." And at the end, "I don't know anymore who I am." And then—"Am I at all?"

and "Who am I?" Then the standard denial: "Above all, I am not the Other."

Who will win the Third World War? Everyone: our dictators with their homegrown intellectuals (adherents of paranoia and anti-West whining); Western regimes and their far-right factions; ISIS and its end of the world. When reason dies, everyone is right.

Dissociative thoughts, because there's nothing more to say after the attacks.

Tunis is struck again. The world will be buried all together.

CAMUS CROSSED OUT

Yale is a temple. Like Herman Hesse's *The Glass Bead Game*. Because around the campus, the city of New Haven is plagued by unemployment, agitated by violence and the race Question (with a capital Q), this unease between skin and flag in the United States. Inside, a universe of stone buildings and giant trees on fire with a brilliant autumn. "Trees are the only visible ancestors in America. The country has no ancient history, and so is attached to its trees," my American publisher tells me. It's here that I come across the manuscript of Albert Camus's *The Myth of Sisyphus*. The university acquired it a long time ago from an Israeli collector. You can access this relic through a rite of documents, searches, and finally silence. A text reconstructed page by page. A surprising penmanship: so much does the style of this man have the rigor of numbers, his calligraphy is an embrace, stifled by ink and abruptness. Handwriting that's gnarled, hurried, flattened, crossed out practically from the inside, born of a short breath, not a long inhale. The man seems to have written by avoiding writing, enduring it as a chore. Grasping at its neck. On the thin paper, the crossed-out bits are more plentiful than the sentences, they are the writing. It's fascinating to see, like a second, twin book, a palimpsest. The scratched-out lines are a dull murmur in the ear. An awakened dream of a second, hidden book, the vigilant reader's myth of the scribe from the Middle Ages, the hermeneutist. Trying to decode the crossed-out words is like surprising time in its imperfections. Coinciding with the present of another time, precisely at the moment of a fundamental hesitation. I try to follow the book back to the man, to his irregular breath. Additions, erasures, deletions in the rhythm of his inhalation. To read the manuscript is to experience this rhythm directly, hear his respiration, perceive within it the noise of the earth beneath his tread. The manuscript is the place where the book hasn't erased its other possibilities. A place that echoes, sonorous but frozen in the blanching of fallen ink. This space offers a retort to the definitiveness of every book, with a certain surprise at its haste toward perfection.

But it wasn't just a simple aesthetic experience. A manuscript is also the most extraordinary embodiment of death. It doesn't decompose; but it decomposes everything else. It's the hard corpus of a permanent ghost. Because the survival of this calligraphy presupposes death. Otherwise it's just a draft. In the penmanship of *The Myth of Sisyphus*, I see the impossible reflection of a face marked by its absence; and I have the impression, at moments, that a man is pulling apart the dense foliage of a thicket of writing to look at me. An hour later, after paging through this relic, I arrived at this certainty, violently, as though through an extreme shortcut, that I was paging through...my own death. Every manuscript is both glory and terror for a writer. Bent arms, fingers gripping the pen, muscle, all that exists no more, and there remains only this radiant tension between choices of words, which is style. A dead man was looking at me. And I, too, was promised to this death, whose corpus I was holding in my hands. A desperate thought: even God couldn't resist writing books that would secure his eternal life. So I took a shot at it: breathe slowly, to find the exact rhythm of this writing. The interplay of his lungs and concentration. Like filling out someone else's body. The manuscript's paper was thin, requiring that I pay attention as I would to a whisper. To turn the pages was to draw closer. The manuscript is what remains of the labyrinth—it's the solution, the hidden tangent. And so to read it is to file away at the mystery of the book, but also to grope in darkness: to touch, with the eyes closed, a desired body, to reconstruct the pleasure that awaits beyond the concealment. A renewed encounter, resuscitation of that moment of reverie before selecting a word. At the exact moment of occurrence of this word, did he hesitate? Was there a shout in the street? An irruption of the quotidian from behind the glass pane of eternity.

On the flipside of one of the pages there's a date: 25 May 1938. It was on the back of a note from the board of directors of *Alger Républicain*, the newspaper of the time, that Camus continued to write his book. It was the censored chapter, which was devoted to Kafka. A two-sided page that had been torn off, picked up again during editing. A palimpsest is a refutation of eternity. In the religion of books, you can be killed for that.

2016

FULL TANKS AND FATWA VALLEY

What can be done about Saudi Arabia? Just after the November 13 attacks in Paris, I published an op-ed in the *New York Times* that offered a reminder of something straightforward: we can't fight ISIS if we don't fight against its ideological womb. In other words, this vast Fatwa Valley of well-fed clerics-in-chief, housed and paid by the Saudi monarchy. It's these clergy who have ensured religious propaganda, with their books, their satellite channels, their courses, their mosques, and their preachers, who are the source of one of the major radicalizations upending the world. It is a source that has formed (or deformed) entire generations, and with satellites and the Internet it has found a way to spread ever faster. There's the black ISIS, the one of November 13, and the white ISIS, the one that invents the jihadists' ideology from the blessed kingdom of God and barrels. In the article I outlined the evidence, but also this astonishing myopia that the West maintains with regard to the kingdom.

The most amusing thing was to see how governments reacted to this evidence after it was printed and reprinted all over the place. How could they both promise a global war on terror and honor their eternal ally in this kingdom, preserve this contradiction that they won't admit to. Going after this regime, they maintain, would provoke a disastrous domino effect, accelerating the insecurity of the oil supply and playing into the hands of their Iranian adversaries. An age-old concern that's understandable. Saudi Arabia an ally? Dismantling this stubborn illusion was easy. This monarchy rests on two contradictory pillars of interest: founded by a warrior (Mohammed ibn Saoud) and a fundamentalist theologian (Mohammed ibn Abdelwahhab) in the middle of the eighteenth century, the kingdom is built around a so-called strategic alliance with the West, but also on an ideological alliance with its religious clergy. The first ensures its international protection, the other its internal legitimacy. Except that these two camps are at war with each other: the monarchy suffers when there are terrorist attacks, and claims it will fight against them; but it is spawning the terrorism. You only have to listen to the Friday sermons in this country, which unite millions of faithful each season, to understand that the king's diplomacy and the violence of his preachers are two different worlds. And the kingdom has no choice but to hastily propose a kind of Muslim NATO against ISIS, all the while incubating this erosive clergy.

One is not born, but rather becomes, a jihadist. And one becomes a jihadist because Wahhabism has a strike force that is both financial and editorial in a way that "modernity" does not. It upends, massacres, and creates "Sahelistans," propaganda, and undercurrents that have lent it and its armies legitimacy and means. This equation must be solved in order to solve the ISIS problem. Otherwise we will continue to tally the deaths, to salute Saudi Arabia's "participation," and to condemn while turning around and around in circles. It's unpleasant to condense this crisis in this way, but that is the essence of it, if you also add Palestine, the wrong turns of decolonization, and the failures of philosophical alternatives to Islamism.

But back to the question, what can we do? Could a younger king, possible only through new rules of succession, allow courageous reforms targeting an aggressive clergy? International pressure that would dry up the profits in Fatwa Valley? Yes, but that's the equivalent of turning this kingdom into a one-legged creature that can't stand up. "To fight ISIS? Ah, well, we must stop driving cars," an American editor friend says. Bush wanted to fill up the tank for free, and Saudi Arabia sells us hydrocarbons for the price of blood. Terrorism, like engines, runs on oil and gas.

JANUARY 18

THE "COLOGNIZATION"
OF THE WORLD

Colognization. The word doesn't exist but the city does: Cologne. Capital of rupture. For several weeks now, the West's imagination has been rattled by an anxiety that is reactivating ancient memory: sex, women, harassment, barbarian invasion, liberty, threats against civilization. That's the best way to define the word "colognization." Invade a country to take its women and its freedoms, submerge it with numbers and crowds. That's what happens during "colonization"— you invade a country to take over its land. And that's what happened at the train station in the German city eponymous with this syndrome, during New Year's Eve celebrations. A crowd of "Others," i.e., North Africans, Syrians, "Arabs," refugees, exiles, and invaders, took to the streets and attacked women passing by. At first a seemingly random occurrence, it became a German national tragedy, and then a Western trauma. "Colognization" will forever denote this event, but also name a game of fantasies. It's difficult to distinguish between what happened at the train station and what's happening now in heads and in the media. The testimonies gush forth, but the analyses are biased by a binary discourse of civilization versus barbarism, which overshadows that other discourse of solidarity and compassion. At the core are the questions of the body, women, public space, life.

For the aggressors this is all evident: they come from these lands where sometimes it's sex, not murder, that's a crime. A woman who

281

isn't "daughter of..." or "wife of..." is loot, potential property. Sex for the taking. A body to sling over your back and head toward the bushes. The spectacle of the free woman in the West isn't seen as the essence of freedom and the West's strength, but as a caprice, a vice, a provocation that can only end in satisfaction. The sexual misery of the "Arab" world is so immense that it has turned into caricature and terrorism. A suicide attack is orgasm by death. And social space is a prison of desire that can only be expressed in violence, degradation, fleeing toward other lands, predation, or concealment. We speak little of this sensual misery in the land of turbans. And, in an unfortunate paradox, it's the Islamists who take charge of how sexuality is expressed, they delineate it, codify it, reduce it to a halal expression of procreation. They kill desire by prescribing it in doses, to the point that it's become an obsession in sermons, a kind of libido-Islamist conquest.

But "colognization" has revived the fantasy of the threatening Other in a West that doesn't know what to do with us or with the rest of the world. These tragic and foul events at the train station have crystallized a fear, a denial, but also a rejection of the Other: the West will use it as a pretext to close its doors, refuse to welcome, and legitimize the arguments of hate speech. "Colognization" is that, too—a fear that stirs up the irrational, killing solidarity and humanity.

THE SOLUTIONS OF CLOWNS

The division of labor is clear: the elites of the South pass judgment on the democracies of the North, the elites of the North surveil the democratizations in the South. Last week's halfhearted fad, for example, was to talk about the Tunisian experience. The January 14 anniversary of the first revolution (and Ben Ali's departure) brought with it a return (discreetly) to the big, tired questions: Is democracy possible in the land of Allah? However, the interest in democracy in the South is different from that in the North: for the South, it's the question, how did the Northern democracies come into being? How can we do the same thing? Is democracy a question of nature or nurture (like the old debates of the Middle Ages)? There's an entire literature grown out of this art of deconstruction in the so-called Arab world. It appeared during the Renaissance, continued through the imitation of Communism, the construction of socialism, and then there was a series of genealogical studies before arriving at rejection of Western regimes, because of the resentment and assault in the Middle East.

Western democracy is a spectacle for us in the South. We derive from it our arguments for our faith in democracy, but we also seek out its weaknesses to feed bad faith. The first bug in the model: that fascism attains power through...democracy. The big lesson there is from the twentieth century: Hitler was elected. And that effect has reproduced itself in our countries through the bug of revolution: we make dictatorships fall in favor of democracy, but it's in the name of democracy that Islamist fascists attain power. That's the democratic model's first contagious disease. The second bug, still being rolled out, is populism. The "consensus of clowns": a metaphor that must be unpacked. Because it's fascinating to see that what's threatening the democracies of the North is not only the election of fascism, but above all a descent into spectacle and show. Exhausted by the lack of solutions, heavy with fear, lobotomized, perhaps, by comfort and remote controls, the great democracies have begun to gorge themselves on these sumptuous clowns, an expression of fatigue with the model and a crisis of confidence. These expressions are more extreme even than Berlusconization: Beppe Grillo in Italy, the UKIP faithful in England, or a triumphant Donald Trump in the United States. It's shocking for us to see this populism rise in the West despite the power of its elites.

What is Trump an expression of? He's been imbued with a thousand meanings. The most obvious is that of the third way: between the illusion of Obama and the nightmare of a return of a Bush type, Trump is a show, a devastating entertainer, something so gluttonous and coarse like junk food, he represents a kind of nervous laughter in the face of fear. With his image of politician as middle finger to politics, the guy advances in the polls. He is the embodiment of voters' resentment and anger. He is also reinventing campaign style for the era of buzz: there is no longer any other way to be heard except through spectacle and provocation. All you have to do is take extreme positions (build a wall with Mexico, ban Muslims from entering the country, confuse Germany and Paris) to save millions of dollars' worth of flyers: the Internet will take care of spreading bad information, having reinvented prophets and prophecies.

For the intellectuals of the South, on a tireless quest for a solution to the democracy-plus-Allah equation, Trump is a source of anxiety, and something to be mocked. It depends on what you're trying to demonstrate, the failures of the West or the limits of its proposal for civilization. Donald Trump is the expression of the (momentary) end of politics, or perhaps its suspension during a hallucinatory intermission; but, seen from the South, it's either a scandal for the model, or evidence that its time has run out. It's the reprint of the escapades of Rome, with the emperor Claudius's solution. But there's also a domino effect that lends credibility to those peddling the end of the world: the Islamists, the conservatives, the anti-West acolytes, or antidemocrats of all types. We say to ourselves that if America can produce Trump, why do we need to explain how we were able to produce bin Laden? What difference is there between folly and foolish laughter? One kills, the other kills through ridicule. In the South, some deem that the West has come down with the illness of the Roman emperors: either its genius or its frivolity.

JANUARY 27

I WANT THE REVOLUTIONS TO FAIL BECAUSE...

There appears to be a kind of intellectual pleasure, for some, in announcing the death of the revolutions in the so-called Arab countries. It mixes together a verdict on the cultural impossibility of such a thing, pronounced by the West about the regions of the South, with the secular fatalism of Southern elites when they look at themselves through affect or the prism of current events. So let's dissect, with sophisticated dismay, the Egyptian, Syrian, and Libyan examples. We'll trace the path between the heady hopes of the first days and the disappointing reversals five years later. In both visions, in the West's as well as in those of the anguished descendants of decolonization, we'll have to invoke some hidden judgments and a simplistic understanding of history.

Because these estimations of failure assume that, at the end of the day, given the current bloodshed, revolutions are a worse ill than dictatorship. And that's a judgment of bad faith. It forgets that the true evil is not revolution itself, but what makes revolution inevitable. If people were free, happy, and lived in a nation of justice, what would push them to go out into the streets shouting demands? We forget that the hostage-taking by Islamists was only possible because the Islamists are the spoiled children of dictatorship. And that emptying out the dictators' palaces isn't enough so long as we don't also have the courage for sexual, religious, and mental revolutions, too.

It is also assumed that revolutions in our part of the world must produce their fruit immediately: a fast-food vision of change, IKEA-style democracy. In other places, people expect revolution to be a tree that promises fruit in a generation; here, we expect magic beans that will grow tonight. In the South we are asked that our revolts please conclude in democracy within the period of that week's business days, which is not the case in the North.

That the revolutions have failed is an observation that proceeds from a studied perception of history: it's assumed that history unfolds in the manner of a Hollywood blockbuster, with a rupture in the beginning stasis, then a quest, an obstacle, a confrontation, and finally victory, happiness, and lots of children. It's a mediatized vision that has nothing to do with the long and inhuman process of historical evolution of countries and their peoples. Man may be horrified by blood, so he believes that history progresses with the same sensibility.

This judgment of failure also comes from a place of self-denigration, of repackaged skepticism: the North's skepticism is reproduced in the South as a cruel jeer at oneself. The revolutions, as soon as they no longer bear much romanticism, are a defeat. Many in the South rush, with a tenacity that says much about our own psychology, to find within this string of bad luck a sense of satisfaction, resentment, denigration, and a desire to justify this sad vision.

That is, these revolutions are botched because they don't correspond to my desires and my vision. I'm not their father nor their tutor, so I can clear my name, and that comforts me from where I sit, I can attribute my unhappiness to others.

We announce the failures of the revolutions also because we confuse our personal lives with the life of the nation: because a revolution doesn't carry its fruits into my own life, it's a fiasco. Whereas in reality, the calculations of national history care little for the random rhythms of our breath.

The conclusion that the revolutions have failed is also intended to prove this version in which history consists of conspiracies, especially theories from the West, hidden neocolonialism. Our fail-ure is proof that they were "imported," fabricated by the CIA and the Mossad. Concluding that the revolutions were a disaster allows us to validate the idea that change and effort are bad, and that our sad fate is not primarily our fault.

The revolutions in the so-called Arab countries are a process, however, not a film or a fairytale. They are a movement, which isn't attuned to the level of each individual's pain. This movement devours and crushes, but it's irrevocable. It may appear to conclude, but it's never definitive: the movement goes on in places where we aren't filming. It's something that goes beyond good and bad, it can't be reduced to our emotions and suffering.

The so-called Arab revolutions aren't a failure, unless we con-fuse history with road movies. They are tragic and disastrous for our homes and our lives, but they are irreversible.

FEBRUARY 15

LETTER TO A FRIEND ABROAD

Dear friend,

I read your letter with care, of course. I was touched by the generosity and the lucidity within it. Strangely enough, your words have reinforced the decision I've come to over the last few days. I took from them, above all, the tender expression of your friendship and support, despite your concern. However, I would like to respond.

For a long time I have written with a spirit that is unencumbered by the opinions of others when they are the dominant ones. This has given me a certain freedom of tone, a style maybe, but also the liberty of insolence and irresponsibility, of audacity. Naïveté perhaps. Some have appreciated this style, others were not into it. I have taunted radicalism, and I have tried to defend my freedom in the face of clichés that I found horrifying. I have also tried to think. To do so by way of newspaper articles, or through literature. Not only because I wanted to succeed, but also because I was terrified of living a life without meaning. During the difficult years in Algeria, journalism allowed me to live the metaphor of writing, the myth of experience. So I wrote often, too much, feverishly, with anger and amusement. I said what I thought about the fate of women in my country, of freedom, of religion, and the other big questions that may bring a person into consciousness, to the point of renunciation or fundamentalism, depending on what one wants in life. Except that today, with the media success that I've had, I've come to understand a few things.

First of all, that we have entered into an age of litmus tests. If you are not on one side, you are on the other. With regard to the Cologne text, I actually wrote about part of it—the piece about women—several years ago. At the time it elicited no reaction, or very little. Today, the temperament has changed: tensions lead people to read into it, and overinterpretation leads to prosecution. I wrote both this article and the one that appeared in the *New York Times* in early January; that the publication of the first was followed so quickly by the second was merely an accident, and not an insistence on my part. I was moved to write out of shame and anger at my own people, and because I live in this country, in this land. I said what I think and offered my analysis of something that we can't bury away beneath the pretext of "cultural benevolence." I am a writer, and I do not write academic papers. What I write is also emotion.

I find it immoral that these academics should now sign a petition against me because of this text. They do not inhabit my flesh, nor my country, and I consider illegitimate if not scandalous that some of them pronounce me guilty of Islamophobia from their Western capitals and their café terraces, where comfort and security reign. All of it served up in the form of a Stalinesque trial, and with the bias of the expert: "I lecture the native because I speak better than he does of the interests of other natives and postdecolonials." It is, to me, an intolerable position. I think it is immoral furthermore to offer me as fodder to local hatred under the verdict of "Islamophobia," a banner that serves today as an Inquisition. It's shameful to accuse me of all this, all the while remaining very far away from my daily experience and that of the people I live with.

There is great beauty in Islam, depending on who carries it, but I like for religion to be a path toward a god, and I want the steps of the man who follows it to resonate along the way. These coddled petitioners have given no thought to the consequences of their actions on the lives of others.

Dear friend, I also understand that we are in a difficult moment.

In another era, it was the writer who came in from the cold; today it is the writer who comes in from the so-called Arab world who is entrapped, ordered around, shoved in the back, and cast off. Over-interpretation follows him everywhere, and the media harass him, on the one hand to reinforce a certain worldview, on the other to reject and deny. The treatment of women is tied to my future and to the future of my people. In our lands, desire is unwell, and the body is under siege. That is undeniable, and I must say it aloud and denounce it. But all of a sudden, I find myself responsible for how this will be interpreted depending on the place and the atmosphere. Denouncing ambient theocracy at home becomes an Islamophobic argument elsewhere. Is this my fault? Partly. But it is also the fault of our time. That is what happened with the article on Cologne. I accept it, but I am also saddened that it could be used to deny the humanity of the Other. Today the writer from the land of Allah finds himself the target of unbearable media solicitations. I can't do much about that, but I can remove myself from it; I had believed I could do so with wisdom, but I can also do it with silence, as I choose to do henceforth.

And so I am turning to literature, and on that point, you're right. I will leave journalism shortly. I am going to go listen to trees or to hearts. Read. Recover my confidence and my tranquillity. Explore. Not give up, but go beyond the trends and the media games. I have resolved to pry deeper rather than perform.

I have for my country the affection of the disenchanted. A love that is secret and strong. A passion. I love the people and the skies, which I try to decipher in books and in glimpses at night. I dream of power, of sovereignty for my people, of consciousness and togetherness. And I am disappointed that I'm not living this dream. It makes me angry, pushes me to chastise lovingly. I do not hate my own, nor the humanity of others. I'm not insulting their reason. But I exercise my right to be free. This right has been misinterpreted, sought out, mistreated, and judged. Now, I also want the freedom to do other things. And I apologize a thousand times, dear Adam, if at any moment I have let you down.

If I now choose to make this letter public, it's because it is addressed to caring people of good faith like you. And above all to you.

MARCH 2

MY LITTLE WARS OF LIBERATION

As a general rule, I don't like speaking in the first person. The "I" is abusive, even more so for a journalist. It bothers me, like a kind of armor or makeup. It makes me think of these outsized egos that are growing in number among the "engaged," the activists, the intellectuals, or the chattering class. Writing is an exercise in lucidity, and it demands that you erase yourself. In place of the "I" I prefer the artifice of "the columnist." A managerial metaphor. It allows me to write while jousting about freely behind the words. It gives importance to the Other. Allows a breeze to enter. Opens a window with a handshake. Lets me listen and stay put awhile to see the unexpected reveal itself through a thicket of verbs. To express ideas without weighing them down with your own ego.

But today, an exception. My subject here is an explanation and a thank you. First, I need to explain why I'm choosing to take a break. My main reason is that I'm tired. To write is to expose yourself, as a colleague said, and it wears you out. In Algeria there is a passion that drains you, kills sometimes, tires you and pushes you into a kind of immobile exile (staying at home, in your own skin), or the exile of struggle (going somewhere else). We are motivated by the emptiness inside ourselves, but also by our fate. It leads us to a violence that sometimes has the appearance of folly. There can be a kind of permanent prosecution, with the word "treachery" always on the tip of the tongue. Algerians' verdicts against themselves have a radical force. And during these years of exercising my profession I experienced this passion. I ended up embodying, without wanting to, these contradictions in the Algerian spirit, its affect, passions, blind spots; Palestine, religion, women, sex, freedom, France, all of these things. I spoke as a free man on these subjects that ate at me and weighed on my life. I provoked both enthusiasm and hatred, and I accepted it as such, right up to the breaking point where people call you a harki, a sellout, or a Zionist. I experienced success to the point where recognition in the world made me afraid at home, because of our distrust and our innate hatred, like that of a domesticated dog. I wrote to a point where I felt myself both going in circles and encircled. And so I decided, a few months ago, that I would rest, and try to understand, to rediscover reading and serenity. As it happens, this decision, which had been slated for the end of March, was accelerated by the "Cologne affair." So I wrote that I was quitting journalism. And this became yet another misunderstanding: some thought I was defeated, others were delighted by my "weakness" in the face of the criticisms coming from this absolutist Paris. And that made me smile. If for so many years I stood up for my freedom when confronted with all this, nineteen academics were hardly going to make me give in! This misunderstanding was funny, but also revealing and tragic: it's symptomatic of our delirium.

In the "Cologne affair," I ended by understanding that I was merely the spark that ignited something that had been brewing, waiting. The delirium came so fast, and was so out of proportion, that it became more interesting than my words that had ignited it. So I decided to stop, not respond, because doing so didn't produce any kind of clarity. It was amusing, but above all diagnostic. What I wrote, however, about our unhealthy relationship with desire, the body, and women, I stand by and defend. What I think about our "cultural" monstrosities is what I see with my heart and my body, and have for years. I am Algerian, I live in Algeria, and I do not accept for other people to think in my place or in my name; not in the name of a god, nor in the name of a capital, nor in the name of some ancestor. And that's why the massive show of support and all the messages of solidarity moved me: they testify to a desire for sharing, understanding. The stakes in this matter were greater than my small person: to be able to speak freely, without falling into compromise in the name of a certain culture, race, or complicity. On my behalf, some people put their own convictions aside, because this was a question of freedom. And some proved their honesty in refusing the inquisitions and the distortions. They understood that this was a question of rights, of my rights and those of the people in my country, and that to stand up against me would demean us in the name of a belief. Postcolonialism doesn't need to mean blindness, and "difference" doesn't excuse barbarism. I'm not an Islamophobe. I'm free.

It also happens that as time goes on one becomes worn: you end by understanding that people's belligerence is hiding something. A sickness in our souls. A secret inability to accept the world, to conquer it, to admire the successes of one's own children. There is the doubt tied to having children. The suspicion of others' success. Putting people's intentions and beliefs on trial. We Algerians suffer from this strange sickness of imprisonment, and when one of our own frees himself from the straitjacket and jumps over the wall, and comes back with other worlds beneath his arm, we throw stones at him, isolate him, are suspicious of him. Independence preceded, and still has not produced healing in our history.

Disappointment? No. It's my country. I live here and I don't lower my eyes, I don't kill anyone; I share it with those who don't want to divide it, and I defend it against those who want to cover it with a veil, eat it, hide it. I'm not a patriot according to the proclamation, but because the people I love are here, my favorite trees and my entire memory are in the land. And I will stay here.

God? It's like my birth and my death: it doesn't concern anyone else. Islam? It belongs to no one, and I claim the right to petition it freely and insolently. And so on. I've never lied and I've always written what I thought. Good faith is better than faith. I repeat this. I don't change the music, as I said to one journalist, only the instrument. I became a journalist because I needed a salary, and so that I could stay within the arena of writing. It became a passion, then a way of living. For me, writing a column is like archery. It's a hundred-meter-long pathway that sends the body sailing toward the fire. I like this exercise, the tense mornings. More still? I'm not a Zionist, nor an atheist, I'm not bought off, nor French, Swedish, or Arab. I am free with this freedom that my ancestors dreamed of and died for in order to give it to me beyond their tombs. I have great flaws. I have my convictions and my books. I like to pit myself against the sky and the chatter of skeletons. I grew up in a village that has become a kite inside my head. I tried to learn fast and I loved the written word. I treated my work at newspapers as though it were a question of life or death. I shared, I betrayed. I found, amidst the chaos of my generation, pathways and possibilities that I seized. I'm no better or worse, only constant. I criticized the regime out of disappointment with its ambitions as a state, its missing grandeur, its greedy men who lack class and clean shirts. And now, I want to take a break from journalism in order to dream of literature.

So today I say my thanks, to those who've always shared my pleasure in writing. Who derived, from the accidents of my verbs, what they needed as reasons or convictions. Because this country is passionate, its children many. Some want to inherit it before death, some steal from it, others submit to it, others respect it with the kind of silent veneration due to a parent. Among them, many have understood me, forgiven me, followed and defended me like their own lives.

I, too, am conducting a war, for my own liberation. And at times I celebrate my independence.

GLOSSARY OF NAMES AND TERMS

AAV Green Algeria Alliance, an Algerian political coalition created in 2012 that brings together several Islamist organizations.

ABANE, RAMDANE (1920–1957) One of the top Algerian revolutionary leaders. He was assassinated by the FLN.

ADAMI, MOHAMED Algerian politician who served as minister of justice under President Liamnie Zeroual, forced to resign in October 1998.

AÏT AHMED, HOCINE (1926–2015) Algerian revolutionary leader who was imprisoned from 1956 to 1962. After independence, he formed the Socialist Forces Front, which became the principal opposition party in Algeria. He was exiled in Switzerland between 1966 and 1989.

ALN Algerian National Liberation Army, the principal armed faction during the War of Independence.

ANSEJ The National Agency for Youth Unemployment, an Algerian government organ tasked with helping young entrepreneurs.

APC Assemblée populaire communale, the equivalent of a city or town council.

APN Assemblée populaire nationale, the lower house of the Algerian parliament.

APS Algérie Presse Service, the public information agency of Algeria.

ARRISSALA A 1976 film by Moustapha Akkad that recounts the life of the Prophet Mohammed.

BACHAGA A civil servant: a term left over from the Ottoman administrative state. Over time it came to have a derogatory connotation, and was used to refer to high-level Algerian clerics loyal to the colonial power.

BAKER, JAMES (BORN 1930) American politician and secretary of state who served in the Reagan and elder Bush administrations. He was the UN representative in the Western Sahara conflict.

BELHADJ, AL (BORN 1956) Cofounder, with Abassi Madani, of the Islamic Salvation Front.

BELKHADEM, ABDELAZIZ (BORN 1945) Algerian politician who served as prime minister. He is a member of the FLN and considered part of the Islamist movement.

BEN ALI, ZINE EL ABIDINE (BORN 1936) President of Tunisia from 1987 to 2011. Initially prime minister, he became president by ousting President Habib Bourguiba. In 2011, following weeks of protests, he fled to Saudi Arabia. A Tunisian court later sentenced him in absentia to life in prison for inciting violence and murder.

BEN BELLA, AHMED (1916–2012) Algerian nationalist politician, the first president of independent Algeria. He was overthrown in a coup in 1965, imprisoned, then kept under house arrest until 1980. He was subsequently exiled in France until 1990, when he returned to Algeria.

BENFLIS, ALI (BORN 1944) Algerian politician and member of the FLN who served as prime minister under Bouteflika before joining the opposition and creating his own party.

BEN M'HIDI, MOHAMED LARBI (1923–1957) An important Algerian nationalist figure, one of the six leaders of the FLN. Head of the Algiers autonomous zone, he was captured by the troops of General Massu on February 23, 1957. He died on March 3, after being tortured.

BENTALHA Town fifteen miles south of Algiers where one of the largest massacres of the Black Decade occurred, on the night of September 22–23, 1997. The massacre, resulting in more than four hundred deaths. was made famous through a series of photographs by Hocine Zaourar, entitled "The Madonna of Bentalha," which received the World Press Photo Award.

BENYOUNÈS, AMARA (BORN 1958) Algerian politician, founding member of the RCD and then the UDR in 2004, which is close to the presidential majority and considered part of the modernist movement.

BETCHINE, MOHAMED (BORN 1934) Retired Algerian army general and former head of the secret service. An influential adviser during the Zeroual presidency, he was forced to resign in October 1998 following accusations of corruption.

BISMILLAH A commonly used religious phrase meaning "in the name of God."

BOUAZIZI, MOHAMED (1984–2011) Tunisian street vendor who attempted suicide by self-immolation after being harassed by municipal officers. He died on January 4, 2011. His act sparked protests across Tunisia, and is considered to be the trigger of the revolution that brought about the fall of the Tunisian regime.

BOUDIAF, MOHAMED (1919–1992) Algerian statesman and founding member of the FLN, assassinated on June 29, 1992, while serving as the head of an interim government.

BOUMÉDIÈNE, HOUARI (1932–1978) Algerian colonel and statesman, president of the republic from 1965 to 1978.

BOURAQ A fantastical courier in the Islamic tradition depicted with the head of a woman and the body of a horse. The *Bouraq* is connected to the Nocturnal Voyage of the Prophet Mohammed, between Mecca and Jerusalem, and then from Jerusalem to heaven.

BOUSSOUF, ABDELHAFID (1926–1980) One of the top leaders of the Algerian revolution, who founded the Algerian secret service. He withdrew from politics when Algeria gained independence.

BOUTEFLIKA, ADELAZIZ (BORN 1937) Current president of Algeria, he took office in 1999, and is now the longest-serving president.

CHADLI, BENJEDID (1929–2012) A former fighter in the War of Independence, he served as the third president of Algeria, from 1979 to 1992.

CHAOUCHI, FAOUZI (BORN 1984) A capricious and popular goalkeeper for the MC Algiers soccer team.

CHEIKH CHEMSSOU A religious preacher who officiates on the private television station Echourouk.

CHOUYOUKH Muslim scholars.

CLAN D'OUJDA A group of Algerian politicians and army officers from the FLN, mostly from western Algeria, who, during colonization, settled in Oujda, a Moroccan town on the border with Algeria. There they established a coalition that took power after independence and became the backbone of the Algerian *pouvoir*—which is still the case today, as President Bouteflika is a member.

CONSTANTINE PLAN A broad economic and social plan initiated by the French colonial government in Algeria after de Gaulle came to power in 1958, which sought to thwart the effectiveness of the Algerian revolutionary movement by constructing housing, redistributing agricultural land, industrializing, and enacting a policy of employing Algerians in high-level management positions.

DAESH The Arabic term for Islamic State (ISIS).

DAÏRA An Algerian territorial subdivision that groups together several towns.

DJILALI, SOUFIANE (BORN 1958) Algerian politician, president of the Jil Jadid (New Generation) party.

DRS Algerian intelligence agency and secret service.

ECHOUROUK Arabic-language daily paper and private TV channel.

ELMAHDY, ALIAA MAGDA Egyptian blogger and member of Femen.

EL WATAN French-language daily newspaper in Algeria.

ENNAHAR Arabic-language daily paper and private TV channel in Algeria.

ENNAHDHA A Muslim political party founded in Tunisia by Rached Ghannouchi in 1981 and inspired by the Iranian revolution and the Muslim Brotherhood. Following the Tunisian revolution of 2011, it became a leading political party.

ENTV Algerian national television network composed of a number of public TV stations.

ESSEBSI, BÉJI CAÏD (BORN 1926) Longtime Tunisian politician who got his start at Tunisian independence and lasted through the revolution of January 2011. He is the current president of Tunisia.

FCE An Algerian association of business owners.

FELLAGHA Armed anti-colonialist militants in French North Africa. They are most closely associated with nationalist movements in Algeria (especially during the Algerian War, 1954–1962) and Tunisia.

FFS Socialist Forces Front, Algerian opposition political party founded in 1963 by Aït Ahmed.

FIS Islamic Salvation Front, an Algerian political organization created in 1989 and dissolved in 1992.

FITNA Discord.

FLN The National Liberation Front, founded at the beginning of the War of Independence in 1954. Now a political party whose honorary president is Abdelaziz Bouteflika.

GHANNOUCHI, RACHED (BORN 1941) Tunisian Islamist politician.

GHOUL, AMAR (BORN 1961) Algerian politician close to the presidential majority, and belonging to the Islamist movement.

GHOZALI, SID-AHMED (BORN 1937) Algerian politician and former prime minister who joined the opposition.

GIA Armed Islamic Group, a terrorist organization founded in 1992 with the goal of overthrowing the Algerian state and taking power.

GIS Special Intervention Group, an Algerian elite special ops unit often referred to as "the Ninjas."

GPRA Provisional Government of the Algerian Republic, formed in 1958 to negotiate independence from France.

HADJ, MESSALI (1898–1974) Algerian politician and pioneer of the independence movement, founder of the PPA, MTLD, and Algerian National Movement (MNA), which opposed the strategy the FLN adopted to fight for independence. He was violently suppressed and sent into exile in France, where he died.

HARAM Used to describe any act that is forbidden or proscribed by Islamic law.

HARGA An undocumented migrant. From an Arabic word meaning "to burn." Plural: *harraga*.

HARKI Native Muslim Algerians who served France as auxiliaries during the Algerian War (1954–1962).

INJAZAT Arabic word meaning "achievements," used to refer to big accomplishments during successive terms of President Bouteflika.

ISLAHATE Term with a religious connotation that refers to reforms or positive achievements.

KAABA The cubic construction at the center of the sacred mosque of Mecca, representing the symbolic center of Islam that the faithful turn to when performing prayers.

KASMA A "section" of the FLN; a local office below the *mouhafadh*.

KATIBA Base unit of the ALN; a battalion. This structure has been appropriated by terrorist organizations.

KHALIFA A caliph.

KHASSA The elite. Literally, "minority."

KHELIL, CHAKIB (BORN 1939) Algerian politician, former president of OPEC, and minister of energy from 1999 to 2010. He resigned after suspicions emerged of corruption.

KHIDR A mysterious mythological figure in Islam, alluded to in the Koran, considered by some to be a saint.

LAAYOUNE The biggest city in Moroccan-controlled Western Sahara.

LE POUVOIR Literally, "the power" in French, this refers to those in power.

LSP Social housing program initiated by the Algerian government during the 2000s to address a housing crisis.

MADANI, ABASSI (BORN 1931) Cofounder, with Ali Belhadj, of the Islamic Salvation Front.

MAKHLOUF, HAFEZ (BORN 1971) Syrian colonel, head of the Algerian intelligence service.

MAKHZEN The Moroccan monarchy and the institutions that form the basis of the Moroccan state.

MALG The Ministry of Arms and General Liaisons, which served as the intelligence service during the War of Independence. Founded by Boussouf. The members of MALG are generally referred to as the "Madagascans."

MAMERI, TAREK A young blogger convicted by the Algerian courts in 2012 for calling for a boycott of legislative elections.

MARZOUKI, MONCEF (BORN 1945) Tunisian politician who served as president of Tunisia from 2011 to 2014.

MEZRAG, MADANI The terrorist leader of the Islamic Salvation Army from 1993 to 1997. He was granted amnesty and now appears regularly in public debates.

MOKRI, ABDERRAZAK (BORN 1960) Algerian politician, president of the MSP since 2013.

MOUHAFADH A regional representative of the FLN.

MSP (OR HAMAS) Social movement for peace, an Algerian Islamist political party founded in 1990.

MTLD Movement for the Triumph of Democratic Freedoms, founded in 1946, which preceded the creation of the FLN in 1954.

MUJAHID Fighter who participated in the War of Independence as a member of the Algerian National Liberation Army or the FLN. Plural: mujahedeen.

NATIONAL DAY July 5 is the Algerian national holiday marking the declaration of independence on July 6, 1962. November 1 marks the beginning of the Algerian War of Independence on November 1, 1954.

OAS Organisation de l'Armée Secrète, an illicit armed terrorist group created in 1961 to fight with all means possible against Algerian independence.

OMRA A minor, noncompulsory pilgrimage to Mecca, in contrast to the hajj, which designates the great pilgrimage.

OUFKIR, MOHAMED (1920–1972) Moroccan army officer and politician. He was the leader of a failed coup d'état against King Hassan II.

OUM DOURMAN City in Sudan where the Algerian soccer team beat Egypt on November 18, 2009, in a qualifying match for the 2010 World Cup.

POLISARIO FRONT A Sahrawi liberation movement that seeks to end Moroccan control in the Western Sahara.

PPA Algerian People's Party, founded by Messali Hadj in 1937. It became the MTLD (Movement for the Triumph of Democratic Freedoms) in 1946, and laid the ground for the creation of the FLN in 1954.

QURAYSH Arab tribe in Mecca to which the Prophet Mohammed belonged.

RADP People's Democratic Republic of Algeria (full name of the Algerian state).

RASD Sahrawi Arab Democratic Republic, the sovereign state of Western Sahara declared by the Polisario Front on February 27, 1976, but unrecognized internationally.

RCD Rally for Culture and Democracy, an Algerian political party founded in 1989.

SAADANE, RABAH (BORN 1946) Algerian soccer player who became head coach of the Algerian national team, which went to the World Cup three times under his leadership (1982, 1986, 2010).

SAÏDANI, AMAR (BORN 1950) Algerian politician, former secretary general of the FLN.

SOLTANI, ABOUDJERRA (BORN 1954) Algerian politician, member of the Islamist movement.

TAKBIR The pronouncing of the formulation *Allahu akhbar*, or "God is great." Also refers to the call to prayer.

TARTAG, BACHIR (BORN IN THE EARLY 1950S) Algerian army general, head of the secret service since 2015.

TPI International Criminal Court.

UGTA General Union for Algerian Workers, the largest labor union in Algeria.

UMMAH The Muslim community around the world.

WAHHABISM Founded by Muhammad ibn Abd al-Wahhab in the eighteenth century, this ultraconservative Islamic doctrine and religious movement is practiced in Saudi Arabia and Qatar.

WAKF In Islamic law, a gift made by an individual to a work of public utility, which therefore becomes inalienable.

WALI An Algerian regional governor, equivalent to a French *préfet*.

WALLAH Algerian exclamation, literally meaning "by God," but used to mean "I swear by God."

WANTOUTRI A colloquialism for the exclamation "One, two, three, vive Algeria!"

ZAOUIS An Islamic religious school or monastery.

ZEROUAL, LIAMINE (BORN 1941) Algerian army general and president of Algeria from 1994 to his resignation in 1999.

CREDITS

Except for "Saudi Arabia, an ISIS That Has Made It" and "Letter to a Friend Abroad," all the essays in this collection were originally published in French. Most appeared in the author's regular column in *Le Quotidien d'Oran*, while others were first published in *Le Point* or on the Web sites Algérie Focus (algerie-focus.com), Yagool (yagool.dz), or Impact 24 (impact24.info).

"Saudi Arabia, an ISIS That Has Made It," translated by John Cullen, from *The New York Times*, November 21, 2015, © 2015 The New York Times. All rights reserved. Used by permission and protected by the Copyright Laws of the United States. The printing, copying, redistribution, or retransmission of this Content without express written permission is prohibited.

"Letter to a Friend Abroad" first appeared in English in the article "Friendship Amid Frenzy: The Correspondence of Kamel Daoud and Adam Shatz," *World Policy Journal* (2016) 33(2): 67–69, published by Duke University Press.

KAMEL DAOUD is an Algerian journalist based in Oran, where he writes for *Le Quotidien d'Oran*—the third-largest French-language Algerian newspaper. He contributes a weekly column to *Le Point* and is a regular contributor to the op-ed pages of the *New York Times*. His articles have appeared in *Libération*, *Le Monde*, and *Courrier International* and are regularly reprinted around the world. A finalist for the Prix Goncourt, Daoud's *The Meursault Investigation* (Other Press) won the Prix François Mauriac and the Prix des cinq continents de la Francophonie.

ELISABETH ZEROFSKY is a writer as well as a translator. Her work has appeared in *The New Yorker*, *n + 1*, *New Republic*, and *Harper's*. She is a graduate of Brown University and was a Fulbright fellow in Paris from 2008 to 2009.

Also by **Kamel Daoud**

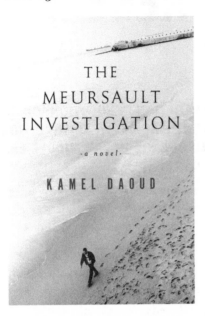

THE
MEURSAULT
INVESTIGATION

· a novel ·

KAMEL DAOUD

"A tour-de-force reimagining of Camus's *The Stranger,* from the point of view of the mute Arab victims."
—THE NEW YORKER

"[A] retelling of Albert Camus's classic *The Stranger* from an Algerian perspective... [this] debut novel reaped glowing international reviews, literary honors, and then, suddenly, demands for [Daoud's] public execution."
—NEW YORK TIMES

"A superb novel... In the future, *The Stranger* and *The Meursault Investigation* will be read side by side."
—LE MONDE DES LIVRES

"Daoud has said that his novel is an homage to Albert Camus's *The Stranger,* but it reads more like a rebuke... Where Camus's godless prose is coolly mathematical in its ratio of words to meaning, Daoud's work conducts waves of warmth. The sand and the sea and the sky and the stars, which, for Camus, seem to negate life rather than affirm it, are, for Daoud, vital witnesses and participants in his existence."
—NEWYORKER.COM

He was the brother of "the Arab" killed by the infamous Meursault, the anti-hero of Camus's classic novel. Seventy years after that event, Harun, who has lived since childhood in the shadow of his sibling's memory, refuses to let him remain anonymous: he gives his brother a story and a name — Musa — and describes the events that led to Musa's casual murder on a dazzlingly sunny beach.

The Stranger is of course central to Daoud's story, in which he both endorses and criticizes one of the most famous novels in the world. A worthy complement to its great predecessor, *The Meursault Investigation* is not only a profound meditation on Arab identity and the disastrous effects of colonialism in Algeria, but also a stunning work of literature in its own right, told in a unique and affecting voice.

▉ OTHER PRESS

www.otherpress.com

⊞ OTHER PRESS

You might also enjoy these titles from our list:

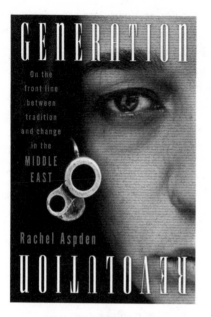

GENERATION REVOLUTION: ON THE FRONT LINE BETWEEN TRADITION AND CHANGE IN THE MIDDLE EAST
by Rachel Aspden

A British journalist unravels the complex forces shaping the lives of four young Egyptian just before and after the Arab Spring.

"The Arab Spring has yielded a bumper crop of books about youth across the region, and *Generation Revolution* is among its more fruitful reads…[Aspden's] stories are always compelling…A sobering tale for anyone with an interest in Egypt's future."
—*The Guardian* (UK)

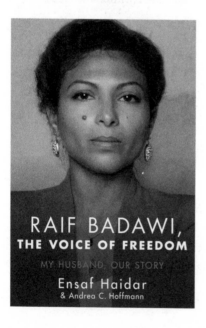

RAIF BADAWI, THE VOICE OF FREEDOM MY HUSBAND, OUR STORY
by Ensaf Haidar and Andrea C. Hoffmann

Ensaf Haidar's account of life with her husband Saudi Arabian social activist Raif Badawi, and her campaign to free him from imprisonment.

"A sobering exposé of Saudi Arabian culture and a tribute to the courage and strength of both the author and her husband."
—*Kirkus Reviews*